PUBLIC

EXPRESSIONS

OF RELIGION

IN AMERICA

Conrad Cherry,

Series Editor

Published in cooperation
with the Center for the Study
of Religion & American Culture
Indiana University–Purdue
University at Indianapolis

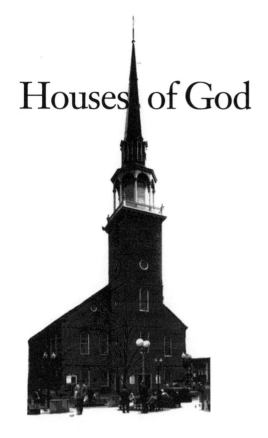

Houses of God

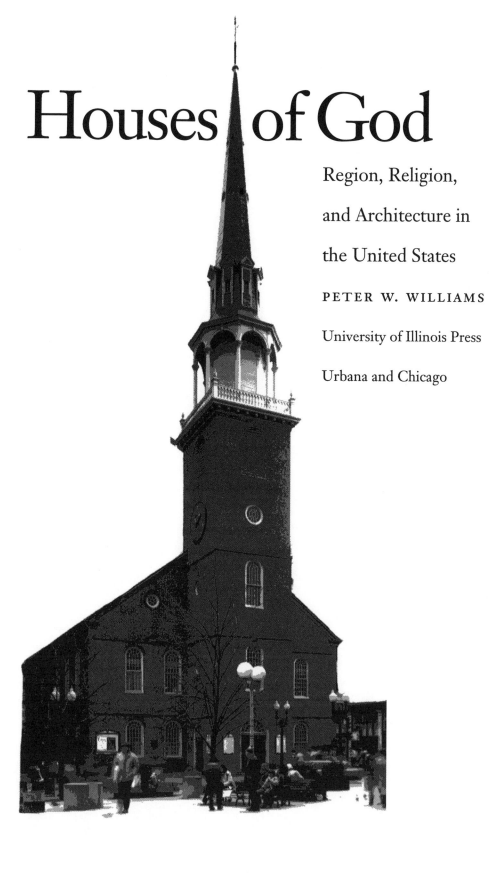

Houses of God

Region, Religion,
and Architecture in
the United States

PETER W. WILLIAMS

University of Illinois Press

Urbana and Chicago

First Illinois paperback, 2000

© 1997 by Peter W. Williams

All rights reserved

Manufactured in the United States of America

⊚ This book is printed on acid-free paper.

Library of Congress

Cataloging-in-Publication Data

Williams, Peter W.

Houses of God : region, religion, and

architecture in the United States / Peter W. Williams.

p.   cm.

(Public expressions of religion in America)

Includes bibliographical references and index.

ISBN 0-252-06917-x (pbk. : alk. paper)

1. Church architecture—United States. 2. Liturgy

and architecture—United States. 3. Synagogue

architecture—United States. 4. Mosques—United States.

5. Temples—United States.

I. Title. II. Series.

NA5205.W55   1997

726'.5'0973—dc20   96-25358

CIP

P   5   4   3   2   1

FOR RŪ   *amore canibusque magnis*

CONTENTS

INTRODUCTION

In April of 1994, the Center for the Study of Religion and American Culture at Indiana University–Purdue University at Indianapolis sponsored a photographic exhibit on the theme of regionalism and American religious architecture at its conference, "The Public Expression of Religion in the American Arts." What follows is a set of essays arising from this exhibit, which was jointly curated by the author and Nannette Esseck Brewer of the Art Museum at Indiana University, Bloomington. The catalogue and checklist for that exhibit have been published separately by the Indiana University Art Museum.

The purpose of this book is to examine the built environment of religion in the United States – its architecture, landscape, and other dimensions of its public physical aspect – with special attention to the importance of geographical and cultural *region* in shaping that expression. Regionalism has always been a powerful, if fluid and somewhat imprecise, category of the way in which Americans have experienced and interpreted their collective lives. The vastness of the continent and its infinite physical variety are part of this regional mystique, captured in our "national hymns" in images of the "woods and templed hills" of New England, "amber waves of grain" of the Great Plains, and "purple mountain majesties" of the Rockies. Distinct cultural patterns have become enshrined in self-mythification, especially the "moonlight and magnolias" syndrome of the South, or through commercial exploitation, such as the "Marlboro man's" embodiment of rugged western virtues (while promoting the dubious harvest of Virginia and North Carolina.) The emergence of transregional "Sun Belts" and "Rust Belts" following major demographic and economic shifts in the twentieth century has altered but not eradicated more traditional patterns of regional identification.

Beginning with the postulate that regionalism remains a valuable organizing principle for examining patterns of American religious building, I have organized what follows into seven chapters, each representing a major cultural region or aggregate of proximate regions. In doing so, I have been guided by standard geographical literature such as Raymond Gastil's *Cultural Regions of the United States* (1975), but have ultimately followed my own instincts as to what "works" in this particular context. The results are something of a mixed bag, reflecting the unevenness of American regional experience. Some broad areas, particularly the South and New England, have coherent narrative threads running through much of their history which make their stories more susceptible to a unified, linear interpretation. Others, such as the Great Lakes/Old Northwest area, are linked more by a shared geography and economy than cultural coherence. Nevertheless, even in such cases, the juxtaposed patterns of proximate religious subcultures make an intriguing mosaic rather than an unending line of slowly evolving meetinghouses on the town green. For the sake of economy, I have in the cases of the Pacific Rim and the Great Plains and Mountains combined quite disparate subregions into single chapters. Even in these cases, though, continuities emerge that render these arbitrary but geographically natural juxtapositions illuminating.

An exploration of regionalism and religious architecture necessitates the consideration of several related themes. The first of these is religious *tradition* or, in its later, distinctively American form, *denomination*. The pluralism of America's religious experience is a given from the beginnings, first for the colonial settlements in aggregate, then later in virtually every town, city, and state. Christians of all sorts have been numerically prominent from the beginning, and for much of our history culturally dominant as well. Christians, however, have for centuries been irreparably divided, as witnessed in the rival and often hostile presences of Spanish Catholics and British Puritans and Anglicans from the early European presence in North America. Sectarian Protestants, ethnic Catholics and Jews, and, later, Buddhists, Hindus, and Muslims have enriched this tapestry in succeeding waves of immigration, each bringing with them and/or adapting for their own purposes a wide variety of types of houses of worship and other sacred sites and structures – cemeteries, shrines, chapels, schools and colleges, convents and rectories. Complexity of tradition and practice has thus been a major theme of the built environment of American religion from the earliest days.

Style is yet another component of the American religious architectural mosaic. For some religious groups – those, like the colonial Anglicans, endowed with wealth and representing social status and political power – this has meant *high style*, the fashionable work of prominent and expensive architects. Such structures, at first in Europe and then in this country, have often provided the patterns for domestic imitation and adaptation. The colonial Anglican churches of Virginia and Massachusetts, for example, were strongly influenced by the neoclassical style embodied in Christopher Wren's "rechurching" of London following that city's disastrous fire of 1666. Wren's successor, James Gibbs, popularized a later version of this style in pattern books widely circulated on this side of the Atlantic that were adopted by a growing number of religious communities, including those hostile to the Church of England. In subsequent decades, native-born designers such as Charles Bulfinch, Henry Hobson Richardson, and Ralph Adams Cram provided successive prototypes that would be imitated widely across the social and denominational spectrum.

It becomes clear here that *social class* is another factor influencing religious design. Only wealthy and usually urban or, later, suburban congregations could afford such creativity, and most have been content to adapt rather than innovate. *Vernacular* church architecture has received practically no scholarly attention, though many of the photographers represented in our exhibit have shown a keen eye for its attractions. Vernacular architecture is often eclectic, combining stylistic elements with various degrees of harmony, as exemplified in many of the

Victorian-era neo-medieval Methodist and Baptist churches in which elements of Gothic, Romanesque, and who-knows-what have been juxtaposed in remarkable ways. The availability of materials has also influenced the process, with wood or brick often substituted for the more monumental medium of stone. Vernacular, however, has not always meant vulgar; the Baptist adaptations of Greek revival that have caught the eye of many a photographer exemplify a striking process of simplification of basic visual elements to the point of starkness, while the "Carpenter Gothic" popularized by Richard Upjohn in the mid-1800s inspired both the painter Grant Wood and a myriad of local builders who were thus able to achieve a dignified and pleasing architectural statement at little expense.

Region, denomination, and stylistic variety are three central factors that complicate and enrich our picture. How do they relate to one another? One way of approaching the question is through the concept of "culture hearths," that is, the entrance of various strains of European culture into the North American social environment through distinctive geographical nodes. New England thus becomes the point of entry for the Puritan Congregational variety of the Reformed tradition of Protestant Christianity, and with it the distinctively Puritan institution, the *meetinghouse.* This structure evolved out of the absence of any previous built environment for worship and the Puritan desire to house their Bible-oriented services in a place uncontaminated with the sacral associations of the term "church." The Quakers of the Middle Colonies employed similar structures for their very different sort of worship, and gave Pennsylvania a distinctive "churchscape" in its early years as well.

The Tidewater South, another major area of colonial settlement, was thoroughly different from New England in its social, geographical, political, economic, religious, and cultural orientation. Thus, the neoclassical Anglican churches of Virginia and Maryland were sited not on village greens but rather at rural transportation nodes among widely scattered plantations. Here was a material expression of another, distinctive Reformation tradition of belief and worship in a very different social matrix. In later decades, however, the Wren-Gibbs style of neoclassicism that had originally entered the British Atlantic colonies via southern Anglicanism began to make its way north. By the third decade of the eighteenth century, Puritan meetinghouses were coming to resemble Anglican churches; by the time of the Revolution, even the Baptists had adopted this once "high style" favored by the slave-holding gentry whose worship was suspiciously "popish" to New Englanders.

New Spain, which included California and today's Southwest, was the point of entry for Spanish Catholicism. The missions of the colonial era in that region reflect a combination of European Baroque high style templates, native workmanship and materials, and an imperial plan of Europeanizing the indigenous peoples in which the mission complex and its activities played an important role. In the mountain region, however, extensive settlement by Europeans did not take place until the arrival of the Latter-day Saints in the 1840s. This indigenous movement created a whole new civilization in the middle of the great desert, and imposed a new religious building type, the Mormon temple, on the transformed landscape, drawing upon a wide variety of traditional stylistic elements to house new and exotic rituals instituted by Joseph Smith and his followers.

Each of these regions has a clear-cut role as a seedbed for a distinctive religious culture, part European, part indigenous, and usually somewhat eclectic in its growth and development. Other regions, such as the Old Northwest/ Great Lakes zone, were settled later and more pluralistically than the four already discussed. The development of this built religious environment and landscape is thus less clearly focused, though the presence of distinctive ethnic groups – German Lutherans and Polish Catholics, for example – and the work of influential architects such as Frank Lloyd Wright provide some points of departure. It is at this point that *ethnicity* – the simultaneous presence of culturally distinct groups in the midst of a dominant culture – becomes particularly important for our purposes.

By the nineteenth century, much of the story of American architecture and religion becomes transregional; our concern now becomes one of tracing patterns of transmission and variations on common themes, such as the national popularity first of the Greek and then of the medieval revivals across regional and denominational lines. In addition, religious developments influencing worship and its physical setting also tend during the twentieth century toward the ecumenical, such as the adoption of the "split chancel" plan by mainline Protestants and the wide impact of the liturgical reforms emerging from Vatican II.

This simultaneous exploration of religion, region, ethnicity, and architecture lends itself to both complexity and richness. The way religious groups have chosen to express themselves in wood, brick, stone, or concrete tells us much about their character: their patterns of worship, their social standing and economic resources, the natural environment surrounding them, their interaction with one another and with the surrounding secular realm, and their participation in the cultural matrixes exemplified in architectural style and regional culture.

This project began in the imagination of Conrad Cherry, director of the Center for the Study of Religion and American Culture at Indiana University–Purdue University at Indianapolis. Fortunately, it was one which fit perfectly with the research interests I had been developing for a decade and a half, so I was easily able to make it my own. Nan Brewer of the Indiana University Art Museum served not only as the co-curator of the exhibit out of which this book grew but as a continuing stimulus to expand my own knowledge of the arts, especially American photography. The exhibition, which appeared in Indianapolis and then Bloomington in the spring and summer of 1994, was the result of a true collaboration, in which each of our individual contributions became inextricably entangled with those of the other to form an original and inseparable whole. Liz Dulany of the University of Illinois Press has been a continuing delight to work with, on this and many other projects. The generosity of the Lilly Endowment, Inc., made the whole project possible. Gretchen Townsend Buggeln, John Buggeln, John Eller, Charles Lippy, Kevin Sweeney, and Dewey Wallace made valuable comments on various portions of the manuscript. James F. White of Notre Dame deserves special mention for having read and commented on the entire work in manuscript form. Countless staff members of churches and synagogues across the country have been patient and cooperative in opening their doors and files to me, as well as in supplying many of the images for this book. The photo credits also indicate many other sources of indebtedness. Miami University's Applied Technologies staff, especially Barbara Wheeler and the three photographers, Bill Hicks, Jeff Sabo, and Virgil Sweeden, worked with me at considerable length to improve the quality of the images. Southern Methodist's Jeremy Adams must be acknowledged for first having given me the odd idea that I might actually have something to say about architecture. Finally, my wife Ruth Ann deserves extensive acknowledgment for putting up, more or less cheerfully, with endless detours off the interstate while I photographed *yet another* church.

BIBLIOGRAPHY

Gastil, Raymond D. 1975. *Cultural Regions of the United States.* Seattle: University of Washington Press.

A NOTE ON THE ILLUSTRATIONS

Although the number of structures discussed in these pages is so large as to preclude their all being illustrated, I have tried to include a wide variety of photographic illustrations of the buildings and landscapes dealt with in the text. When possible, I have tried to use the images by distinguished American photographers that constituted the exhibit on which this book might be viewed as an extended commentary, and hope that the viewer will take the opportunity to reflect upon the varied interpretations of these structures that their images reflect. Some are sharply focused and detailed, drawing the eye to the design itself. Others are idealized, representing the buildings and sometimes their surrounding landscapes as icons of the American and/or religious experience. Some capture the buildings in their social context, depicting them as players in the bustling life of a modern city. Still others are tinged with humor or irony, reflecting on the contrast between the real and the ideal. I have also included a number of interior shots to give a sense of the way in which these buildings accommodate the worship patterns of their respective traditions and congregations.

My sources in drawing together these images have been diverse. In many cases, I have utilized the vast collection of the Historic American Building Survey Series at the Library of Congress. Still others have been furnished through the generosity of the congregations of the houses of worship themselves, as well as by an array of professional photographers, libraries, archives, and historical societies. My thanks to all who have made these images available; they are enumerated more fully in the Photographic Credits section.

Houses of God

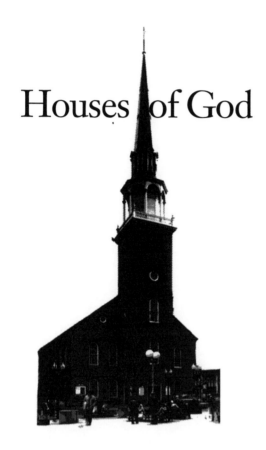

1 : New England

In November of 1942, the meetinghouse at Groton, Massachusetts, was pictured on the cover of *Life* magazine, in conjunction with a photo essay entitled "The Puritan Spirit." Two years later, for the 1944 Thanksgiving issue, *Life* again featured a similar though somewhat more ornate meetinghouse, this one located not in New England but rather in the suburbs of Akron, Ohio (see figure 1). These traditional houses of worship and their transformation here into icons of American democracy are good starting points for an examination of the development of religious architecture in the regional culture of New England.

An appropriate beginning theme is the disentangling of the character of Puritanism in the colonial New England of history from the web of mythology that grew up around it during the two centuries that have ensued since its demise as a coherent religious force. The disestablishment of the Congregational churches in Massachusetts in 1833 was the final legal blow to the intricate alliance of religion and society that was essential to the Puritan experiment as it had developed distinctively in New England. Since then, the Puritans had been hailed by their filiopietistic descendants as well as progressive-minded historians as forerunners of a democracy with its remote origins in medieval German forests and its more proximate beginnings in Calvin's Geneva and the town meetings of New England. Others, such as the acerbic Baltimore journalist H. L.

Mencken and the literary historian Vernon Louis Parrington, had by the 1920s begun to deride the Puritans as repressed bigots who had begotten the prohibitionists and book censors they saw as blights on the contemporary American cultural landscape.

The 1942 *Life* article evokes both sides of this tradition of historically innocent representation. Although mindful of the violence against the aboriginal peoples committed by the early British arrivals on New England soil, the text of the essay focused primarily on the role of the Puritans as progenitors of the major themes of American culture. "Eventually the Puritan dies out," wrote the anonymous author of the brief text accompanying the illustrations,

> and a new, all-American type – the Yankee – took over New England. But the Puritan Spirit lived on and expanded and has always been a pervading influence in American life and in the individual American conscience. It was with the Minute Men at Lexington and Bunker Hill. It rode with the pioneers across the mountains to settle new lands in Ohio and Michigan and Illinois and Kansas. The Puritan Spirit was with John Brown at Harpers Ferry, and again it was with Marcus and Narcissa Whitman when those New England [Methodist] martyr-missionaries founded their school in the State of Washington, and were murdered by the Indians they wished to teach. It speaks from the pulpits and hearts of Americans today; the official statements of American leaders are filled with it. [Episcopalian] President Roosevelt might have been speaking for the Puritan Fathers on this page when he closed his first radio address of the war, on Dec. 9, 1941, with the words that our cause and our hope were for "liberty under God." (*Life*, 13, no. 21 [Nov. 3, 1942], 74ff.)

What follows these inspirational words during wartime are several pages of reproductions of nineteenth-century artistic interpretations of early New England, from the sentimental "Embarkation of the Pilgrims from Southampton" by Edward Moran to Thomas Satterwhite Noble's romanticized and in fact rather misleading "The Salem Martyr," in which an innocent-looking young woman, hands bound before her, is led to the gallows by a stern-looking hangman accompanied by a group of smug Puritan elders. (Most of the twenty executed at Salem as witches were older women; the appeal of the maiden in jeopardy, however, presumably had more cultural resonance, as it still does in the formulas of made-for-television features.) At the article's close, striking contemporary photographs evoke the lasting Puritan legacy of hard work and prosperity, schools and learning, and, of course, religion. Last among them is a chiaroscuro image of some of the Puritan gravestones whose carvings have generated a veritable cottage industry of reproduction, display, and interpretation by later generations of Americans.

The iconic character which some of the surviving artifacts of New England culture have acquired in more recent times is part of the broader colonial revival that took place during the 1920s and 1930s. This revival was a more sweeping version of an earlier wave of enthusiasm for matters colonial that had arisen in the late 1800s, and took on a new significance during the wartime years of the early 1940s. After many decades of neglect as putative products of a primitive epoch, New England's buildings, furniture, and grave markings began to be re-

habilitated in the American imagination through a variety of means. The Congregationalist minister-turned-photographer Wallace Nutting began during the
1920s to produce a series of books following a standard format, with the title
Connecticut [or some other state] Beautiful. These were highly romanticized inter-
weavings of text and pictures, the latter consisting of photographs carefully staged
by Nutting and sometimes featuring young female models in period costume.
The static, posed quality of his work was taken up in following decades by Samuel Chamberlain, who turned out a lengthy series of photographic studies, including many meetinghouses, with titles ranging from *Beyond New England
Thresholds* to *The Yale Scene*. The atmospheric, sometimes tinted photographs of
both, redolent with the play of light and shade, transformed their subjects into
iconic reflections of a vanished age – an age which could, however, be reevoked
through a tasteful acquisition of historic objects, a process which considerably
enriched the entrepreneurial antique-dealing Nutting (Robinson 1980, 172–75
and 192–94; Nutting is represented in his photograph "The Old Dutch Church,"
which accompanies the text of chap. 2).

Other aspects of the colonial revival were the Cape Cod–style houses that
proliferated throughout the country during the wave of suburban building that
followed World War I; the Massachusetts Bay tercentenary, the celebration of
which in 1930 resulted in the erection of numerous historical markers around
the Bay State and generated considerable interest in America's past as the object
of tourism; Harvard's own tercentenary six years later, which generated historical and institutional enthusiasm among its far-flung influential alumni; and, in
another cultural region, the restoration of Colonial Williamsburg through the
impetus of a local Episcopal priest and massive infusions of Rockefeller family
funding. The latter would subsequently provide a model for similar postwar "living museums" in New England such as Plimouth Plantation, Old Sturbridge
Village, and Mystic Seaport (Kammen 1991, chap. 11 and passim).

However interesting the rediscovery and renovation of houses, barns, and
gravestones might be, the meetinghouse holds particular interest for us as the
epitome of New England's earliest European-derived religious culture. The
images on the wartime *Life* covers, chosen for their presumed inspirational resonance for Americans of all regions, religious persuasions, and ethnic origins,
continue to reverberate through the popular culture, appearing frequently today – usually in crisp color – on calendars, tourist posters, postcards, and souvenir photographic books, now valued perhaps as much for their picturesque and
nostalgic quality as for their implicit religious content. Whatever their contemporary uses, these meetinghouses tell a story about a past very different from the
present-day landscape they continue to adorn and to which they continue to draw
tourists.

THE PURITAN MEETINGHOUSE

One of the first things to note about the meetinghouses on the 1940s *Life*
covers is their siting in both time and space. Temporally, they come closer to

the end of a tradition of building than to its beginnings. Dating respectively from 1755 and 1825, the buildings, with their neoclassical features, bear little resemblance to their earliest predecessors, now represented by Hingham's "Old Ship" meetinghouse alone. Geographically, they are a mixed bag. While Groton, Massachusetts, the site of the earlier structure, is in the heart of Puritan country, the 1825 building reposes in the suburbs of Akron, Ohio, a city associated with heavy industry and immigration from eastern Europe during the late nineteenth century.

The answer to this apparent enigma lies in the character of the early settlement of northeastern Ohio. Set aside by the federal government as Connecticut's "firelands" – that is, compensation for losses suffered from malicious damage carried out by the British during the Revolution – this segment of the Old Northwest was originally colonized by Nutmeg State emigrants, one of whom designed for them a meetinghouse that would have passed muster as eminently fashionable in his home state. This westward movement was part of the "Yankee Exodus" that took place in the late eighteenth and especially the early nineteenth centuries, when New Englanders by the tens of thousands fled the impoverished soil of their native region for the more fertile regions first of upstate New York, then of the extensive territory further west that was opened by the government for settlement on highly attractive terms. These New England–style churches, accompanied by Greek revival homes and place names derived from identifiably New England families (e.g., Cleveland, a corruption of the name of Connecticut settler Moses Cleaveland) or locales, are characteristic of the band of territory that bounds I-80 on either side for some distance; eventually, it trails off into lands settled from Virginia and Pennsylvania to the south and wooded, infertile upland only thinly populated by later immigrants in the north.

These particular meetinghouses also raise some other issues illustrating the complications emerging from a building's existence over several decades or even centuries. First, though both were raised as houses of worship in the New England Calvinist tradition, neither is now affiliated with a denomination even close to Puritan Calvinism in its theology. The Groton congregation long ago joined with the large majority of the Congregational churches in eastern Massachusetts in espousing the Unitarian cause, which emerged amidst the Congregationalists during the decades following the Revolution and, by the time of the disestablishment of Congregationalism in 1833, had established itself as a separate and distinctly liberal denomination. Though Unitarianism took its name from its unorthodox rejection of the doctrine of the Trinity, its repudiation of the notion of predestination, a particular hallmark of Calvinist theology, was really more central to its new vision of humanity and its relationship with a benevolent deity. The Ohio congregation, on the other hand, is now affiliated with the United Church of Christ, a group almost as liberal as the Unitarians in many ways, which resulted from a merger of the Trinitarian Congregationalists and the German-American Evangelical and Reformed Church in 1957. The physical shells remain, as do, perhaps, some descendants of the stock of the Puritan; the content of preaching, however, has radically changed in the intervening decades.

Still another factor to take into account when "reading" these buildings is stylistic change. While the Tallmadge, Ohio, church remains roughly the same as
always, a viewer with even a modicum of knowledge of architectural history will
experience severe cognitive dissonance when comparing the 1942 *Life* cover with
the information contained within, that is, the brief paragraph giving a 1755 date
for the building. The triangular pediment and the Doric columns and pilasters
of the Groton meetinghouse can only be read as Greek revival, a style that would
not be incorporated as an essential part of the vernacular architectural repertory
of Americans until the 1830s.

The resolution of this conundrum is not surprising: like many colonial or early
nineteenth-century houses of worship, that at Groton was both remodeled and
moved in 1839. Originally, it had been of a piece stylistically with its contemporaries; entry was through a porch on one of the long sides, and a narrow tower
with steeple and spire adjoined it at a short end. The radical face-lifting it later
underwent brought it into harmony with the high style of its time, for better or
worse. It was also split into two levels, the lower of which was used as a town hall
for some time, and its interior was subsequently altered yet again in 1877 and
1916. Many other meetinghouses received stained glass windows during the
Victorian era, an anachronistic touch later repented of by many congregations
who in the later twentieth century restored them to something resembling their
original appearance (Sinnott 1963, 166–67).

The very name of these buildings, which we have strenuously been calling
"meetinghouses" till this point, is yet another, and extremely important, key to
understanding their character. The term "meetinghouse" (also written as two
words or with a hyphen) persisted as standard usage into the nineteenth century, when it was gradually replaced by the more familiar "church." Originally,
however, it was carefully chosen by the English Puritans as a deliberate alternative to the older term, which to them implied that the building itself possessed a
sacred character, that it was somehow the place in which the deity was present.
The Puritans, who held to the Calvinist notion of the Real Presence in the Eucharist while denying the traditional Roman Catholic teaching of transubstanti-
ation, nevertheless regarded the preached Word as the chief point of intersection between the sacred and secular realms. This intersection conferred no sacral
character on its sheltering environs and in turn required no special setting for
its performance (Turner 1979, 227–30; Zimmerman 1979, 124–25).

Given this theology, and a more generalized detestation of the Church of
England as morally corrupt and too closely attached to "Popish" (Roman Catholic) ways, the first European New Englanders set out consciously to devise a
housing for their worship that could not be regarded as itself a holy place. Re-
jecting both parish church and cathedral as prototypes, they turned instead to
secular places of public assembly such as the late medieval guildhalls of their
ancestral land as models for places of religious gathering. (The Hellenistic Jewish adoption of the Greek synagogue and the post-Constantinian Christian appropriation of the Roman basilica provide practical though not ideological parallels.) The term "meetinghouse" implied a neutral public space, where "church"

had conveyed a notion of intentional sacrality reinforced by the rites of conse-
cration through which a Roman or Anglican church came to possess its distinctive identity. (Marian Card Donnelly advanced the idea that the New England
meetinghouses were based on market or guild hall prototypes in *New England
Meetinghouses*, chap. 6. This argument is not universally accepted by scholars
today.)

The predecessors of the New England Puritans in Zwingli's Zurich and
Calvin's Geneva generally had made do with the conversion of older Catholic
structures into halls appropriate for preaching by iconoclastically removing all
artwork – banned by Calvin on Old Testament grounds as idolatrous – and replacing altars with pulpits as the central fixture for worship. In Britain, the Puritans gained what was to prove a short-lived ascendancy only several decades after the New England "holy commonwealths" had begun; here, Calvinistic
dissenters under Elizabeth and the early Stuarts had to meet more covertly, utilizing whatever domestic buildings they might appropriate for the purpose. In
New England, however, organized opposition was lacking, and the aboriginal
inhabitants had been reduced by something like 90 percent from their precolo-
nial number by an epidemic of unknown character that had preceded the land-
ing of the "Pilgrims" at Plymouth Rock by a few years. Since these Algonkians
had led seminomadic existences, the British newcomers quite literally had the
opportunity to build from the ground up (Turner 1979, 206ff.).

The result was a new architectural creation – the meetinghouse – which was
to lead a short but exemplary existence as the center of Puritan communal religious life. Like their Catholic and Anglican nemeses, the New England Puritans
had little use for dissent, and sent their theological challengers, such as the in-
trepid Quakers who made occasional forays into Massachusetts, off packing with
a whipping or worse. The religious monopoly implicit in the notion of the Puritan church-state or "Holy Commonwealth" continued until toleration was ultimately imposed upon them decades later by an unamused new regime in Britain in the wake of the Glorious Revolution. In the intervening decades, the
meetinghouse stood unchallenged as the physical symbol of Anglo-Calvinist
religious hegemony.

The meetinghouse was the physical focus of a religious culture in which church
and state, though formally separate, nevertheless collaborated in the proclamation and enforcement of God's Word, as revealed in Scripture, as the basis for
civil and divine law alike. It was erected when possible at the center of the town,
often on an elevated site, for both symbolic reasons of social centrality and practical considerations of access. (What was originally the meetinghouse's lot later
metamorphosed into the greens or commons that became such a picturesque
characteristic of the nineteenth-century New England town.) Attendance at
worship was compulsory for saint and reprobate alike, and the latter was pun-
ished by the secular arm for failure to carry out such weekly obligations. Lengthy
worship services were held twice on the Sabbath – the Hebraized Puritan term
for Sunday, or the Lord's Day – as well as on Wednesday evenings. The sermon –
the public proclamation and exposition of God's revealed Word – was the focus

of this extended public worship (Winslow 1952, 1; Sinnott 1963, 10; Donnelly 1968, 16).

The structure and appearance of the seventeenth-century meetinghouse were designed positively to accommodate the specific character of Calvinist worship and negatively to avoid as far as possible the sacral character of Anglican and Roman practice. Where the church, or cathedral, thrust its spires upward toward the heavens, the meetinghouse was horizontal in its lines. One entered the church through one of its short ends – traditionally the west, since the church was "oriented" so that the altar would lie at the east end, the legendary direction of Christ's second appearance. Access to the meetinghouse, on the other hand, came through one of the long sides. Where the church and, especially, the cathedral – the seat of the bishop, whose office had been rejected by the Puritans as unscriptural – was monumental in scale, the meetinghouse was domestic. With its hipped roof and unornamented plain wooden construction, it was deliberately designed to resemble nothing so much as a good-sized house (Pierson 1970, 55).

Upon entering the meetinghouse, the worshiper was confronted not with the altar upon which Jesus's sacrifice was to be reenacted but rather with a massive central pulpit from which the Word of God was to be lengthily proclaimed. This was often surmounted by a sounding board, which augmented the acoustical properties of the sermon while simultaneously accentuating the pulpit's visual prominence. Communion, administered monthly, was celebrated in early years with domestic cups and plates from a kitchen-style table or a dropleaf board affixed to a wall for the purpose. (In later decades, vessels of high quality would be used instead.) Neither, obviously, was intended to attract much attention. Sermons, the buildings for their delivery, and the vessels for communion were all intended to emphasize the message rather than to call attention to its medium, thus exemplifying the Puritan aesthetic: "the plain style." With the passage of time and the coming of prosperity, however, the "plainness" of the plain style persisted only in the absence of iconography, while the quality of materials and workmanship increased dramatically in wealthy congregations (Benes and Zimmerman 1979, 35–44 and 83ff.; Garvan 1960; Zimmerman 1979, 132; James F. White has, in an as yet unpublished discourse, challenged the use of the term "plain style" on the grounds that later colonial meetinghouse furnishings were quite ornate, though never representational).

Seating within the meetinghouse was not in the "slip pews" familiar to modern worshipers. Originally it was on wooden benches, which in the eighteenth century were superseded by square or box pews which enclosed an entire family within their hinged doors. The arrangement of the pews, which were sold or leased to families on the basis of social standing assigned by a municipal committee appointed for the purpose, reflected neither piety nor wealth in isolation but rather a more complex notion of collective prestige. (A similar system determined class ranking at Harvard College, which had been founded by the Massachusetts Bay Puritans in 1636 as a vehicle for educating an indigenous clerical and political elite.) The system of pew rent or sale was shared by the Puritans' Anglican counterparts in the South, and its abolition was not completed in some places until well into the twentieth century. In the galleries, or balconies, which spanned all sides but that of the pulpit, young men and maidens faced one another across the building's main expanse, while Indians, black slaves, paupers, and others who did not fit into the categories of respectable Christian society were relegated to a separate section (Benes and Zimmerman 1979, 55–56).

The meetinghouses of the seventeenth century are largely preserved only in engravings. The sole surviving example of the genre is the Old Ship meetinghouse at Hingham, Massachusetts, on Boston's South Shore, built by Puritans in 1681 but now sheltering the liberal Unitarianism which most eastern Massachusetts congregations had embraced by the early nineteenth century (see figure 2). "Old Ship" acquired its familiar name through a fancied resemblance of its interior to that of a ship's hold. Though altered and added to in subsequent years, it still exemplifies the iconoclastic style and pulpit focus of its dozens of now vanished contemporaries (Pierson 1970, 55–58; Sinnott 1963, 33–35).

FROM MEETINGHOUSE TO CHURCH

During the eighteenth century, a kind of architectural dance took place between New England's Puritan Congregationalists and the Anglican church they had reviled and abandoned in coming to the New World. By the early 1700s, an Anglican presence in Boston had been assured through the imposition of a royal governor who by definition had to be loyal to the established church of the mother country. The result was, among other things, the erection in Boston in 1723 of Christ Church – better known as the "Old North Church" of Paul Revere legend (see figure 3).

Christ Church still serves a functioning Episcopal parish not too far from Paul Revere's house in the now heavily Italian North End of Boston, but represented in its heyday both a religious and an architectural challenge to New England Puritanism. In some ways, such as its galleries, box pews, and prominent pulpit with sounding board, it shared with the Puritans a common structural language of worship. On the other hand, Christ Church is clearly a *church*, with an altar situated in a small recessed apse at the center of the church's east end and fenced off from the congregation with a rail. Though eighteenth-century Anglicanism may have shared some of Calvinism's theological emphases, especially in the southern colonies, its arena for worship focused on the celebration of the sacraments – baptism and the Eucharist – as well as the preaching of the Word (Pierson 1970, 98–100).

Aesthetically, Christ Church contained a challenge as well. Although remarkably simple and even awkward in contrast with its high-style London contemporaries, it nevertheless represented an elegance that had hitherto been anathema to devotees of the plain style. The contrast between Old Ship and Old North is most vivid in a comparison of the facades. Where Old Ship was deliberately made to resemble a large two-story house, Christ Church is fronted by a four-staged brick tower capped by a steeple composed of belfry and lantern and, finally, a graceful spire topped by a weather vane. This visually complex upward thrust is a principal feature of the neoclassicism exemplified in the London churches of the great Sir Christopher Wren, who was commissioned to rebuild literally from the ground up the city's ecclesiastical fabric after the Great Fire of 1666. With the elaborations of Wren's successor, James Gibbs, whose designs were printed in the 1720s and widely circulated in the colonies, the "Wren-Gibbs style" set for generations the tone of "high style" church building in England and its transatlantic colonies (Pierson 1970, 68–69 and 131–34).

Boston's Puritans were perhaps understandably ambivalent about these developments. After decades of more or less benign neglect, the British presence represented an unwelcome intrusion into colonial affairs, and set in motion grievances that would eventually culminate in a successful revolution. The unified religious culture they had fashioned, far from England's censorious eye, was now being challenged on its own grounds by a new style which, while theologically highly incorrect, made Boston's old-style meetinghouses look downright dowdy. As the saying has it, the Puritans came to do good, and many wound up doing very well indeed in the prosperous trade that involved New England commercially with the mother country as well as with Africa and the West Indies. Though Christ Church would have appeared almost laughably provincial in sophisticated London circles, it stood for a previously unknown elegance in faraway Boston. The exact motives for the resultant changes in New England religious architecture can never be known with any certainty, but a growing cosmopolitanism among an increasingly worldly and status-conscious urban elite cannot be discounted. Nor was Anglicanism the only influence; the Brattle Street church of 1699 had already boasted a tower and spire (Kennedy 1989).

An enduring example of the resultant change in fashion precipitated by the advent of Old North was the appearance in Boston six years later of the Old South Meetinghouse. Old South, now preserved as a museum years after its congregation fled the downtown for Copley Square in the Victorian era, is an early example of the second phase of meetinghouse design that dominated New England building till after the Revolution (see figure 4). At a very casual glance, Old South follows the general contours of Old North: a rectangular building with a pitched roof and a tower, steeple, and spire at one end. Closer examination, however, reveals some important differences. The main entry is not through the short tower side but rather one of the long sides, as was the custom in the preceding century. Entering the main door, the viewer confronts a dominant central pulpit, again as in the old style. Old South, in short, is still very much a meetinghouse, though the attached tower gives it the outward contours of a Wren-style church. Clearly, a process of cultural transition and ambivalence is being expressed here visually (Pierson 1970, 102–5; Sinnott 1963, 43–46).

The eighteenth century saw both the proliferation of the new meetinghouse style and an unfolding religious pluralism spurred by the excitements generated by the Great Awakening, the revivals of the 1740s led by Jonathan Edwards, George Whitefield, and other, considerably less well credentialed preachers of all sorts and conditions. Splits in congregations were frequent, with Awakening proponents often raising a meetinghouse of their own. By the time of the similar New Light Stir of the 1770s and 1780s, New England saw not only Congregationalists and Anglicans – still the elite – but a wide variety of popular groups such as Free Will Baptists, Universalists, Friends (Quakers), Shakers, Methodists, and adherents of smaller, evanescent sects contending for the allegiance especially of those in the newly settled and still culturally volatile areas of the north and west. All of these groups erected their own vernacular variations on the basic meetinghouse theme; some, like Providence's substantial Baptist community, had become sufficiently sophisticated to erect a handsome structure in the style of James Gibbs in the proximity of their own Brown University in 1774 (see figure 5; Pierson 1970, 136–39).

For all its flourishing and diversity during the colonial era, the New England meetinghouse did not reach the form that would later attain iconic status in the American pictorial repertory till after the turn of the nineteenth century. It was then that the Federal style, the American counterpart of the neoclassical refined elegance popularized by the Adam brothers in Britain, was the basis for still another transformation of the religious built environment of New England. The time was right for a new wave of building, following the Revolution and an ensuing depression. The ecclesiastical building trade was also promoted by the schism in Massachusetts between conservative Congregationalists and liberal proto-Unitarians, in which the latter usually wound up in the majority and therefore claimed the local meetinghouse as their own. Their displaced opponents set up new places for worship, generally in the style of the times. Congregations untroubled by dissent hurried to keep up with fashion; many in smaller towns unable to afford an entirely new structure renovated the old, often in curious and retrospectively not very satisfactory ways.

The meetinghouse of the Federal era was no longer a meetinghouse in name or form. Gradually the term began to fall into disuse, as did Puritan itself, which yielded to Congregational(-ist). The churches of this new time continued in the neoclassical Wren-Gibbs tradition, but differed in their degree of ornamentation, as well as in a number of other, less important particulars. Typical of these new churches was a porch or portico, often of considerable scale, which featured columns in one of the classical orders. Rising above this, though partially perched on the roof of the main part of the building, was a multistaged steeple, with a belfry, a clock (at times), a lantern, and an open or closed colonnaded area in different combinations, all richly ornamented with columns or pilasters, urns, and other classical motifs (Pierson 1970, 235–39).

The typical Federal-era Congregational church interior was similar in some ways to the basic plan of its predecessors, with a central pulpit emphasizing the importance of the preached word. However, access to the central auditorium space was now through the porch or portico at the opposing short end, rather than the traditional (in New England) entry through a long side. Though still a space designed primarily for preaching, and lacking the visual arts that the Puritans had banished when they had rejected the iconography of medieval Catholicism as idolatrous, these churches now radiated an elegance that their prede-

cessors had never known, which in the colonial period had been more associated with the pretensions of Anglicanism.

Instrumental music in the form of an organ – once also shunned as popish –
now became de rigueur for the fashionable Yankee, as an accompaniment to hymn
singing or for solo performances. Other interior elaborations, such as a finely
carved mahogany pulpit with lavish hangings, undermined in practice the Puritan ideal of unpretentious iconoclasm. Today's familiar slip pews gradually displaced the older square box pews that had isolated families and categorized them
according to rank and wealth. Finally, by the Victorian era, stained glass windows
and Gothic pointed arches were often added to create an aesthetic hodgepodge
with little discernible theological or liturgical rationale (Benes and Zimmerman
1979, 101–6; Nylander 1979).

A good illustration of these changes, which reflected the growing cult of genteel manners and aesthetic refinement among the middle classes, can be found
in the heart of present-day New Haven, Connecticut, on the town green that
adjoins the Victorian Yale campus on one side and faces an array of governmental and commercial structures of a variety of styles and periods on the others. Here
three churches, all built during the second decade of the nineteenth century,
coexist harmoniously, in an aesthetic as well as an ecumenical manner. One of
these, Trinity Episcopal, is an early example of the Gothic revival in American
architecture, and also represents the accepted status that Anglicanism had by now
attained in once Puritan Connecticut.

United and Center (First) Churches, however, are both Congregational in
background, and today both are affiliated with the United Church of Christ. Built
at virtually the same time, the two are both substantial brick urban churches
reflecting a once-prosperous and now sadly numerically diminished constituency. (Center Church is supported mainly today by a substantial endowment rather than its elderly and dwindling membership.) The seeming redundancy of two
denominationally identical churches side by side stems from the split of the congregations in the aftermath of the Great Awakening, a physical illustration of the
difficulty of healing a communal break even after the original issues have long
since been forgotten – as they had by and large been even at the time the two
current structures were erected.

The two are both clearly neoclassical in inspiration, though differing considerably in detail. The taller Center Church, more Georgian than Federal in inspiration, is the more imposing of the two, and the elaborate ornamentation of
its frieze, pediment, and steeple provide a striking visual contrast with its more
restrained but nonetheless elegant neighbor (see figure 6). The interiors are remarkably similar, though Center Church retains a Victorian-era Tiffany stained
glass window behind its pulpit illustrating the founding of New Haven by John
Davenport, who had provided the biblically inspired nine-square grid plan that
still serves as New Haven's fundamental spatial model (Pierson 1970, 235, 238;
Brown 1965).

Center Church is also interesting in the presence of a crypt underneath, which
still contains over a hundred grave markers from the burying ground that orig-

inally lay on its site. At the time of the construction of these churches, a controversial communal decision had been made to remove these markers, which had been placed rather haphazardly around the older churchyard in typical Puritan fashion, to the newly opened Grove Street Cemetery a few blocks away. Only those directly under the new church were preserved, though no bones were disturbed; the remainder were allowed to lie unmarked. This removal of the last visible evidence of the presence of these dead was part of a broader program of what might now be called the "gentrification" of the Green, in which burial of the dead and pasturage of livestock – part of the round of normal activity of a colonial village – would now yield to an urban desire for a genteel townscape (Brown 1965, 14).

Grove Street, which acquired an imposing Egyptian revival gateway designed by local architect Henry Austin in 1845, was a forerunner of the "rural cemetery" movement best exemplified in Mount Auburn in Cambridge, Massachusetts. (Old Granary burying ground, across Park Street from Boston's King's Chapel, boasts a similar entryway; the Egyptian revival was largely restricted to cemeteries, prisons, and medical schools, and only a handful of churches echo its monumental lines.) Reflecting the Romantic sensibilities of the age, the rural cemetery was landscaped to take away the sting of death represented in the chaos of the Puritan burying ground, and replace the ancient clutter with a soothing parklike environment as conducive to picnicking as to contemplating the ravages of death and the wrath of an unforgiving God (Linden-Ward, 1989; Brown 1976, 128).

The center of New Haven thus became an American "high style" version of a transformation of the landscape later enshrined in the iconography of nostalgia represented on the wartime *Life* covers. The picture postcard white frame meetinghouse on the neatly kept village green was the New England of John Quincy Adams, not that of Cotton Mather. Even the whiteness of the meetinghouses was new; the reds, browns, and yellows of an earlier time had yielded to the uniformity of taste of another cultural era. George Tice's 1963 photograph, "Village of East Corinth, Vermont," illustrates nicely the iconic role which the meetinghouse on the green has assumed in the American pictorial vocabulary (see figure 7).

NINETEENTH-CENTURY CONGREGATIONALISM

The penultimate phase of the meetinghouse's development began in the late 1820s, and reached its heyday during the ensuing two decades. The Greek revival, a much simpler mode than its Federal predecessor, featured a portico of imposing and largely unornamented Doric columns with a similarly plain pediment above. Its inspiration was nothing from Christian history but rather derived from the "pagan" temples of Hellenic antiquity, of which it was a modern-day appropriation. Many, if not most, of these meetinghouses were capped with a steeple, which rests on the body of the church itself rather than extending partly over the portico in the Federal mode. That on the town green in Madison, Con-

necticut (ca. 1838), which still shelters an active parish of the United Church of
Christ, is a particularly elegant example (see figure 8; Sinnott 1963, 26, 136; Pierson 1970, 440–41).

The Greek revival style, with its associations of a democratic polity, manifested itself across all lines of function and denomination. Greek revival buildings housed almost every form of activity, from countless houses with columned and pedimented porches to Boston's Fanueil Hall Marketplace. In the religious realm, the Swedenborgian Church in Bath, Maine (1843), is a steepleless representative, as is the Episcopal Cathedral Church of Saint Paul in Boston (designed in 1820 by Alexander Parris, also the architect of Fanueil Hall Marketplace [Myers 1974, 81–83; Southworth and Southworth 1987, 11–12]).

The meetinghouse style manifested itself occasionally during the Colonial revival of the twentieth century, in such consciously historicizing buildings as Harvard Yard's Memorial Church of 1931. The tenuous final phase – or, perhaps, last gasp – of its organic evolution as a style indigenous to New England was a sort of footnote to the Gothic revival of the 1840s. Richard Upjohn, the English immigrant architect and genius of the movement, was a committed Anglican who began his American career in Boston but soon moved to New York City. Upjohn's best-known work – particularly his Trinity Church on Wall Street of 1839–46 – is located in New York and other mid-Atlantic states, and was primarily designed for his fellow Episcopalians.

Upjohn's influence, however, was confined neither by region nor denomination. His plans, many of which he supplied gratis to poor parishes, were carried out through much of what was then the nation. Other denominations were eager to emulate the new fashion, which in its more vernacular form came to be known as "Carpenter Gothic." A good example of the countless churches either designed by Upjohn or inspired by his plans is Saint Paul's Episcopal in Lancaster, New Hampshire, built in 1875–76 by an unknown designer. This 1936 photograph by Arthur Rothstein highlights the powerful aesthetic effect of the style's vertical elements (see figure 9; Tolles 1979, 325–26).

Upjohn himself did important work in New England, especially in the college town of Brunswick, Maine. One of his three fine churches there was the chapel (1845–55) he designed for Congregationalist Bowdoin College in the *Rundbogenstil* (literally, "round arch style"), the version of the Romanesque revival then popular in Germany and imported by visiting American architects. Another was nearby Saint Paul's Episcopal Church (1845), a small, handsome parish church in which Gothic detailing such as pointed-arch windows was executed in wood rather than stone. The entire structure is given a distinctive, Gothic-like verticality through the board-and-batten method of construction, in which wider vertical boards were joined together by alternating thin wooden strips ("battens") (Myers 1974, 111–12; Anderson 1988, 23–28).

Upjohn's regional masterpiece, however, was Brunswick's First Congregational Church of 1845–46 (see figure 10), in which today a marker designates the spot in which Harriet Beecher Stowe was seated when she experienced a vision of the death of Uncle Tom. In the past, Congregationalists and Episcopalians had kept their distance on stylistic grounds, with the former attracted by the elegance and exoticism of such early Gothic examples as New Haven's Trinity Church on the Green but still repelled by their "popish" associations. By the 1840s, however, the Romantic vogue of love for the exotic and the picturesque, popularized by writers such as Andrew Jackson Downing, had sufficiently domesticated the Gothic for proper Protestant usage.

Upjohn's First Church was liturgically a meetinghouse rather than a sacramental church, with a prominent stage and pulpit in the visual center and with no evidence of popery in the form of saints' statues or pictures. The exterior continued what had become the meetinghouse tradition in its frontal tower and white wooden construction, but the departures were obvious. A transept, unknown in the tradition previously, gave the structure a cruciform shape, and pointed-arch lancet windows and pinnacles arising from the corners of nave, transept, and tower all bespoke the fact that something strange and perhaps wonderful was at hand. Though lacking in specific iconography, the interior has been gothicized by the elaborate maze of open trusswork that at once supports the roof and provides the eye with an endless play of form, reminiscent of the Hampton Court palace of the early Tudors (Pierson 1978, 433–45).

Other Gothic revival Protestant churches would be built in New England towns, and even more meetinghouses would be haphazardly gothicized in the wildly eclectic fashion typical of the Victorian era. The Gothic revival, however, was clearly more appropriate to Episcopalians (and, of course, Roman Catholics), whose architectural and liturgical heritage embraced churches in this style. The medieval revivals – Romanesque and, in a later phase, Gothic – would return to New England later in the century in a more urban context, where they would result in masterpieces such as Boston's Trinity and New Haven's Christ Church.

POPULAR PROTESTANTISM IN NEW ENGLAND

The meetinghouse, though known elsewhere, was without question the dominant and distinctive architectural form of colonial and antebellum New England. Quakers, as already noted, utilized a version of the form adapted to their own distinctive theology and worship; the "culture hearth" of their society, however, was in the Philadelphia area, and their meetinghouses had best be examined in that context, since the New England versions offered little of novelty beyond the basic pattern. The non-Calvinistic popular denominations that arose in the region in the post-Revolutionary era, such as the Universalists and Methodists, similarly offered little to distinguish themselves architecturally, and their places for worship were either refurbished buildings abandoned by the more elite denominations or adaptations of the "high styles" of the era, especially the Greek revival, into a vernacular mode.

One notable regional exception to this principle was the Methodist camp meeting, an institution with origins on the southern frontier which, by the early middle years of the nineteenth century, had been appropriated and domesticated by the Methodists. By the middle of the century these seasonal rural gatherings for song and prayer had taken on a life of their own; tents yielded to frame cottages and open-air torchlight worship to permanent tabernacles. Although examples of the camp meeting-turned-pious-vacation-community can be found throughout much of the eastern part of the country, from the Jersey shore to that of Lake Erie, one of the premier examples of this genre of built religious environment still exists on Martha's Vineyard, the island off the coast of Massachusetts once famous for whaling but now as an elite summer vacation enclave.

Wesleyan Grove, founded in 1835 and later incorporated, is still a visual wonder, consisting of several hundred colorful Victorian gingerbread single-family frame cottages arranged in a semicircle around a gigantic iron tabernacle constructed in 1879. Architectural historian Ellen Weiss argues that, in its inspiration of the adjacent planned community of Oak Bluffs, Wesleyan Grove provided a prototype for the Romantic secular suburb, an alternative middle-class dwelling space to the cities that were growing crowded with commerce and immigrants and perceived by those with the means to escape as both physically and spiritually insalubrious. The forest, portrayed by Nathaniel Hawthorne in his *Scarlet Letter* as the moral antithesis of the rigidly civilized Puritan commonwealth, was now, in domesticated form, offering a spiritual balm to post-Puritan Evangelical New England (Weiss 1987).

Another variation on the meetinghouse theme in popular religion found in New England as well as in other, scattered locales was its adaptation by the Shaker communities. The United Society of Believers in Christ's Second Appearance – better known as Shakers – began to flourish in the years following the Revolution with the coming of their founder, "Mother" Ann Lee, and a handful of her English followers. From an original settlement in Watervliet, New York, the Shakers spread as far south and west as Bowling Green, Kentucky. Their greatest strength in their heyday in the decades preceding the Civil War was in the northeastern states. Though they are now nearly extinct, their final outposts have been in New England, at Canterbury, New Hampshire, where the last surviving member died early in the 1990s, and in Sabbathday Lake, Maine, where a handful of believers still maintain a presence with the help of many sympathetic outsiders fascinated both with their lifestyle and their material culture.

The Shaker communities, which numbered around two dozen at the group's peak, were centrally planned by the sect's leadership and intended to be socially and economically self-sufficient. Dormitories were symmetrical, with separate but parallel entrances and quarters for men and women, reflecting the group's beliefs in both sexual equality and celibacy. Central to the communal life of each settlement was a meetinghouse, the only building to be painted white. Inside was a clear space flanked with benches for spectators, in which participants conducted the at times ecstatic dancing that begot their nickname of "Shakers." (An early example, here illustrated in an 1878 stereographic view, is the 1792 meetinghouse at Canterbury, New Hampshire, which features a gambrel roof, a row of dormers, symmetrical chimneys, and separate entrances for men and women [see figure 11].) Although Shaker design, in furniture and crafts as well as architecture, has become highly esteemed (and priced) in the antique market, their aesthetic was basically an extension and adaptation of the Puritan "plain style" and Yankee craftsmanship, in which austerity was promoted to the status of a religious and aesthetic virtue (Hayden 1976, chap. 4; see also Stein 1992).

CATHOLICISM AND ETHNIC DIVERSITY

The advent of the camp-meeting-as-suburb was an indirect token of the dramatic changes that New England was undergoing during the middle decades of the nineteenth century. The region's decline in prominence as an overseas trading center, hastened by the embargo and ensuing War of 1812, was compensated for in the following years by its emergence as the nation's premier center of manufacturing. The "dark satanic mills" of Lowell, Lawrence, and Holyoke were economic magnets for those young country people, especially women, whom the rocky land could not adequately support and who had not yet left for literally greener pastures to the west. The milltown soon became even more alluring to thousands upon thousands of immigrants, few of them Protestant, who were instrumental in the process of transforming New England, especially its southern tier, into a densely urban society and culture.

Many of these immigrants – Irish, French Canadians, Poles, Cape Verdeans, and Italians – were Roman Catholic by tradition. This faith had scarcely been represented at all in colonial New England, given the hostility toward "popery" that had been a driving force in Puritanism. The Irish, overwhelmingly poor and Catholic, began to arrive in vast numbers in the wake of the potato famine of the 1840s. Given the patterns of oceanic transportation then available to the poor, Boston proved to be one of the most accessible of North American cities for them, and their advent would transform the city's social, economic, and religious character within a few decades.

One of the earliest Roman Catholic structures in New England was one of its least typical. Boston's first bishop was not Irish, as most of his successors would be; rather he was the French émigré Jean Lefebvre de Cheverus, a genial and urbane man who rapidly charmed the city "establishment" with his grace, cultivation, and learning. In part as a result, John Adams and a host of other distinguished citizens subscribed generously to the building of Holy Cross Church (1800–1803) to provide Cheverus's flock with a place for worship other than the hand-me-down meetinghouse to which they had been forced to resort.

The design for Holy Cross Church was the work of Charles Bulfinch, the region's preeminent architect of the Federal period who would later distinguish himself with his meetinghouse at Lancaster. Holy Cross Church, demolished during the Civil War years, was a sort of jeu d'esprit on the architect's part, in which he fronted what was basically a meetinghouse with a Baroque facade topped with a small cupola. Though this particular building is unfortunately long gone, Bulfinch's work and the Catholic community would later intersect in the purchase

of his New North Church, a considerably more elaborate work, by the diocese
in 1862. Renamed Saint Stephen's and refurbished for Catholic worship, it continues in use as a North End parish with stations of the cross and other pious accoutrements that would have shocked the neighborhood's original residents beyond expression (Kirker 1969, 161–64, 168–72).

The subsequent history of Roman Catholic church architecture in New England reflects that of many immigrant communities. In the pre–Civil War decades, make-do was the rule, and Catholic worship was frequently held in buildings abandoned by various Protestant denominations. As the community grew in size, independent undertakings became possible. These new churches expressly designed for Roman use were often realized through the work of Patrick Keeley, a seemingly ubiquitous Irishman who is said to have designed over six hundred churches, mostly Catholic and many of them in New England. Preeminent among these is his Cathedral of the Holy Cross (1867–75) in Boston's South End. Gothic in style with twin square towers of unequal height, the cathedral sent a strong visual message that the Catholic community, hitherto scorned as illiterate "micks," was beginning to come of age as a civil presence to be reckoned with (Southworth and Southworth 1987, 324–35).

Although a variety of styles associated with the Catholic past were utilized in building the myriad of typically urban Catholic churches in New England and elsewhere in the northeastern quadrant of the nation during the latter half of the nineteenth century, the Gothic emerged as the preeminent Catholic mode. Since the Irish, who dominated the clergy and hierarchy nationally and especially regionally until well into the twentieth century, detested all things English and had little indigenous architectural tradition, continental versions of the style, especially the French, were most common. (Many Irish clergy had been trained at the seminary at Maynooth by French priests fleeing the Revolution.) Though few of these structures are memorable as individual examples of the Gothic revival, they collectively shape the skyline of New England's smaller cities, as a glance from the various interstate highways today will readily reveal.

The built environment of Roman Catholicism, however, did not stop with churches. As the tradition took root among the region's – and the nation's – immigrants, the church rapidly began to develop a vast institutional complex providing not only facilities for the celebration of the sacraments but also those for comprehensive educational and social services and the personnel to staff them. In an age when governmental functions were minimal and those maintained by other religious groups untouchable, the Catholic church attempted to create an infrastructure that would socialize and minister to its constituency especially at its most vulnerable stages – youth, illness, penury, and death.

Most of this complex was executed in the style of the Victorian "total institution," with convents, elementary and later secondary schools, shelters, and hospitals erected on a massive scale in some variant on the Italianate or Second Empire modes popular at the time. They were notable not so much for their architectural distinctiveness as their vast scale and scope, overwhelming neighborhoods such as the Boston suburb of Brighton. In many cases, convents, rectories, college buildings, and other residential and administrative structures were intended to project gentility more than utility, and mansions or estates of the wealthy were acquired through donation or purchase and converted to ecclesiastical use.

The Second Empire style John C. Anderson house (1882) in New Haven, Connecticut, is a good example of what was originally built as a luxurious dwelling being adapted into Saint Mary's Convent. Similarly, in adjoining Hamden, Albertus Magnus College's Rosary Hall, its central administration building, was designed as a private residence by the Boston firm of Peabody and Stearns in 1905. Eventually Catholic firms of prestige were to emerge; Boston College's English collegiate Gothic campus, for example, was the work of the eminent architects Maginnis and Walsh. Construction of the new Chestnut Hill campus commenced in 1909, ironically on an estate originally owned by the Yankee entrepreneur Amos A. Lawrence (Brown 1976, 149, 158; Tucci 1978, 76, 176).

Since World War II, the emergence of Roman Catholics into positions of political and social prominence, exemplified in the Kennedy family; the participation of many more Catholics in the suburbanization process; and the liturgical reforms long promoted by the Benedictine order and then mandated as normative by Vatican II have all resulted in a newer Roman Catholic architecture exemplary of broader contemporary trends in church building. The cathedrals at Hartford (1962) and Burlington (1977), both of which incorporate modern materials and the play of geometric shapes to achieve the traditional vertical thrust associated with the Gothic tradition, are good examples. An even better one is the chapel (1961) at Portsmouth Priory, a preparatory school staffed by Benedictine monks. Pietro Belluschi, the Italian architect whose reputation as a church designer was established primarily in the Pacific Northwest and in New Saint Mary's Cathedral in San Francisco, here superimposed one octagon upon another with a thin soaring spire rising from the center (Smith 1989, 14–15, 144–45, 158–59).

THE JEWISH PRESENCE

The Jewish presence in New England has followed a familiar demographic pattern since the Civil War years. An early, primarily German Jewish settlement in Boston's South End was soon swelled by the vast "New Immigration" of the late nineteenth and early twentieth centuries. These newcomers joined their predecessors, who had now largely moved to the immigrant-dominated North End. During the twentieth century, the growing and rapidly assimilating community migrated collectively first to the West End, then to the nearby enclaves of Dorchester and Roxbury, and, following World War II, to more prosperous suburbs such as Brookline. Similar movements took place in New Haven and other cities both within and far beyond the region. Synagogue architecture generally reflected styles developed in New York, Cincinnati, and other centers of Jewish settlement. As in the rest of the nation, Jewish patterns of residence in New England have been predominantly first urban and then suburban, with most of the region's population concentrated in the cities of the three southernmost states.

One major exception to this last generalization, however, needs mention.
Possibly as early as the 1650s, a group of Spanish- and Portuguese-speaking Sephardic Jews settled in Newport, Rhode Island, the kind of seaport town that attracted the mercantile talents for which these earliest Jewish settlers were noted. Joined by a number of their Ashkenazic (German-speaking) counterparts, this prosperous community was able by 1763 to erect the first Jewish house of worship in what would become the United States. The Touro Synagogue, as it has come to be known, was designed by Peter Harrison, often called America's first professional architect, who also planned Boston's King's Chapel (see figure 12).

The synagogue, which today functions both as a museum and a house of worship for an Orthodox congregation, resembles on the exterior nothing so much as the house of a prosperous merchant. This was in keeping with the general attitude of the colonial Sephardim, who did not particularly wish to call attention to their presence, even though anti-Semitic feeling in the colonies was negligible. The interior is an elegant combination of neoclassical forms adapted to the specific needs of Jewish worship: a platform (traditionally known as a bema) from which the Torah might be read and a framework for the Ark of the Covenant, in which the Torah scrolls were stored. Also typical of Orthodox practice was the seating of men on the ground level and the women in the gallery, a practice easily accommodated by traditional meetinghouse design. With the Anglican Trinity Church and the Quaker meetinghouse nearby, the Touro Synagogue stands as a still elegant testimony to the religious pluralism that prevailed in colonial Newport and alone in Rhode Island among the New England colonies (Smith 1989, 142–43; Pierson 1970, 147–48).

THEOLOGICAL INNOVATION

Roman Catholics, Jews, and, to a smaller degree, Eastern Orthodox swelled the ranks of the region's nineteenth-century population and contributed substantially to its religious diversity. Lutherans and Presbyterians, numerous in other regions, gained little foothold here due to patterns of population distribution and immigrant settlement. Among indigenous movements, Unitarians maintained considerable continuity with the Trinitarian Congregationalists from whom they formally split in 1825. They continued substantially their predecessors' polity, their style of worship, and their architecture, frequently in the parent denomination's own buildings, over which the liberals gained control after winning some decisive legal victories. With national headquarters at 25 Beacon Street in Boston, near Charles Bulfinch's gold-domed state house, the denomination still is deeply imbued with its regional origins, though its churches and fellowship groups outside of New England have developed a nontheistic identity and architectural expression of their own. The Universalists, a more rurally based liberal movement that also repudiated Calvinist predestination, continued in the meetinghouse tradition, adapting for their more vernacular uses the succession of styles popular in nineteenth-century church building, and eventually merged with the Unitarians to form the Unitarian Universalist Association (UUA) in 1961 (*Souvenir Portfolio* 1906).

Another, considerably more novel religious movement with solid New England origins was Christian Science, which Mary Baker Eddy "discovered" in the 1860s and expounded in a series of editions of her *Science and Health* beginning in 1875. Eddy, a native of Bow, New Hampshire, at first pursued her career as a preacher of religious healing precariously in a series of locales in the Boston area. By the latter decades of the century, however, she had attracted a significant following, especially among middle-class urban women who found little relief from their sufferings in the medical orthodoxy of the time. Even during her lifetime, Mrs. Eddy, as she was generally known, became the object of an almost cultlike devotion, and her various residences have been maintained as shrines by her devotees (Adams 1948).

The success of Christian Science found material expression most notably in the Mother Church, now a neighbor of Boston's towering Prudential Center (see figure 13). The original building (1893–94) was in the style of a Romanesque church with an adjoining square tower with a pyramidal cap. A decade later, however, it was overshadowed by a monumental Classical revival domed structure superficially reminiscent of Saint Peter's Basilica in Rome. Boasting "the largest pipe organ in the Western hemisphere," this "addition," as it was called by Scientists, has an interior designed as a gigantic auditorium capable of seating five thousand. Its twin reading desks on the central stage represent an adaptation of the auditorium church design popular among "mainline" Protestants of the era, but suited to distinctive Christian Science uses featuring pairs of male and female "readers" (Southworth and Southworth 1987, 295).

Christian Science churches throughout the region and beyond have generally taken the Mother Church as a prototype. Usually urban and often monumental in scale, they were built in the revival styles popular in the early twentieth century. (A good regional example is the church in Concord, New Hampshire, built by the Boston firm of Allen and Collens in 1903–4 in an eclectic mixture of Gothic and Romanesque revival styles.) Small Christian Science "reading rooms," a distinctive denominational institution, can be found regionally and beyond in downtown commercial districts and suburban shopping malls. Architecturally indistinguishable from their surroundings, they provide a quiet place for the passerby to peruse Christian Science literature. At its Boston headquarters, however, the organization maintains a much larger institutional complex adjacent to the Mother Church, which since the early 1970s has featured I. M. Pei's high-rise Colonnade Building and a nearby seven-hundred-foot-long reflecting pool (Tolles 1979, 208–9; Southworth and Southworth 1987, 295).

THE VICTORIAN CITY

This striking complex adjoins and parallels another, slightly earlier cityscape that ranks with the New Haven Green as a paradigmatic example of the impor-

tance of houses of worship in the delineation of a distinctive regional cityscape.
Copley Square, now dominated vertically by the reflective-walled John Hancock
Building, is part of the broader development created during the middle part of
the nineteenth century by the filling in of the Back Bay. This project was planned
to provide a gracious setting for the transplanting of Boston's "Brahmin" upper
class away from the older locus of settlement, now fatally encroached upon by
newcomers. Though no longer primarily a single-family residential area, the Back
Bay has retained much of its distinctive character into the present day as an attractive urban environment (Southworth and Southworth 1987, 210–13).

The first of the neighborhood's churches was Arlington Street Unitarian, built
in 1859–61 in a neoclassical mode reminiscent of James Gibbs. This was the
successor to the Federal Street Church whose pulpit had been graced by William Ellery Channing, the preacher and theologian who had helped launch the
liberal movement as a distinct denomination in its formative years. Channing is
commemorated by a nearby statue adjacent to the Public Garden, one of the city's
splendid central park spaces directly across the street (as well as by a church and
chapel in his name in Newport, Rhode Island, where he had lived during an earlier stage of his career [Southworth and Southworth 1987, 236–37]).

Other congregations flocked to the new area after an attempt to develop the
South End as a fashionable residential neighborhood came to naught. (In John
P. Marquand's *The Late George Apley*, Apley's Brahmin father rapidly sells his house
there when he notices a neighbor appearing in public in his shirt sleeves.) One
abortive attempt at relocation was that of the Brattle Square Church (Unitarian), whose congregation in 1870 commissioned New Orleans–born architect
H. H. Richardson to build them a new home in the Romanesque revival mode
then becoming popular. The congregation was unable to afford this handsome
brown stone structure with its impressive campanile (bell tower), and it was
bought instead by Northern (later American) Baptists, who still precariously
maintain it (Southworth and Southworth 1987, 253–54).

Impressive as the "Church of the Holy Bean Blowers" (as it is sometimes called
after the trumpet-blowing angels sculpted on its tower) may be, it pales before
the even more monumental Trinity Church that Richardson built for the Episcopalians at Copley Square later in the same decade (see figure 14). The result
of a national design competition, Trinity for several years was chosen by the
American Institute of Architects as the finest building in the nation. Based on
Romanesque churches in France and Spain, Trinity set a precedent not only for
religious but for civic building as well, giving rise to "Richardsonian Romanesque"
as the generic name for a whole new style that would grace libraries, academic
buildings, city halls, and railroad stations across the county for decades (Southworth and Southworth 1987, 217–22).

Stylistically, Trinity is notable for the massive round entry arches that have
come to be associated with the name of Richardson, as well as for its polychro-
matic checkerboard patterned brickwork, its elaborate ornamental stonework,
pyramidally capped towers, and its massive central tower that gives the whole
structure visual definition in contrast with its neoclassical and Gothic counter-

parts. The interior, composed of an arrangement of squares, was originally designed as an auditorium to showcase the oratorical talents of Phillips Brooks, the
handsome young preacher who would later become Episcopal bishop of Massachusetts. The current and more ornate chancel area is the result of a later remodeling by the Roman Catholic firm of Maginnis and Walsh, who brought it into
line with the liturgical dimensions of the Anglican tradition more fully exemplified in Russell Sturgis's "High" Church of the Advent (1875–88) in nearby
Beacon Hill.

Trinity is also noted for the convergence of arts brought to bear in its ensemble. Outside is a 1910 statue of Brooks by Augustus Saint-Gaudens, a premier
public sculptor of the era also responsible for the relief carving of Robert Gould
Shaw and his black Civil War regiment at the nearby Boston Common. (Shaw's
story has since been retold in the film *Glory*.) Inside, a series of murals depicting
biblical scenes was executed by John Lafarge, who also contributed to Trinity's
elaborate program of stained glass windows. This fusion of arts was also exemplified in Charles Follen McKim's Boston Public Library (1887–95), which still
faces Trinity across Copley Square. Designed in a monumental Italian Renaissance mode that would, together with Richardsonian Romanesque, become extremely popular as a style for libraries especially, the public library emulated
Trinity in its employment of many of the finest artists of the day in the execution of its complex details. John Singer Sargent, portraitist of the wealthy, was
commissioned to execute there a series of murals on the overtly religious theme
of Judaism and Christianity (Southworth and Southworth 1987, 226–28).

The third monumental anchor of Copley Square is the New Old South
Church, built by the congregation who found "old" Old South no longer appropriate in siting or scale for their purposes (see figure 15). (Old South, fortunately, has been preserved as a museum.) New Old South was an embodiment of the
ideals of John Ruskin, the English essayist whose writings on architecture, especially his *Seven Lamps of Architecture* and his extended meditation "The Nature
of Gothic" in *Modern Painters*, helped legitimate the medieval styles in the minds
of Protestant Americans as morally redemptive. Conspicuous for its polychromy –
that is, stonework featuring alternating bands of muted colors – New Old South
was designed by the firm of Cummings and Sears in 1874–75, and soon became
a vehicle for George Angier Gordon, a liberal Congregationalist honored along
with Brooks with the title of "Prince of the Pulpit." Together, these three buildings help define a distinctively Victorian notion of the city, in which church and
learning jointly participate in the moral redemption of the commonwealth, not
only through their respective services but through the uplifting visual message
conveyed by their architecture (Southworth and Southworth 1987, 228).

Similar cityscapes began to appear in other, smaller New England cities being transformed by the same social and cultural forces. Springfield, the "capital"
of western Massachusetts, has a town square dominated by a handsome 1819
Congregational church in the Federal style; a courthouse by Richardson, now
unfortunately modified; and two Classical revival civic buildings of the late nineteenth century divided by a campanile. On nearby Chestnut and State Streets is

a cluster of civic and religious buildings, including an Italian Renaissance public
library, the Episcopal and Roman Catholic cathedrals, and several museums in a variety of late nineteenth- and early twentieth-century modes. At the corner stands Saint-Gaudens's famous 1883–86 statue of Deacon Samuel Chapin, better known as "The Puritan" (Federal Writers' Project 1937, 362–63).

Though Saint-Gaudens's imposing, resolute Puritan still exerts a certain spell in defining Springfield as a New England city, the lineal descendants of that tradition expressed themselves in very untraditional material fashion during that city's Victorian era. One of Richardson's few other churches, the Church of the Unity (Unitarian), was more Gothic than strictly Romanesque in inspiration. It stood on a corner opposite the Chestnut-State Street complex from its completion in 1869 until its unfortunate demolition in 1961. A short walk down Maple Street brings one to another bastion of Congregationalism, Springfield's South Congregational Church. Designed by William A. Potter and completed in 1875, this massive example of Victorian medieval eclectic polychromy houses not simply an auditorium space for worship but an entire parish plant. Its 120-foot tower, with a pyramidal cap marked by alternating bands of differently colored shingles, combines with its rose window and interior open-beam construction to produce an array of shape and color at once somber and playful. Victorian, certainly, but hardly Puritan (Ochsner 1982, 24–27; Smith 1989, 94–95).

Nearby Christ Church Cathedral (Episcopal), completed in 1876, is a good example of the style that began to prevail among members of that tradition in New England's cities by the 1870s. Small-town Episcopalians had by now thoroughly appropriated the earlier wooden Gothic mode popularized by Upjohn. Those in resort areas sometimes worked a variation on the small church theme with shingled chapels echoing the Shingle Style then in vogue in the building of summer "cottages" along the coast. (Richardson designed some massive examples of these latter for his well-to-do constituency.) Christ Church, Springfield, which was elevated to cathedral status in 1929, differed in its interior design from the Low Church (that is, preaching-oriented in the Protestant manner) proclivities which Phillips Brooks had Richardson reflect in his plans for Boston's Trinity. The cathedral of the Western Massachusetts diocese has as its focus not a pulpit but rather a high altar of Italian marble, which stands before an elaborately carved reredos (decorative screen). Throughout the cathedral are stained glass windows by English designers and statues of figures not only from the Bible but from all phases of Christian history, including Brooks himself (Kalvelage 1993, 30).

ANGLICANISM AND MEDIEVALISM

Just as Congregationalism was embracing a new and more decorative setting for worship, so was the Episcopal church being challenged by a newly invigorated High Church movement that emphasized sacramental liturgy and an appropriately ornate, symbolic setting for that style of worship. The prophet and interpreter of this movement in the architectural realm was the Boston-based convert to high Anglicanism Ralph Adams Cram. For part of his career in partnership with the brilliant designer Bertram Grosvenor Goodhue, Cram designed a myriad of churches and wrote dozens of books and articles in which he attacked the individualism and materialism of Protestant-inspired American culture and argued for a return to a localized, guild- and church-based medieval-style civilization.

Cram was a much better architect than he was an effective writer or practical thinker. His books are largely forgotten, but his churches have mostly survived. Although much of the best work stemming from his collaboration with Goodhue is found outside the region, especially in New York City, a number of gems from Cram's firm still grace the New England landscape. One of these is All Saints Ashmont, an Episcopal church in the Dorchester section of Boston (see figure 16). All Saints is a parish church on the English model with a massive square tower, reflecting in its massing and in the surrounding grounds a pre-urban social ideal. Inside, its chancel (the part of the church in which the altar sits) is divided from the congregation-seating nave both by steps and by a screen, emphasizing the holiness of the place. At the top of the screen stands a cross with a corpus – a representation of the body of Christ – characteristic of High Church worship and designed by Cram himself. Stained glass windows, wood carving, and metal work are all the products of fine craftspeople whom Cram enlisted to produce not just a building but an artistic ensemble. All Saints is what one might call a "jewel church," an organic unity of architecture and decorative arts. Its inspiration lay in the aesthetic ideals of the Arts and Crafts Movement (of whose Boston chapter Cram was an active member), which argued for an eschewal of the tawdry productions of mass-produced industrial goods in favor of hand crafts, as well as in the Anglo-Catholic or High Church interpretation of the Anglican/Episcopal tradition (Tucci 1978, 171–75).

Another interesting work by Cram in nearby Cambridge is the chapel for the monastery of the Society of Saint John the Evangelist, or Cowley Fathers. This was an Anglican religious order, a movement revived first in England and then in the United States after a long hiatus following the suppression of the monasteries by Henry VIII. Another institutional manifestation of resurgent Episcopalianism was more associated with the "muscular Christianity" associated with other wings of the church, namely, the "prep school" enthusiasm that transformed elite secondary education during the Victorian era. Collectively known as the "St. Grottlesex" complex after a humorous fusion of their names, these private boarding schools were frequently conducted under the supervision of Episcopal clergy. Backed by the patronage of the wealthiest classes, they often built handsome campuses with ornate chapels in the Gothic mode of the time (Rettig 1969, O21).

Saint Paul's School in Concord, New Hampshire, is a good example of this development in northern New England. Its Chapel of Saint Peter and Saint Paul was designed in 1886–94 by Henry Vaughan in the English Perpendicular mode, a late phase of medieval Gothic. Cram and Goodhue were both involved in later modifications, and Cram himself designed chapels at other schools of this group, such as Saint George's in Newport, Rhode Island. Vaughan, whose output was

considerably more limited than Cram's, was also the architect of the splendid
Christ Church (1895) in New Haven, which is also designed in the Anglo-Catholic or High Church mode in dark red-brown stone with a dominant Perpen-
dicular-style tower on one side. Since the center of town remained delineated
by the ensemble of churches erected during the century's second decade, however, Christ Church occupies a less conspicuous triangular site that now faces
Eero Saarinen's Yale Co-op and Stiles and Morse Colleges (Morgan 1983, 58–
64 and 89–100).

THE MODERN AGE

The final phase in New England's development in the realm of religious architecture belongs to the post–World War II period. The impact of modern approaches to architecture largely cut across denominational and regional lines, so
that the contemporary houses of worship in New England are not always readily identifiable as expressions of that area's distinctive character and traditions.
However, certain social developments characteristic of parts of New England have
provided the basis for these buildings, and thus are worth noting.

As New England's traditional extractive (lumbering, farming, fishing) and
manufacturing industries began to wane in importance in the twentieth century, other economic resources began to take up at least some of the slack. In the
region's far southeastern segment, great wealth began to accumulate as a result
of this part of Connecticut's pleasant natural environment and close proximity
to New York City. As Manhattan and its immediate suburbs began to fill up,
commuters began to settle farther and farther away, eventually reaching as far as
New Haven. The smaller cities of Stamford, Darien, Fairfield, and Greenwich
became especially popular as addresses for would-be suburbanites, and their residents' high income bases and combined social and religious needs provided the
infrastructure for a new wave of church building, especially during the 1960s.

Particular beneficiaries of these trends were the region's traditionally high-
status denominations – Unitarian, Congregational, and Episcopal – and two others that had made social inroads, the Presbyterians and Roman Catholics. One
example of new building among these groups that attracted national attention,
at least briefly, was the "Fish Church" – Stamford's First Presbyterian of 1958,
designed by Wallace Harrison. Built of a translucent amalgam of limestone and
other minerals and finished in rough slate inset with special glass, this highly
original structure is made of interlocking geometrical forms to resemble a large
fish, a traditional symbol of Christ. (In Greek, the letters of the word form an
acronym of a title of Jesus.) Nearby are a 260-foot bell tower and a walkway
composed of slabs each bearing the name of a notable figure in Christian history (Smith 1989, 32–33).

Other modern churches in the region embody somewhat less literal effects in
their attempt to adapt traditional (or not-so-traditional) approaches to the faith
in a contemporary idiom. Unlike First Presbyterian, which is near an urban cen-

ter, several others are more deeply ensconced in suburbia proper, often in secluded wooded areas. Three notable examples are the United Church (Congregational) in Rowayton (1962), the shingled surfaces of which seem to be continually twisting to form one kind of geometrical curve after another; Saint Barnabas's Episcopal (1958–61), Greenwich, in which ever-changing light plays over the brick walls and wooden beams of the worship space; and Victor Lundy's Unitarian Church in Westport (1964), in which the curved wooden ribs of the roof turn and thrust vertically to a height of fifty-six feet. Lundy's Unitarian Church in Hartford (1964) is a similar but less dramatic play with curved wooden forms in an area also notable for innovative religious architecture, especially Roman Catholic (Smith 1989, 12–13; see also Hayes 1983).

Two other New England resources that began to achieve their full economic potential during the second half of the twentieth century have been tourism and education. Each attracts a transient population of natives and outsiders, and each has generated variations on a particular theme in religious building: the chapel. New England's numerous, diverse, and frequently outstanding colleges and universities have made many creative contributions to this architectural genre. We have already encountered the Bowdoin and Harvard chapels as examples respectively of the *Rundbogenstil* and Colonial revival styles. Other, newer institutions have more recently come up with creative responses to the question of a pluralistic religious presence on a secular campus. Brandeis University in Waltham, Massachusetts, is unique in its nonsectarian Jewish identity and deliberate appeal to Gentile as well as Jewish students. Its approach to the varying worship needs of its students has taken the form of three parallel brick units (1955) each with a glass wall facing a common reflecting pool. Eero Saarinen's contribution to MIT in the same year took the shape of a brick cylinder with a skylight focused on a simple marble cube. Framing this altar is a hanging sculptural screen of small metal rectangles suspended on wires to provide a shimmering effect. The chapel is capped by an abstract aluminum composition. The overall effect is an attempt to capture the spiritual potentials of the technological culture represented by the institution (Smith 1989, 72–73 and 100–101).

The recreation industry has also benefited New England, with millions of tourists annually coming to enjoy the region's manifold natural, cultural, and historic attractions. We have already mentioned the adaptation of the shingle style of the late nineteenth century to religious purposes, as exemplified in Sacred Heart Catholic Church in Yarmouthport and Saint John's Episcopal in Sandwich, both on Cape Cod and dating to 1899. Similar small-scale, seasonal structures in turn-of-the-century styles, often deliberately built to appear rustic and "cozy," can be found in Bar Harbor, Maine, and other summer enclaves. A modern approach to this particular need is exemplified in Olav Hammerstrom's 1958 Saint James the Fisherman Episcopal chapel in Cape Cod's Wellfleet. Purely seasonal, its octagonal wooden base is illuminated by a skylight and capped by a pyramidal bell tower elevated on supporting wooden beams, leaving an open space between the two geometric solids (Vuilleumier 1974, 12, 21, 39; Smith 1989, 102–3).

The history of the built landscape of religion in New England provides a framework or paradigm for looking at the development of religious building over a lengthy period. First, New England was a culture hearth – a point of entry into this country, or its colonial predecessors, of a distinctive culture firmly grounded in a specific and novel religious commitment. The Puritan emigrants soon upon arrival devised a distinctive new building form, the meetinghouse, that reflected their peculiar positive and negative emphases on the issue of how worship was to be conducted, and how the sacred might be experienced by those here on earth.

The evolution of the meetinghouse form from the seventeenth through the nineteenth centuries involved a number of variables. Most meetinghouses were built of wood, though the handful of brick structures especially in cities reflects the limitations placed on stylistic development by both natural and financial resources. The "dialogue" between Puritan and Anglican involved questions not only of theology and liturgy but also of political power, social status, aesthetic taste, and cultural fashion originating in the mother country and then filtered to the provinces. The siting and size of the meetinghouse was a mirror of the transition from Puritan town to the city as it developed from the Federal to the Victorian era. The use of the meetinghouse form reflected both the development of religious pluralism and the commonality of assumptions about worship shared within the spectrum of British Evangelical Protestantism. The proliferation of meetinghouses in the early nineteenth century resulted not only from an increase in wealth and population but also from legal considerations arising in the disestablishment of religion in the New Republic, as congregations divided and claims to property ownership had to be adjudicated.

From the early eighteenth century on, the meetinghouse was flanked by other forms of houses of worship, that is, the church and the synagogue. While the presence of the first Anglican churches had mainly to do with the balance of political power between home country and colony, the coming of Catholicism and Judaism and their respective structures mirrored developing patterns of immigration and population movement. Methodists and Baptists represented the force of popular religion and its symbiotic relationship with the elite churches, including their architectural forms. The various phases of the medieval revivals had to do with changing patterns of social status, liturgical theology, notions of community, and ideological interpretations of work and building. Twentieth-century developments bespoke international trends in architecture as well as changing interregional residential, educational, and recreational patterns.

Nevertheless, New England as a region has resisted in the realm of religious building, as in other ways, the relentless pressures of recent times toward homogenization. By acquiring the status of a national cultural icon, the New England meetinghouse has insured its survival as a communal treasure, regardless of its original theological message. Later styles exemplified in the region, though less closely associated with a distinctive regional identity, have been recognized by subsequent generations to be of such aesthetic and historical significance that their survival in many cases has been assured. Despite its decline in the national political and economic realm, the stock of the Puritan endures.

NEW ENGLAND: BIBLIOGRAPHY

Adams, George Wendell. 1948. *Landmarks from Bow to Boston.* 2d ed. Boston: Christian Science Publication Society.

Anderson, Patricia McGraw. 1988. *The Architecture of Bowdoin College.* Brunswick, Maine: Bowdoin College Museum of Art.

Benes, Peter, ed. 1979. *New England Meeting House and Church, 1630–1850.* Boston: Boston University.

Benes, Peter, and Philip D. Zimmerman. 1979. *New England Meeting House and Church: 1630–1850, a Loan Exhibition Held at the Currier Gallery of Art, Manchester, New Hampshire.* Boston: Dublin Seminar on New England Folklife/Boston University/ Currier Gallery of Art.

Boston Architecture. 1970. Cambridge, Mass.: MIT Press.

Boston Society of Architects. 1976. *Architecture Boston.* Barre, Mass.: Barre Publications.

Brown, Elizabeth Mills. 1965. *The United Church on the Green, New Haven, Connecticut: An Architectural History.* New Haven: United Church.

———. 1976. *New Haven: A Guide to Architecture and Urban Design.* New Haven: Yale University Press.

Cheney, Liana, Donna Cassidy, and Nancy Gill. 1984. *Religious Architecture of Lowell.* 2 vols. Lowell, Mass.: Landmark Printing Co.

Coit, Richard M. 1974. *Churches in Episcopal Connecticut.* Edited by Kenneth Walter Cameron. Hartford: Transcendental Books.

Donnelly, Marian Card. 1968. *The New England Meeting Houses of the Seventeenth Century.* Middletown, Conn.: Wesleyan University Press.

Downing, A. F., and Vincent J. Scully. 1952. *The Architectural Heritage of Newport, Rhode Island.* Cambridge, Mass.: Harvard University Press.

Federal Writers' Project of the Works Progress Administration for Massachusetts. 1937. *Massachusetts: A Guide to Its Places and People.* Boston: Houghton Mifflin.

Garvan, Anthony. 1960. "The New England Plain Style." *Comparative Studies in Society and History* 3:106–22.

Hartford Architecture Conservancy Survey. 1978, 1980. *Hartford Architecture.* 2 vols. Hartford: City of Hartford.

Hayden, Dolores. 1976. *Seven American Utopias: The Architecture of Communitarian Socialism.* Cambridge, Mass.: MIT Press.

Hayes, Bartlett. 1983. *Tradition Becomes Innovation: Modern Religious Architecture in America.* New York: Pilgrim.

Hitchcock, Henry-Russell. 1939. *Rhode Island Architecture.* Providence: Rhode Island Museum Press.

———. 1981. *Springfield Architecture 1800–1900.* Springfield: Springfield City Library/ National Endowment for the Humanities.

Kammen, Michael. 1991. *Mystic Chords of Memory: The Transformation of Tradition in American Culture.* New York: Alfred A. Knopf.

Kalvelage, David A. 1993. *Cathedrals of the Episcopal Church in the U.S.A.* Cincinnati: Forward Movement Publications.

Kelly, John Frederick. 1948. *Early Connecticut Meetinghouses*. 2 vols. New York: Columbia University Press.

Kennedy, Rick. 1989. "Thomas Brattle, Mathematician-Architect in the Transition of the New England Mind." *Winterthur Portfolio* 24, no. 4.

Kirker, Harold. 1969. *The Architecture of Charles Bulfinch*. Cambridge, Mass.: Harvard University Press.

Linden-Ward, Blanche. 1989. *Silent City on a Hill: Landscapes of Memory and Boston's Mount Auburn Cemetery*. Columbus: Ohio State University Press.

Maine Writers Research Club. 1937. *Historic Churches and Homes of Maine*. Portland, Maine: Falmouth Book House.

Mallary, Peter T. (text), and Tim Imrie (photography). 1985. *New England Churches and Meetinghouses 1680–1830*. Secaucus, N.J.: Chartwell Books.

Morgan, William. 1983. *The Almighty Wall: The Architecture of Henry Vaughan*. Cambridge, Mass.: Architectural History Foundation and MIT Press.

Mutrux, Robert H. 1982. *Great New England Churches: Sixty-five Houses of Worship That Changed Our Lives*. Chester, Conn.: Globe Pequot Press.

Myers, Denys Peter, comp. 1974. *Maine Catalog, Historic American Buildings Survey*. N.p.: Maine State Museum.

Nylander, Jane C. 1979. "Toward Comfort and Uniformity in New England Meeting Houses, 1750–1850." In Benes 1979.

Ochsner, Jeffrey Karl. 1982. *H. H. Richardson: Complete Architectural Works*. Cambridge, Mass.: MIT Press.

Pierson, William H., Jr. 1970. *American Buildings and Their Architects: The Colonial and Neoclassical Styles*. Garden City, N.Y.: Doubleday.

———. 1978. *American Buildings and Their Architects: Technology and the Picturesque, the Corporate and the Early Gothic Styles*. Garden City, N.Y.: Doubleday.

Place, Charles A. 1922, 1923. "From Meeting House to Church in New England." *Old Time New England* 13:69–77, 111–23, 149–64; 14:3–20.

Rettig, Robert Bell. 1969. *Guide to Cambridge Architecture*. Cambridge, Mass.: MIT Press.

Robinson, William F. 1980. *A Certain Slant of Light: The First Hundred Years of New England Photography*. Boston: New York Graphic Society.

Sinnott, Edmund W. 1963. *Meetinghouse and Church in Early New England*. New York: McGraw-Hill.

Smith, G. E. Kidder. 1989. *The Beacon Guide to New England Houses of Worship*. Boston: Beacon.

Southworth, Susan, and Michael Southworth. 1987. *A.I.A. Guide to Boston*. Chester, Conn.: Globe Pequot Press.

Souvenir Portfolio of Universalist Churches in Massachusetts. 1906. Boston: Massasoit Press.

Stein, Stephen J. 1992. *The Shaker Experience in America: A History of the United Society of Believers*. New Haven: Yale University Press.

Swarthout, Egerton. 1927. *An Architectural Monograph: Some Old Time Churches of Vermont*. New York: R. F. Whitehead.

Sweeney, Kevin M. 1993. "Meetinghouses, Town Houses, and Churches: Changing Perceptions of Sacred and Secular Space in Southern New England, 1720–1850." *Winterthur Portfolio* 28, no. 1:59–93.

Tolles, Bryant E., Jr., with Carolyn K. Tolles. 1979. *New Hampshire Architecture: An Illustrated Guide*. Hanover: New Hampshire Historical Society/University Press of New England.

Townsend, Gretchen Carol. 1995. "Protestant Material Culture and Community in Connecticut, 1785–1840." Ph.D. dissertation, Yale University.

Tucci, Douglas Shand. 1978. *Built in Boston: City and Suburb 1800–1950.* Boston: New York Graphic Society.

Turner, Harold W. 1979. *From Temple to Meeting House: The Phenomenology and Theology of Places of Worship.* The Hague: Mouton.

Vuilleumier, Marion Rawson. 1974. *Churches on Cape Cod.* Taunton, Mass.: W. S. Sullwold.

Weiss, Ellen. 1987. *City in the Woods: The Life and Design of an American Camp Meeting on Martha's Vineyard.* New York: Oxford University Press.

Winslow, Ola Elizabeth. 1952. *Meetinghouse Hill, 1630–1783.* New York: Macmillan.

Wood, J. S., and M. Steinitz. 1992. "A World We Have Gained: House, Common, and Village in New England." *Journal of Historical Geography* 18, no. 1:105–20.

Zimmerman, Philip D. 1979. "The Lord's Supper in Early New England: The Setting and the Service." In Benes 1979.

———. 1985. "Ecclesiastical Architecture in the Reformed Tradition in Rockingham County, New Hampshire, 1790–1860." Ph.D. diss., Boston University.

1. Congregational church, Tallmadge, Ohio

2. Old Ship Meetinghouse, Hingham, Massachusetts

3. Old North (Christ) Church, Boston, Massachusetts

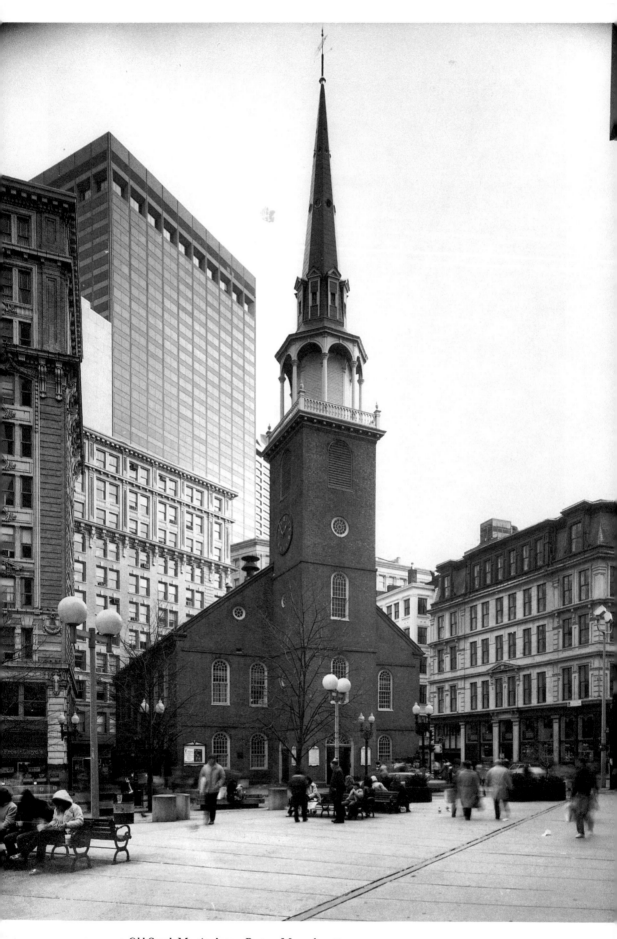

4. *Old South Meetinghouse, Boston, Massachusetts*

5. First Baptist, Providence, Rhode Island

6. Center (First) Church, New Haven, Connecticut

7. *"Village of East Corinth, Vermont"*

8. First Congregational Church, Madison, Connecticut

9. *"Church in New England (Lancaster, New Hampshire)" (St. Paul's Episcopal Church)*, 1936

10. First Parish Church, Brunswick, Maine

11. "The Old Church—Built 1792" (stereoview 1878) (Shaker meetinghouse, Canterbury, New Hampshire)

12. Touro Synagogue, Newport, Rhode Island

13. "View of the Mother Church and Christian Science Center," 1973

14. Trinity Church, Boston, Massachusetts

15. New Old South Church, Boston, Massachusetts

16. All Saints Episcopal Church, Ashmont (Boston), Massachusetts

2 : The Mid-Atlantic States

The states that lie along the eastern seaboard between New England and the South traditionally have not shared a great deal other than a common geography. Colonial New England was united by a common religious commitment, and the southern colonies by a growing investment in the "peculiar institution" of slavery, especially after its rejuvenation in the early nineteenth century by the invention of the cotton gin. Although neither Calvinism nor slavery was unknown in these intermediate regions, neither was formative in their collective character. Nor was anything else.

The colonies that eventually coalesced to form the states of New York, Pennsylvania, New Jersey, Delaware, and Maryland were *proprietary* colonies – that is, their territories were awarded by the British Crown to individuals or groups to divide up and govern to a considerable degree as they saw fit. Only two of these colonies had serious religious motivations underlying their founding: Maryland, which was settled as a haven for English Catholics under the leadership of the Calvert family – the Lords Baltimore – and Pennsylvania, which took its name from a reluctant William Penn, a wealthy convert to the "Friendly persuasion." New York had been seized by the English from the Dutch, largely as a commercial entrepôt. Thus it became an outpost of Anglicanism, with some persistence of the Dutch Reformed Church. Delaware during the colonial era was a political extension of Pennsylvania, and New Jersey to this day reflects a cultural division between the metropolitan regions of New York City and Philadelphia.

In the late twentieth century, the political divisions that had emerged by the time of national independence remain, as do some of the more local traits rooted in culture and geography. Quakers, for example, still abound in the Philadelphia region, and the maritime culture of the Chesapeake gives Baltimore, Annapolis, and other Maryland cities a distinctive regional flavor. Overall, however, the eastern seaboard in this area constitutes the core of America's "megalopolis," an extended urban continuum that stretches with little rural interruption from Baltimore and Washington, D.C., in the south through southern New England and ultimately to the Boston metropolitan region. Washington, Philadelphia, and New York City – together with Boston – are its primary urban foci; this megalopolis constitutes a major national core region for finance, communications, government, and education, rivaled only by California in the west and exceeded by no comparable aggregate. Though the southern stretches of this zone would more accurately be included in the category of "South" during the colonial era, the emergence of the District of Columbia as a transregional governmental center and magnet for a truly cosmopolitan, if somewhat transient, population, makes it more fitting to include it in the "Middle Atlantic" category. In terms of religious architecture, this chapter will concentrate on the metropolitan regions of Philadelphia, New York, and Washington, D.C., with periodic attention to some smaller cities and the western hinterlands.

THE QUAKERS IN THE DELAWARE VALLEY

Perhaps the clearest example of a regionally based religious culture in colonial America outside of New England was that of the Society of Friends, or "Quakers," established by William Penn in the Delaware Valley in the 1690s. Although the Pennsylvania colony was the heart of the Friendly experiment in governance based on the principles of the "Inner Light," the zone of Quaker settlement and influence also included West (that is southern New) Jersey and the three southeasternmost counties of Pennsylvania that were eventually reconstituted as the state of Delaware. Ethnically, the Quakers were primarily of British stock – Welsh and Irish as well as English, with a few German-speaking converts as well. These rapidly displaced in influence the earlier Swedes and Dutch who had attempted to establish a colonial foothold during the earlier seventeenth century, and were joined by large numbers of "Dutch" – that is, *Deutsch*- or German-speakers – who shared the Friendly commitment to peaceful ways and were encouraged by Penn to join in settling his colony. These Amish, Mennonites, and other sectarians soon constituted another significant ethnic cultural core in the counties west of Philadelphia, with their own distinctive building styles. Presbyterian emigrants from northern Ireland – the "Scotch-Irish" – also arrived in growing numbers, but were encouraged by the Quakers to take themselves and their pugnacious ways as far west from Philadelphia as possible.

By 1750, the Quakers were third in the colonies in number of houses of worship: their 250 meetinghouses were exceeded only by the 465 of the Congregationalists in New England and the 289 churches of the Anglicans scattered along the whole stretch of seaboard. Although they differed with their New England counterparts fundamentally on many issues of both faith and practice, Friends and Puritans shared a common aesthetic that manifested itself in their houses for worship and in their material culture more broadly. Both groups shared an attachment to the ideal of the "plain style" – that is, the eschewal of explicit iconography and excessive ornament in favor of a sparely expressed functionalism. Ornament was of the world; it was an expression of vanity, self-centeredness, and

attachment to the transient rather than the eternal. The values that the Friends
rejected were those they associated with the Anglicans who had so often persecuted them in Britain. Quakers thus repudiated what they called "steeple-house
ways"; like the Puritans, their persecutors in the New World, they adopted the
term "meetinghouse" over the traditional usage of "church," which implied the
sacrality of earthly places and structures as well as the oppressive institution of
the Church of England (Fischer 1989, 422, 427).

The Quaker meetinghouse was, if anything, even more austere than its New
England counterpart. The external building, which varied in size according to
local numbers and resources, was built on a domestic model, with no steeple or
other elements that would suggest a traditional church. Colonial meetinghouses had two doors, which enabled men and women to enter separately for their
respective business meetings; meetings for worship, however, were integrated by
the removal of an interior partition. Worshipers sat on benches facing one another, with elevated benches for those overseeing the meeting. Quaker meetings
consisted of testimony from individual Friends; there was no formal liturgy nor
preaching, so that a pulpit was unnecessary. Galleries were sometimes provided
for children. In general, plainness was the primary aesthetic virtue, and no elements were introduced that did not serve an immediate function. As in New
England, this plainness was itself a powerful statement of communal values (Rose
1963, 71).

Aside from the distinctive Quaker requirements for houses of worship, the
exterior development of their meetinghouses ran roughly parallel to that of other
religious groups. Some of the earliest services took place in private houses. William Penn and his wife, for example, were members of the Monthly Meeting held
at the home of William Biles in "The Manor," an area along the Delaware that
took its name from the large tract of land where Penn had built his summer residence. Before long, Friends were erecting wooden structures for worship, which
in turn gave way to more substantial ones of brick or, more usually in this area,
stone (see figures 17 and 18). Like the early New England meetinghouses, these
buildings were sometimes oddly shaped. The first meetinghouse in Burlington,
New Jersey, one of the earliest sites of Quaker settlement, was built in 1692.
Philadelphia local-color historian John Faris described it as "a curious hexagonal structure, with high pitched roof, surmounted first by a lantern, and then by
a conical finial." Although the fieldstone characteristic of eastern Pennsylvania
and environs was the most common building material, local variants were also
known; the Lower Alloway's Creek meetinghouse, for instance, was built of native clay bricks and oyster shell mortar, with benches of local yellow pine (Faris
1926, 126; Rose 1963, 98, 126; Wilson 1981, 7, 22).

During the eighteenth and early nineteenth centuries, meetinghouse design
followed in general ways the fashion of the times, although always avoiding excessive ornament. The smaller houses were often gable-end structures, with the
traditional pair of doors frequently on a long side. Georgian (also known as Wren
Baroque) decorative features made an appearance on many eighteenth-century
meetinghouses, indicating the growing accommodation of Philadelphia's Friends

as they began to constitute a prosperous mercantile elite. One odd deviation from the anti-churchly norm was that built by Welsh Quakers in Lower Merion Township, part of the Welsh Tract (or Welsh Barony) west of Philadelphia. Begun in the 1690s, the Merion meetinghouse was enlarged in 1711–13 in such a way as to become cruciform in shape. This is the only known example of this form, common among Anglicans and therefore offensive to Quakers, in the whole realm of meetinghouse history; presumably it arose from practical needs for more room and a moment of obliviousness to symbolic considerations (Faris 1926, 164–65; Rose 1963, 362–63).

Later Quaker building in the Philadelphia area reflected the larger stresses the society underwent as it periodically dealt with the exigencies of living, and for many decades governing, in a broader pluralistic world that was all along part of the nonpacifistic British Empire. In 1781, a group who called themselves the Free Quakers, including Betsy Ross of flag-making fame, split from the larger group in order to take up arms in the Revolutionary cause. These "Fighting Quakers," as they were known by contemporaries, erected a meetinghouse at Fifth and Arch in Philadelphia, a brick pedimented gable-end structure with keystones on the lintels. The Free Quakers dwindled after the Revolution and had disbanded by 1836; their building, however, is still preserved as a historical site (Faris 1926, 225–27; Rose 1963, 349–50).

Another schism that had an impact on the built environment of the Friends was the split that occurred in 1827 between Orthodox and Hicksite Quakers. Although theological issues involving fidelity to the movement's origins were ostensibly the issue, a significant cause of the rift lay in the social distance that had developed between the prosperous Philadelphia mercantile elite and their less affluent country cousins. As a result, the minority faction in each meeting affected by the schism was compelled to build new quarters, usually in conservative versions of the styles of the era (Wilson 1981, 76–77).

An interesting footnote on the broader reach of Friendly influence can be found in the Long House of the Seneca Indians in upstate New York. Quakers had long been active among the Seneca in a fashion more reminiscent of the Peace Corps than the more aggressive Protestant missionaries, and helped negotiate a treaty between them and the new national government in 1794. As a result of this Friendly influence, the Long House of the Seneca – a modest frame gable-end structure with two doors on the long side – demonstrates a clear influence of the Quaker meetinghouse plan (Wilson 1981, 74–75).

The built environment of the Delaware Valley experiment was not confined solely to meetinghouses. Indeed, Quaker principles and influences manifested themselves in a wide variety of aspects of planning and building. William Penn himself exercised a major role as a city planner, incorporating ideas current in Europe with his own community's ideals expressed in the name of the "city of brotherly love," the urban core of a "Holy Experiment."

Penn had originally intended settlement in an area bordering the Delaware known as the "Liberties," which would assure its occupants access to the advantages of the river. When this proved impractical, a new plan to bring about Penn's

vision of a "Greene Country Towne" became the basis for what emerged as Philadelphia's urban core. At the center was the intersection of High (later Market)
and Broad Streets, the city's major axes. Subordinate streets were arranged on a
grid pattern based on Richard Newcourt's plan for the rebuilding of London after
the Great Fire of 1666. Other parts of the plan included subordinate squares
placed symmetrically and freestanding houses on spacious lots with abundant fruit
trees. The intention was not simply the implementation of an Enlightenment-
era aesthetic but the creation of a community whose inhabitants would be free
from the pressures of life that contributed to the conflict the Friends sought to
eliminate from the human sphere. In many ways, this conception had much more
in common with the other Mid-Atlantic metropolises of New York and Washington than with the religiously inspired but essentially medieval higgledy-pig-
gledy of Boston's eternally picturesque but confusing meander of streets (Teitelman and Longstreth 1974, 1–2; Wurman and Gallery 1972, 79).

Quaker houses also reflected both the cultural origins and the theological
principles of the community. Built largely of the fieldstone abundant in the region, houses in the Delaware Valley closely resembled those of northern England,
the place of origin of many Friends. Some of their distinctive features, such as
the small pent roofs that overhung windows and doors on housefronts, were
regional English idiosyncrasies that had no religious significance. The latter was
more readily evident in the austerity of the interiors, which appeared bright and
spacious while studiously kept free of superfluity of ornament. The region soon
came to abound in what came to be called "Quaker-plan" houses in cottagelike
and grander versions, both based on northern English prototypes (Fischer 1989,
475–81).

Another dramatic way in which the Friendly presence manifested itself in
Philadelphia's built environment was in the realm of benevolent institutions.
Quakers had from early on been concerned with philanthropy, at first directed
toward the persecuted among their own number, then later toward the broader
community. The Friends Asylum for the Insane, for example, was founded in 1817
to provide a humane setting for the emotionally distressed and to promote their
rehabilitation rather than simply isolating them. Like other institutions of the
period, it began as a large houselike structure, with wings added on to give it the
ambience of what Erving Goffman has called the "total institution" in which all
aspects of the life of the residents are encompassed. Almshouses, begun with a
1702 bequest, and the Pennsylvania Hospital, founded in 1751, were further
examples of the emergent Quaker preoccupation with benevolent institutional-
ization, later encouraged by civic-minded non-Friends such as Benjamin Franklin
as well (James 1963, 49–50, 205ff.; Rothman 1971, 44–45; Wilson 1981, 115ff.).

The most famous institutional experiment associated with Quaker Philadelphia lay in the realm of punishment. The Walnut Street Jail of 1790 was built in
the form of a large house, but soon proved inadequate to the city's needs. Its
successor, Eastern State Penitentiary, was a minor wonder of the world in its day
and drew interested Europeans such as Alexis de Tocqueville to the United States
to study what was then the last word in reform. A grim affair consisting of a

quadrangle with castellated gates and long corridors radiating from a central polygonal axis, Eastern State represented a distinctively Friendly approach to the task of punishment and rehabilitation in a nation now too large to depend on local jails or other small-town institutions for effective care of the needy or deviant. The first radial prison in the world, it was based on a philosophy of solitary confinement that would provide the incarcerated with an opportunity to meditate at leisure on their transgressions and hopefully rehabilitate themselves spiritually in the process. Although such institutions may seem harsh by modern standards, it is not clear that their successors have been notably more effective or humane. In their day, they were visible testaments to the humanitarian reform impulse to which the Philadelphia Friends, though no longer solely in control of the city, gave considerable impetus (Baltzell 1979, 310; James 1963, 290; Rothman 1971, 90, 94–95, 98; Teitelman and Longstreth 1974, 139).

Although many of the philanthropic institutions inspired by the Friends' humanitarian concerns passed into public hands, other endeavors remained within the private sphere. Early Quakers were ambivalent about or even hostile toward higher education; however, their gradual accommodation to the ways of the broader world had by the mid-nineteenth century permitted them to found what would become one of the finest clusters of private colleges in the nation: Haverford (1833), Swarthmore (1864), and Bryn Mawr (1880). Friends also founded a number of preparatory schools in the region, beginning with the Friends Academy of 1763. Most of these educational institutions reflected Quaker values in their spacious green settings and their appropriation of the styles of the day, from Georgian to Collegiate Gothic, in an understated, decorous manner. The evolution of the Quaker adaptation to "worldly" culture is reflected in the architectural evolution of these campuses. Montgomery Schuyler, the prominent turn-of-the-century architectural critic, wrote first of Haverford:

> The tenets of the Friends no more tend to grace and becomingness in architecture than in costume. A "Quaker meeting house" is, almost proverbially, the negation of architecture, being the simplest and baldest satisfaction of the material requirements of the case, with a complete abnegation of ornament. . . . And, as in what it would be absurd to call "ecclesiastical" architecture, so in domestic. The old Quaker Philadelphia, of which there are hardly any quarters now left unmodified and unmodernized, showed in its building no higher an ideal than that of vivid cleanliness, attained by painting the bricks, until "Philadelphia pressed brick" came in, the reddest red, and scouring the marble to the whitest white, the same vivid color scheme, by the way, to which the architects of the University dormitories have now reverted, and one which would have been a reproach to the Philadelphian housekeeper if it had been allowed to take "the tone of time." Not much was to be hoped, architecturally, for a Quaker college founded in 1830. . . . Of all the buildings one can say that they do nothing to spoil the landscape.

Of Hicksite-sponsored Bryn Mawr, however, the critic waxes almost rhapsodic:

Bryn Mawr comes last on our list of Pennsylvania colleges. It is lucky that it
is latest in the chronological order, for it should also come last, according to the order of the wedding feast in Cana of Galilee . . . Bryn Mawr is all of one piece. Not quite all, to be sure, for young as it is, it had time to get at least one building in a bad old fashion before it entered on its architectural career. . . . But there is nothing else at Bryn Mawr which one could with any fervency wish away. The site is only a mile or so outward from Haverford, and the country is of the same prettily rolling and pastoral character. The college architecture, a monochrome of gray stone, fits it perfectly. . . . In the later buildings there is no lack of playfulness or fantasy. But one would not think, as he can hardly help thinking sometimes at the university, of calling the fun unscrupulous.

Where Haverford, in Schuyler's view, was dowdy to the point of offensiveness, Bryn Mawr is architecturally sophisticated even to the point of "playfulness" (Schuyler 1910, 203–4, 207–11).

Still later additions to this institutional complex included Pendle Hill, a retreat house near Swarthmore (1930); Friends Center, in downtown Philadelphia, consisting of an 1856 meetinghouse and a modern headquarters for the Philadelphia Yearly Meeting as well as a number of other Quaker-affiliated national organizations; four golf clubs, the first of which was founded in 1901; and, most recently, a number of retirement homes. Graveyards, perhaps needless to say, were established from the very beginnings of the colony. (Sixteen acres were donated by George Fox in 1691 for this purpose.) This blending of religious, philanthropic, educational, and recreational facilities is certainly not without parallel among other religious communities, but its concentration in the Philadelphia area is indicative of the central role this region has always served in the cultural identity of the Friends, as well as the permeation of Friendly ideals through all aspects of the Quaker lifestyle and life cycle (Wilson 1981, 17, 91ff.).

GERMAN-SPEAKERS IN THE PHILADELPHIA CULTURE HEARTH

Although the Pennsylvania colony did not guarantee universal religious freedom, it came as close as any colony save possibly Rhode Island in this regard. William Penn not only tolerated other religious groups but actively encouraged immigration by members of other "peace churches," especially from the Rhine Valley. During the early nineteenth century, considerable numbers of the German-speaking sectarians known as Anabaptists began to settle in the southeastern counties of the colony, attracted by the fertile land and the promise of freedom from the persecution they had experienced in central Europe.

The built environment of these Anabaptists is best described in terms of landscape rather than specific buildings. The Amish, the stricter of the two major Anabaptist strains, built no specific buildings for worship at all; rather, on the model of the earliest Christian community, they held worship in private homes. The sacred was for them not confined to worship but rather was a quality inherent in the totality of their lifeways. Gradually, as the industrial revolution began to have an impact on the agricultural style they shared with many of their neighbors, their patterns deviated more and more intentionally from the mainstream. With sixteenth-century Switzerland as their "strong time" – the time and place of origins that provided their ongoing archetypes – they shunned both the encroachments of technology and those among them who rejected their tight communal discipline.

The Mennonites, who took their name from the early Reformation-era leader Menno Simons, rejected the ultra-strict disciplinary practices of the followers of Jakob Amman (that is, the Amish), and resembled the Friends more in their pacifism and suspicion of excessive worldliness. They first settled Germantown, now part of Philadelphia, in 1683; their first log building, built in or around 1708, was replaced in 1770 with a stone meetinghouse of Germantown Avenue, the only such structure surviving from colonial times. It is a small one-room gable-end building with shuttered windows, a pedimented hood projecting over the single doorway, and a surrounding graveyard. Later and larger but similarly austere meetinghouses abound, particularly in Lancaster County, the heart of the misnamed "Pennsylvania Dutch" country, where German-speakers of all religious stripes settled in considerable numbers during the eighteenth century. George A. Tice's image of the Lancaster meetinghouse evokes the genre well (see figure 19; Faris 1926, 35; Rose 1963, 350–51).

The Brethren – or Dunkards, after their distinctive baptismal practices – were another German-speaking sect whose original meetinghouse can also still be found on Germantown Avenue in Philadelphia. In terms of material culture, the Brethren represent another step closer to the "churchly" norm; their Germantown church, also built of stone in 1770, is perceptibly more ornate than its Mennonite counterpart, as illustrated in its more fashionable round-topped windows and the circular light over the portico that shelters its main door (Faris 1926, 35–36; Rose 1963, 351).

Another theme that distinguished some German-speaking communities from the Reformation mainstream was the communitarian impulse. Though the Amish particularly lived as a distinct, physically and culturally set-apart community, the single-family farm remained the norm. One small, rather short-lived group that rejected this norm was founded by Johann Konrad Beissel in 1735 as a split-off from the Brethren. Beissel's "Society of the Solitary" was part of the Pietistic tradition but carried its injunctions to holiness back toward the medieval Catholic ideal in its practice of celibacy. Men and women lived chastely together in community at what has become known as the "Ephrata Cloister," only two of the buildings of which survive today as a museum in the town of Ephrata, near Lancaster, Pennsylvania (see figure 20). The Saal (1741) has provisions for cooking and dining, worship, and, in its upper stories, small individual rooms for the women members, or "sisters," who also lived in the adjoining "Sharon"; a similar accommodation for men is lost (Rose 1963, 385–87; De Visser and Kalman 1976, 101, 114–16).

Another community which has, through gradual adaptation to mainstream norms, survived in good health to the present day is the Moravian Church. Although their roots lie in the Hussite movement in pre-Reformation Central Europe, the modern history of the Moravians begins in the Pietistic era of the early eighteenth century and the work of Count Nicholas von Zinzendorf in what is now the Czech Republic. The early Moravians founded several settlements along the Atlantic seaboard, especially Bethlehem, Pennsylvania, and Salem, North Carolina (now Old Salem Village in Winston-Salem).

The Bethlehem settlement was based on the *choir* system, in which cohorts based on age and marital status lived together in dormitory-like structures similar to those at Ephrata in basic communal design as well as in architectural details – gambrel roofs, small, double-rowed dormers, red-brick window arches, walk-in fireplaces. The community, now surrounded by downtown Bethlehem, was sited along a central square – *der Platz* – with choir residences at one end and industrial buildings for the processing of livestock at another. Barns, stables, and "God's Acre" – the Moravian term for cemetery – stood further off (Gollin 1967; Murtagh 1967, 9, 12, 36–37, 114–27).

By the time of Independence, the Moravians had experienced what Max Weber has called a "routinization of charisma." Unable to sustain the intense original impulse inspired by the charismatic Zinzendorf, they began to abandon the communal ideal of the first generation. Symbolic of this transition was the abandonment of their old chapel, which had adjoined the *Gemeinhaus*, or original common residence. In its place was built in 1806 the Central Moravian Church, a Federal-style house of worship that is scarcely distinguishable from other Protestant churches of the era. It is still used by the community, which has evolved from a sect into a denomination – that is, from an exclusivistic, tightly disciplined group whose practices contrast sharply with those of their contemporaries, to a more "normal" community not dramatically different from others in belief and lifestyle. The original communal buildings, fortunately, still stand as a well-preserved reminder of the Moravians' early history (Murtagh 1967, 54–55, 124–27).

Until the arrival of German-speaking Roman Catholics in substantial numbers during the nineteenth century, the most "churchly" of the non-British traditions represented in the Middle Colonies was that of the Lutherans. The Lutheran version of Protestantism arrived with the Swedes, who for a few decades of the mid-seventeenth century established a settlement in the Delaware Valley. Among the earliest of their religious buildings was the Cranehook Church, built in what is now Wilmington, Delaware, in 1667, out of horizontal logs; this and similar Swedish buildings were the prototypes of the "log cabin," the archetypal American frontier structure that was really of Old World origin (Rose 1963, 61).

Although the English displaced the Swedes in 1665 as the ruling authorities, the Swedish presence continued uninterrupted, and more permanent houses of worship followed in what are now Delaware, New Jersey, and Pennsylvania. Notable among them is Gloria Dei, or Old Swedes' Church in Philadelphia, begun in the late 1690s to supersede an older wooden blockhouse used for worship (see figure 21). Here is a structure that is clearly a church rather than a meetinghouse. Cruciform in shape with a pedimented square tower and classically ornamented steeple and spire, Old Swedes' is built of brick in the "Flemish bond" pattern. This ornamental design alternates "stretchers" and glazed "headers." (This is a method in which bricks are arranged with their length and width alternately exposed, a pattern frequently used in the elegant Anglican churches of the Virginia colony as well.) The roof's steep pitch and the dimensions of steeple and spire indicate a distinctively Swedish building tradition. As the Swedish community began over the generations to become Anglicized, Old Swedes' – with permission of the king of Sweden himself – became affiliated with the newly formed Protestant Episcopal Church in 1789. Two years later a similar fate befell the similarly named Old Swedes Church in Wilmington, Delaware, built of stone at the same time as its Philadelphia counterpart (Faris 1926, 119ff.; Rose 1963, 132–33, 337–38).

The more widespread German-speaking version of Luther's *evangelische Kirche* was first organized in the Atlantic colonies by Henry Melchior Muhlenberg, who held his first service in Philadelphia in 1742. Muhlenberg, who gathered the scattered Lutheran congregations of the area into a *Ministerium*, eventually became rector of Saint Michael's Church in Philadelphia, a large brick building in the Georgian mode, which in 1790 boasted the largest organ on the North American continent. (Lutherans were a significant force in popularizing the use of such instruments for worship, working against an ingrained Reformed suspicion of such extrabiblical devices.)

Lutheran churches flourished during the nineteenth century especially in the Pennsylvania German country around Lancaster, York, Hanover, and adjoining towns; their building modes were conservative, generally following neoclassical lines. One other early German Lutheran church deserves mention here, however. The Old Trappe Church – originally known first as New Providence, then as Augustus Lutheran Church – was built in 1743 in Trappe, Pennsylvania. Designed by Muhlenberg himself and built of stone, it is notable for its double-pitch "bonnet" roof built around an octagonal apse and sanctuary. Though not in active use since 1852, its interior arrangements reflect social gradations similar to that of colonial Anglicans and Puritans. Old Trappe is furnished with high-backed box pews, with those owned by the wealthier members having doors with locks. Men and women sat separately at worship, as did servants and boys, who were relegated to plain benches in the gallery under the watchful eye of the sexton (Faris 1926, 168; Rose 1963, 365–67).

MORE DIVERSITY: ENGLISH-SPEAKING RELIGIOUS GROUPS AROUND PHILADELPHIA

Another major ethnic and religious strain that molded the mid-Atlantic colonies was Presbyterianism, the version of Calvinism brought by emigrants from Scotland and northern Ireland during the eighteenth century especially. Theologically, Presbyterians shared a great deal with the New England Puritans; they

differed primarily in ethnic and geographical origin as well as in polity. Presbyterian governance, then as now, was based on a system in which lay and clerical
delegates from individual congregations form regional executive bodies known
as *presbyteries*. Presbyterianism in this region can be loosely divided into northern and southern zones, with the former closely allied with coreligionists of New
England whose influence pervaded especially Long Island and East Jersey.

Colonial-era Presbyterian churches in the region do not differ dramatically
in style from their New England counterparts, although the materials from which
they were built reflect local circumstances. First Presbyterian Church (1784) of
Huntington, New York, for example – the third building on the site – is located
in eastern Long Island, once part of the Connecticut sphere of influence. Covered with shingles, this two-story structure has a square tower set into the body
of the building itself and topped with a small belfry and spire. Where the Huntington church is built in the rather awkward mode of later colonial meetinghouse design, its namesake in Newark, erected only three years later, is a much
more graceful example of the Wren-Gibbs style; however, it is built of local stone
rather than the brick or wood characteristic of New England. (Its mortar, incidentally, is made of lime from clam shells left behind in large piles by the area's
aboriginal inhabitants.) The Newark congregation also had close ties with Connecticut, and an earlier structure had been built in the saltbox shape indigenous
to New England. Its urban constituency was obviously both wealthier and more
sophisticated than its Long Island counterpart, as reflected in this handsome
downtown church (Rose 1963, 264–65, 301).

Another strain of Presbyterianism took shape further south in the Delaware
Valley, which eventually precipitated a short-lived schism within that tradition.
The early eighteenth century witnessed the beginnings of the systematic practice of revival preaching intended not so much to instruct hearers in doctrine or
morals but rather to bring about a change of heart and consciousness. The Great
Awakening, as the more intense eruption of revivals in the 1740s came to be called,
led to schism in New England as well, evidenced in the side-by-side Congregational churches that still abide on the New Haven town green. In Philadelphia
the "Grand Itinerant," the Calvinist Anglican George Whitefield, preached frequently during his peripatetic American career.

That city's First Presbyterian Church had been organized in 1698 by a mixture of English Dissenters, Welsh Calvinists, and French Huguenots. Their first
building, erected in 1704 and enlarged in 1729, was described by a Swedish traveler with a clearly "high church" perspective as a plain building with a hexagonal roof which ran north and south, "because the Presbyterians are not particular as to the points of the compass in placing their Church." First Presbyterian
became known as "Old Buttonwood" from the trees that surrounded it, and
Benjamin Franklin, who was only nominally associated with organized religion,
was nevertheless a pewholder. (Franklin later frequented the Anglican Christ
Church, in whose graveyard he is buried.) When First Presbyterian and other
local churches proved inhospitable to Whitefield's message and style, the city's
Second Presbyterian Church was organized in 1742. Originally meeting in an

auditorium built expressly for Whitefield's preaching, it six years later erected a new brick church at Third and Arch, which boasted a multistage steeple taller than that of nearby Christ Church. Critics of this alleged pretentiousness circulated the following verse:

> The Presbyterians built a church
> And fain would have a steeple:
> We think it may become the church,
> But not become the people.

To the presumed approval of the verse's perpetrators, the steeple was eventually removed for structural reasons. One early description gives some insight into the liturgical arrangements thought appropriate for New Side Reformed worship in this era:

> The front entrance was on Third Street, and the pulpit was placed on the north side: over it hung a large sounding-board, suspended in such a way as to cause profound anxiety among the younger worshippers lest it should fall on the preacher's head. Below the pulpit, and directly in front, was a reading desk for the precentor, or the "setter of tunes." An aisle ran through the middle of the church from east to west, and another from north to south, paved with brick, in which were placed slabs to commemorate the dead who were buried underneath. One pew was set apart as the President's or Governor's pew. It was surmounted by a canopy, supported by carved columns.

John Adams, who attended the church in 1774, described the administration of communion then common, in which partakers took their places in a row of seats on either side of a table, and presented tokens before being given the sacrament (Faris 1926, 39–51).

Second Presbyterian relocated in 1837 and then again around 1870, finally settling into the High Victorian Gothic structure that still stands at Walnut and Twenty-second Street. Although Whitefield had provided the occasion for its founding, its real moving force had been the local revivalist Gilbert Tennent, whose sermons on "the Dangers of an Unconverted Ministry" would provoke considerable controversy in their implicit attack on many settled clergy. Elsewhere in the Delaware Valley, one of the earliest moving spirits behind the revivalist impulse had been Gilbert's father, William Tennent, an Anglican from northern Ireland who switched allegiance to Presbyterianism upon arrival in the New World. After various ministries in New York and Pennsylvania, Tennent settled near Hartsville in Bucks County, Pennsylvania, and began to train young men, including his sons, for ministerial action according to "New Side" – that is, revivalist – principles.

Tennent's "Log College" in Neshaminy, built across the road from his house on the York Road, was emblematic in its rough-and-ready character of the revivalist spirit, which frequently expressed itself in disdain for the more formally educated settled ministry that dominated much of colonial religious life. (That the Log College eventually metamorphosed into what would become Princeton is indicative of the evanescence of this phase of revivalism.) Tennent and his followers also exemplified the material form that the Awakening spirit often took when in 1741 they broke away from the congregation that worshiped in an original 1726–27 building and built their own stone church in 1742. Long after the factions had reunited, the church was drastically remodeled in 1842, with an oddly eclectic result combining Greek and Gothic revival features (Teitelman and Longstreth 1974, 102; Rose 1963, 374–75; Faris 1926, 171–77).

In addition to precipitating short-lived schisms among the Calvinist denominations, the Awakening also stimulated the emergence of yet newer institutionalized versions of Protestant Christianity. The pietistic movement John Wesley had created originally as a spiritual supplement to the formalistic services of the Church of England began to be spread in the colonies first by self-appointed preachers, then soon afterwards by official Wesleyan emissaries such as Francis Asbury. Although Methodism, as Wesley's movement soon came to be known, rapidly spread in all directions to become a national popular religion, its origins were firmly anchored in the mid-Atlantic region.

Early Methodism was by a combination of necessity and design a peripatetic phenomenon, similar in strategy to that devised by Wesley's old Oxford colleague, George Whitefield. Much Methodist preaching took place wherever an audience could be found – in the open air, in churches of other denominations, or in secular buildings such as private homes. Before too long, Methodist chapels, larger or smaller but architecturally unpretentious gable-end structures with minimal ornament, began to be constructed. These included Wesley Chapel on John Street in New York City; Bush Forest Chapel near Aberdeen, Maryland; and Barratt's Chapel near Fredericka, Delaware. This area of Delaware and Maryland's Eastern Shore is historically one of the most intensely Methodist areas of the country, where circuit riders once flourished and small white-frame churches still abound.

Two particular sites deserve further discussion. The first was Saint George's Church, organized in Philadelphia by followers of Wesley and Whitefield in the 1760s, who originally held worship services in a sail loft (see figure 22). In 1769, they acquired an unfinished German Reformed church whose congregations had not been able to muster sufficient resources for its completion, and some of whom actually wound up in jail for debts incurred in the process. Called originally the Georg Kirche after the reigning monarch in England, Saint George's wound up with a somewhat more ecclesiastical name, reflecting the Anglican origins of the Methodist movement. Saint George's, where services are still held, is a two-story pedimented brick structure with rectangular windows and access via a stone porch. Though it was first used for worship while unplastered, unpainted, and with a dirt floor, it rapidly attained, in Asbury's word, "cathedral" status among American Methodists, and was the first such congregation to employ the term "church" rather than the earlier "chapel" in self-description. As its constituency prospered, Saint George's was soon enhanced by trappings such as galleries, chandeliers, and a broken-pediment altarpiece, all modeled on the nearby Anglican Saint Paul's Church at which the congregation had originally taken communion. The large building is aesthetically unprepossessing, but has an almost sacred quality in the Wesleyan imagination as one of the tradition's historical shrines at which American Methodism's first conferences took place (Bilhartz 1984, 17, 19, 21, 26; Faris 1926, 197–200; Rose 1963, 344–45).

FURTHER DIVERSITY IN THE EARLY MID-ATLANTIC REGION

The other most prominent shrine of early American Methodism was the Lovely Lane Meetinghouse in Baltimore. In this modest 1774 double-entry gable-end stone building with a semicircular fanlight sixty Wesleyan preachers met on Christmas Eve in 1784 to form the Methodist Episcopal Church, the first group in the tradition to constitute itself as formally separate from the mother Anglican Church. The original Lovely Lane was destroyed by fire in 1796. Today the name is borne by a very different edifice (1882–87), designed by Stanford White of McKim, Mead and White, the firm responsible for the Boston Public Library (see figure 23). Romanesque in inspiration with an auditorium-plan interior, the "new" Lovely Lane Church is distinguished by a massive square tower culminating in a pyramidal spire. (Judson Memorial Baptist Church, designed by the same firm in 1892, is an interesting parallel example of the appropriation of this medieval style by an Evangelical denomination in New York's Greenwich Village.) Its design by an architect known primarily for his elaborate houses for the Gilded Age elite is indicative of the movement of Methodism from social marginality to bourgeois respectability during the intervening decades (Bilhartz 1984, 28–30; Dorsey and Dilts 1973, 160–62; *Maryland Guide* 1940, 230–31; Howland and Spencer 1953, 136; White and Willensky 1978, 68).

Although the Chesapeake Bay was one of the primary loci for the establishment of Methodism in the colonies, the Maryland colony had been first settled in 1634 by aristocratic English Roman Catholics seeking, like many other colonists, a refuge from the uniformity imposed by the Established Church. Although the original Maryland charter established broad religious liberties, the Catholics found themselves displaced from power after England's Glorious Revolution ejected the Catholic-sympathizing Stuarts from the throne. Maryland's Catholics thus remained a distressed though sizable minority until independence, unable to worship freely in public in what had once been their own colony. As a result, worship had to be conducted privately and discreetly, usually in chapels at Catholic-owned estates such as the Carroll family's Doughoregan Manor near Ellicot City, or "Priest Neale's Mass House," a 1764 domestic structure near Poole acquired by the Jesuit order, who constituted most of the colony's Catholic clergy. Scarcely any other Roman Catholic houses of worship survive from colonial days, and few are recognizable as churches per se (Rose 1963, 27ff., 173, 184).

After independence, the situation of Roman Catholics, like that of all religious groups, was rapidly transformed as a result of the universal religious liberty guaranteed by the First Amendment, at least as far as concerned the federal government. Catholics now found themselves faced with the pleasant task of reorgani-

zation, and the rather complicated challenge of dealing with a genuinely novel
situation in which they were neither favored nor persecuted by the state. In 1790 John Carroll, part of the old Maryland Catholic family already cited, was designated bishop (later archbishop) of Baltimore by Rome, the first resident of the United States to hold that title. (North American Catholic affairs had previously come under the episcopal jurisdiction of Quebec.)

John Carroll was much in sympathy with the ethos of the New Republic, an enthusiasm he evidenced when challenged with the task of building the new nation's first cathedral. Benjamin Henry Latrobe, a Protestant architect of great distinction, offered Carroll two sets of plans, one in the Gothic style, the other Roman revival. Although both had resonance with Catholic tradition, Carroll selected the latter as being more in harmony with the ideals and iconography of the new nation, as expressed for example in the architectural designs of Thomas Jefferson. The Baltimore Cathedral – now known as the Basilica of the Assumption, since a new cathedral has superseded it – of 1814–18 thus features a portico, two small domed towers, and a much larger dome over the crossing (see figure 24). It was a startlingly modern building in the context of its times, and a dramatic proclamation of the place claimed by Roman Catholics in a nation in which suspicion about their loyalty had deep roots in English Protestant mythology (Pierson 1970, 360–72).

If Maryland owed its colonial origins to English Catholics, New York was in its beginnings the province of the Dutch. Like those of the Swedes, however, Dutch ambitions for a share of North America were unable to stand up against the superior force and determination of the English, and New Netherland in 1664 was transmuted into New York. A number of Dutch Reformed churches of colonial provenance still exist along the Hudson, where the *patroon* system of large landholdings once prevailed. Most of the handful of surviving eighteenth-century Dutch churches in New York feature large square towers, either set into the body of the church itself or abutting it. The First Reformed Church in Fishkill, Dutchess County (1731), is one of the most visually distinctive because of the red brick quoins set into the white stucco of the walls to ornament the church's corners and the rims of its doors and windows.

Perhaps the best known Dutch Reformed site in American lore is that at Sleepy Hollow, near Tarrytown, New York, whose cemetery was the reputed site of Ichabod Crane's encounter with the Headless Horseman as narrated by Washington Irving. Built in 1699, this stone church illustrates well the social structure of the Dutch colonial settlement in the Hudson Valley (see figure 25). The church was built for the Philipse family, who numbered among the most influential patroons of the region. Inside were family pews; servants and slaves were relegated to a gallery in a manner reminiscent of both colonial Virginia and New England. The stone building material is characteristic of the region, and the double-pitch roof is typically Dutch. The pointed arch windows, visible in the Wallace Nutting photograph taken probably in the second decade of the twentieth century, are almost certainly later additions to this frequently remodeled structure (Rose 1963, 305).

These two churches are among the handful of remnants of the colonial Dutch presence in the New York-New Jersey area. This remains the major demographic focus of the Reformed Church in America, the more "mainline" branch of the tradition which closely resembles Presbyterianism except for its now vestigial ethnic heritage. (The more conservative Christian Reformed Church, which maintained strong Dutch ties until well into the twentieth century, is discussed in the context of the ethnic variety of the Old Northwest.) Although the Dutch Reformed were more successful in maintaining their distinctive identity in the New World than their French Huguenot coreligionists, the community along the eastern seaboard was overshadowed by its other fellow Calvinists, the Presbyterians, whose architecture was remarkably similar.

ANGLICANISM

During the colonial era, the Church of England was by definition the established church for all lands that lay within British hegemony, and its rights could not be denied. However, its actual status varied considerably from colony to colony, depending on the religious inclinations of the colonists and the provisions on religion embodied in the very different colonial charters. After the Glorious Revolution, British supervision of the colonies became more focused, and an Anglican presence was imposed upon grudging New England Puritans. In the southern colonies, including Maryland, the Established Church had legal priority, and minority traditions were at best tolerated even while growing significantly in strength, as in eighteenth-century Virginia. In the middle colonies, Anglicanism was "established" only in four counties of New York; in the remainder of this territory, its adherents constituted a minority, but one that was conscious of its favor in the eyes of the Crown as well as its generally high social and economic status, particularly in urban areas. Its building patterns reflected this rather mixed picture.

The successive versions of the neoclassical style of Christopher Wren and his successor, James Gibbs, had become normative for Anglican church building for decades following Wren's rebuilding of London's ecclesiastical fabric following the Great Fire of 1666. Neoclassicism thus became normative for colonial Anglicans, though its precise execution varied considerably according to local building materials, communal wealth, and the influence of other cultural presences. Interior arrangements, which will be discussed at greater length in the context of the colonial South, were fairly uniform, and included provision for four basic liturgical functions: a desk and pulpit for the proclaimed and preached Word, and a font and table for the administration of the two sacraments. The king's arms usually adorned a wall, indicating the political role that the church played in the British scheme of things (Friary 1971).

One of the most distinctive Anglican churches in the Middle Colonies was Christ Church, Philadelphia, at which the Protestant Episcopal Church was formally organized in 1785 after American membership in the Church of England had become politically impossible. The gathering here of the Continental Congress for fasting and prayer following the Battle of Lexington further links Christ Church with the patriot cause, an association not always present with colonial Anglican churches. (William White, its rector, served as chaplain to the Congress, and later became the first Episcopal bishop of Pennsylvania and presiding bishop of the Episcopal church.) Christ Church was built of brick in phases beginning in 1727; its steeple was paid for a lottery, a common fund-raising device during the eighteenth century. The church was at least in part designed by one of its vestrymen, Dr. John Kearsley, and is rich in the Palladian motifs that characterize the Anglo-American neoclassicism of the era. Although it is a monumental building by colonial standards, the plan of Quaker Philadelphia does not permit it to dominate the cityscape as Anglican churches often were designed to do (Faris 1926, 62–65; Friary 1971, 312ff., 388; Rose 1963, 340–41; Teitelman and Longstreth 1974, 40).

Rural Anglican churches were generally smaller and less stylish than urban counterparts such as Christ Church, which itself might be viewed as something of a country cousin of its London models. Saint David's Church (1715) in Radnor, Delaware County, is domestic in size and contours and built of the fieldstone so common in eastern Pennsylvania. Erected in response to a petition for a Welsh-speaking Society for the Propagation of the Gospel missionary to serve settlers in the Welsh Tract, its design probably reflects Welsh cultural influences rather than those emanating from London (Faris 1926, 203–7; Rose 1963, 356–57).

Following independence, the newly established Protestant Episcopal Church underwent a marked decline in popularity, reflecting in part the cloud overhanging it from the Tory sympathies of many of its colonial clergy. By the 1820s, Anglican fortunes began to recover through strong episcopal leadership, especially in New York and Virginia. However, the "churchmanship" associated with these two foci differed considerably. Where Virginia and much of the South were decidedly "Low Church" – that is, essentially Protestant in theological identity – New York, New Jersey and eastern Pennsylvania had by the 1840s become a hotbed of "High Church" theology, influenced by the Oxford Movement, which emphasized the "Catholic" themes of hierarchy and sacraments. This region also came under the spell of a related movement known as "Ecclesiology." Led by a small group of propagandists at Cambridge University, British and American Ecclesiologists argued that the only proper architectural setting for sacramental worship was the Gothic, particularly the "Decorated" style that flourished during the late thirteenth and early fourteenth centuries in England (Pierson 1978, chap. 4, part 1).

Churches with Gothic features had been present in the American colonies as late medieval survivals, including the earliest version of New York's Trinity. During the early decades of the nineteenth century, a tentative revival began to manifest itself in churches such as Trinity Episcopal on the New Haven Green. These churches, however, were essentially in the Wren-Gibbs lineage, with Gothic accoutrements such as pointed-arch windows added on to what was essentially a neoclassical form. The coming of "true" Gothic principles to American shores was the result of two intersecting forces: the founding of the New York Ecclesiological Society in 1848 and the earlier arrival of the English architect Richard Upjohn in 1829.

The first American church to be built according to designs specifically furnished by the Cambridge Camden Society (the English Ecclesiologists) was Saint James the Less (1846–48) in what is now Philadelphia (see figure 26). Built by a local businessman and based on the Church of Saint Michael in Longstanton, Cambridgeshire, Saint James is the quintessence of the English country parish church transplanted to American soil. One distinctive feature required by the principles of Ecclesiology which the church exhibits is a *chancel* – the area in which the Eucharistic liturgy is conducted – that is visibly distinct from the *nave*, or main body of the church. Other features resonate with the Romantic pursuit of the picturesque that was so influential in American design at the time: random ashlar (fieldstone) construction, rural setting in a churchyard surrounded by a stone fence and, instead of a full tower and belfry, a bellcote – a thin vertical unit rising at one end of the church with a gabled top and three openings in which bells could be placed. Surrounded today by a stable but less than prosperous neighborhood, this lovely diminutive Anglo-Catholic church and its walled-in surrounding burying ground stand as a refreshing anachronism in an otherwise dreary cityscape (Pierson 1978, 184–95; Stanton 1968, 98ff.).

Although Saint James the Less was a purist expression of a theological and architectural orthodoxy, the Ecclesiological gospel was to prove highly influential but not entirely normative in American Anglican practice. The architect who would popularize an authentic version of Gothic revival throughout the entire nation and among denominations other than the Episcopal was the Anglican emigrant Richard Upjohn, who began his American practice in New England but soon relocated in New York City. Upjohn's first major triumph was Trinity Episcopal Church on Wall Street, the third in a line of churches for a parish dating from the earliest days of British occupation in New York, and still the owner of enormously valuable Manhattan property (see figure 27). Trinity, completed in 1846, is in some ways very different from Saint James. Reflecting the later Perpendicular phase of English Gothic, it is both more monumental and symmetrical, and is distinguished by a single, centrally placed tower and high-soaring spire. Trinity also embodies both a profound knowledge of fundamental Gothic structural and design principles, and features the "divided chancel" so stressed by the Ecclesiologists as essential to proper sacramental worship (Pierson 1978, chap. 4, part 2).

Upjohn went on to design a myriad of churches throughout the country and invented the distinctly American form that came to be called "Carpenter Gothic," examples of which are discussed elsewhere in the context of other regions. Although many of his creations, including Trinity, were monumental structures designed specifically for urban settings, one of his distinctly rural churches might also be mentioned. George Washington Doane, the High Church bishop of New Jersey, was the first American patron of the Ecclesiological Society, and had observed at first hand the ideological ferment taking place in England. Though a bishop, Doane also served as rector of Saint Mary's Church in Burlington, New Jersey, a parish dating back to Society for the Propagation of the Gospel days in the early 1700s.

In 1846 Doane engaged Upjohn to design a new church. Upjohn had available detailed drawings of the Church of Saint John the Baptist in Shottesbroke, Berkshire, by the English Gothicist William Butterfield, which he used as the basis for this new parish church in a setting equally as picturesque as that of Saint James the Less. The original, which dated to the "Decorated" or "Middle" period of English Gothic design, was cruciform and featured a square tower with high spire at the crossing. Upjohn improved upon this original by streamlining the spire into a "broach" design – one in which the bases of the triangular parts extend out and curve to meet more gracefully the square base of the tower, and by reducing the elements of the interior to their essentials. Although Saint Mary's was liturgically "correct" by Ecclesiological standards, the English advocates of the movement sneered at Upjohn for not following plans that they themselves had furnished and other minor offenses against authority (Pierson 1978, 177–84; Faris 1926, 16–19; Rose 1963, 286–87).

Although Ecclesiology helped launch the first Gothic revival in the United States, with its axis in the New York-Philadelphia region, its popularity spread for reasons well beyond the narrow confines of ecclesiastical dogmatism. During the later nineteenth century the Episcopal church became the quintessential elite urban denomination in an age of growing Anglophilia and vast new fortunes in the days before the graduated income tax. Although virtually all of the cities of the northeastern quadrant saw handsome Gothic revival Episcopal churches rise during the decades between the Civil War and the Great Depression, it was in Manhattan that their role in shaping the cityscape was most conspicuous.

Manhattan's "churchscape" during the years following independence was virtually a tabula rasa. Although New York, with Boston and Philadelphia, was a major port during colonial days, much of its built environment from that era was destroyed either by fires or by the relentless pace of urbanization as it rapidly rose to the status of becoming the nation's premier city, as well as its most important point of entry for immigrants. Today only one church survives from the colonial era. Saint Paul's Chapel (1764) at Broadway and Vesey Streets is one of what were once several "chapels of ease" of Trinity, built to provide access to worship for parishioners not sufficiently close to the mother church in an age when transportation over even what now seem very short distances could be formidable. Saint Paul's is built in the high Gibbsian style of the time, but of local micaschist and brownstone (Rose 1963, 295–97).

A number of early nineteenth-century churches in a variety of styles and denominations still stand in the socially and architecturally mixed neighborhoods of lower Manhattan. The progress of the city, however, was to be relentlessly northward; as new immigrants began to push into the Lower East Side and other downtown areas, the middling and wealthier classes began inexorably to drift uptown. Episcopal churches – "the spoor of the rich," as one parish historian called them – became a good indicator of where the fashionable resided at a given moment. A few, such as Saint George's in Stuyvesant Square (1856), stayed put, even as their clientele moved outward. A stout brownstone building of pre-Richardsonian eclectic Romanesque design, Saint George's became known as the archetypal "institutional church" under the leadership of its rector, the Irish-born William Rainsford, and his staunch supporter and warden, the fabulously wealthy J. P. Morgan. Confronted with the influx of poor newcomers as the "New Immigration" from southern and eastern Europe reached its floodtide during the late nineteenth century, Saint George's stood its ground and responded to changing conditions not by flight but rather by beginning myriad outreach programs and establishing chapels for immigrant speakers of different languages (Moulton 1964; Goldberger 1979, 105; White and Willensky 1978, 118–19).

Unlike Saint George's, the congregation of Saint Thomas Episcopal Church represented the tendencies both to relocate as well as periodically to rebuild, often necessitated by the fires which were an omnipresent part of pre-twentieth-century American urban life. The first Saint Thomas stood at Broadway and Broom Streets; built in 1823, it apparently was a rather odd early attempt at Gothicism, with painted and pointed windows and battlemented towers. When this architectural curiosity burned in 1851, it was replaced on the same site in the same style due to the wishes of an eccentric but well-to-do parishioner. In 1870 the congregation relocated at Fifth Avenue and Fifty-third Street, having engaged Richard Upjohn to design an elegant Gothic revival building with a corner tower. This third Saint Thomas was graced not only by Upjohn's attention but also by that of two of the most prominent artists of the day: the sculptor Augustus Saint-Gaudens executed the reredos and the painter John La Farge the murals (DeMille 1958).

This Victorian ensemble, alas, was destroyed by yet another fire in 1905. Phoenixlike, it became reincarnated in even greater splendor on the same site in 1914 through the enormous wealth of the fashionable congregation and the design genius of Ralph Adams Cram and Bertram Grosvenor Goodhue. Cram, the Boston Gothicist, appears to have provided the overall scheme for the building which, like its predecessor, makes optimal use of its midtown corner site with a single tower. Unlike Saint Patrick's Cathedral, which lies only a block or so down on the opposite side of Fifth Avenue, Saint Thomas does not attempt to dominate its space, but rather blends in with its high-rise commercial surroundings with an understated dignity (see figure 28; Allen 1974).

Although its exterior is elegant enough, the real glory of Saint Thomas becomes apparent only upon entrance. The interior, designed by Cram's partner, Bertram Goodhue, is one of the nation's most truly splendid spaces. Resplendent in dark carved stone and wood, its reredos stands as one of the most massive liturgical sculptural schemes in the world. Designed by the German-born sculptor Lee Lawrie, who was also responsible for the great Atlas statue outside nearby Rockefeller Center, these reredos embody the liturgical and aesthetic philosophy that underlay this last and grandest phase of the Gothic revival. Arising out of the coincidence of the Arts and Crafts and Anglo-Catholic movements, it affirmed the collaboration of the building and decorative arts in honoring God through the most elaborate and beautiful setting for worship that was possible. Here in Saint Thomas it was realized as fully as it might be in a parish church. The persistent rumor that a dollar sign is carved in its "Brides' Door" – associated with the Consuelo Vanderbilt–duke of Marlborough wedding – bespeaks the financial undergirdings upon which such opulence necessarily rested (Goldstone and Dalrymple 1974, 202; Oliver 1983, 65, 69–70; Grove 1965, 19).

Episcopal churches abound in Manhattan, indicative of the early Anglican presence and the role the denomination played among both the city's well-to-do and, eventually, those poorer folk to whom outreach became an important priority. One other Episcopal parish church, only a stone's throw from Saint Thomas at Park Avenue and Fifty-first Street, deserves special mention in any architectural tour of the city. Like Saint Thomas, Saint Bartholomew's had emerged by the Victorian era as a church of wealth and fashion (its members included several Vanderbilts) that had also developed a vigorous program of social outreach. Its earlier homes included an 1835 neoclassical hybrid on Lafayette Place and a Victorian Romanesque creation by James Renwick, Jr., the designer of Saint Patrick's Catholic Cathedral, at Madison and Forty-fourth. Working with a monumental arched porch by Charles Follen McKim carried over from the second church, Bertram Goodhue created a splendid domed structure in a Romanesque-Byzantine blend that he himself characterized as more evocative of the Arabian Nights than of the Christian past. Unlike Saint Thomas, Saint Bartholomew's was based on Goodhue's theory of the primacy of solid geometrical shapes rather than complex Gothic interlacings (see figure 29). The sharp volumes of the exterior contrast dramatically with what lies within. Here, Goodhue combined a variety of materials of different textures and colors – limestone, marble, and tile – to evoke an almost dreamlike atmosphere (White and Willensky 1978, 150–51; Oliver 1983, 151; Smith 1988, 6–7, 44, and passim).

The mixture of aesthetic opulence and social outreach exemplified in this parish's history has continued, sometimes controversially, into Saint Bartholomew's later history. The splendor of the interior today is set off by the narthex, which is lined with cots to accommodate some few of the city's legions of homeless. During the 1980s, the parish was torn by a bitter conflict over a multimillion dollar offer it had received for the air rights to the space above its parish house. Although the church itself was not in physical danger, a substantial minority of the parish allied with preservationists to oppose this move, which its proponents justified on the moral basis that the funds obtained could be put to benevolent use. The "Battle of St. Bart's" ultimately reached the United States Supreme Court, which sustained the position of the opponents of the sale. (For a highly partisan account of these developments, see Brolin 1988.)

Although Manhattan boasts many other fine examples of Episcopalian building – Saint Mark's in the Bowery, Saint Mary the Virgin, and James Renwick's Grace Church, to name only a few – one such church in particular deserves mention. At the top of Central Park, near the lower reaches of Harlem and not too far from Columbia University, rises the world's largest cathedral. The Cathedral Church of Saint John the Divine has a complicated history, arising in its conception quite possibly from the scandal of the upstart Roman Catholic community's being able to boast a cathedral as fine and monumental as Saint Patrick's on Fifth Avenue. Although the original design competition in 1889 was won by a hybrid Gothic-Romanesque entry from the firm of LaFarge and Heins, the death of the former partner ended the agreement, and Ralph Adams Cram received the new commission in 1907.

"Saint John the Unfinished," as it is both ironically and fondly known, must certainly rank among Cram's finest achievements. The cathedral is so vast as to seem cavelike, and has to be explored component by component in order to take in its awesome complexity. In contrast with Washington's National Cathedral, which is fundamentally rectilinear and can be "read" at a glance in its essential outlines, Saint John's is architectonic rather than transparent. Even the quality of light in the two great buildings is sharply different: where the National Cathedral seems clear and airy, Saint John's is heavy and contemplative. To comprehend its richness, the viewer must circumambulate the great nave, looking into the side chapels, studying the stained glass, and contemplating the great rose window that links it to the tradition of French Gothic.

The role of Saint John's in the community is similarly complex. Originally conceived, one may assume, as a tangible expression of the central role of the Episcopal church in the power structure of the city, the cathedral's assembly slowed with the depression and halted with World War II. When peace came, the diocese put a halt to further construction in recognition of the overwhelming needs of the surrounding community. Eventually, however, another shift of direction took place: construction resumed, but through the work of local young stone carvers learning their craft in the process. Building and outreach thus proceeded in tandem. In addition, Saint John's – still unfinished, but progressively less so – has become a center for the arts, a forum for public debate on social issues, and a celebrant of the ongoing vitality in such events of the annual "blessing of the beasts," at which creatures ranging from gerbils to elephants assemble for a benediction. In these ways, Saint John's has tried to redefine the role of a cathedral in a complex and troubled urban society.

URBAN VARIETY IN NEW YORK

Restaurants and churches are two of the most accurate gauges of social variety in a city; New York abounds in both. The five boroughs abound in houses of worship of almost every variety conceivable, from Russian Orthodox cathedrals to neighborhood *botánicas* where devotees can purchase the materials for Santería worship at home. Exhaustively cataloguing New York City's religious richness would be a futile task; the best we can aim for here is a sampler of some representative examples.

As already indicated, Saint John the Divine, Manhattan's most spectacular house of worship, may well have been inspired by a desire to excel the growing reality of a Roman Catholic presence exemplified most fully in Saint Patrick's

Cathedral (1853–79). Saint Patrick's was the creation of two men: Archbishop
"Dagger John" Hughes, who had actively organized and armed his Irish followers against the threat of nativist violence, and James Renwick, Jr., the Episcopalian architect responsible for such socially prestigious churches as Calvary and
Grace as well as the Smithsonian Institution's "castle" in Washington. Hughes
wanted, in his own words, "to erect a Cathedral in the city of New York that may
be worthy of our increasing numbers, intelligence, and wealth as a religious community, as a public architectural monument, of the present and prospective
crowns of this metropolis of the American continent." To this end he chose, instead of a "safe" Catholic architect such as Patrick Keeley, a non-Catholic of
reputation and imagination who could satisfy his wishes (Pierson 1978, 211).

Renwick, presumably, was intrigued by the possibility of creating a truly monumental structure rather than even a fashionable parish church, as well as expressing what he had learned from his study of the Cologne Cathedral, an incomplete
medieval undertaking then being brought to a conclusion in the heyday of Romantic revivalism on the Continent. The result, expressed grandly in white
marble, was unlike anything the city had yet witnessed. To be sure, it speaks of
Catholic triumphalism; in its splendor, it seems like a great wedding cake, somewhat excessive in its unnuanced intricacy. Still, Saint Patrick's stands firmly against
its towering secular neighbors, such as the Rockefeller Center that stands directly
across Fifth Avenue; like its Anglican neighbor, Saint Bartholomew's, it helps
remind New York of another set of priorities besides the endless acquisition of
wealth and fame (see figure 30).

In addition to Saint Patrick's, of course, there are hundreds of Roman Catholic churches in New York, built mainly during the late nineteenth and early
twentieth centuries; many of them now serve constituencies substantially different from those for whom they were built. Like churches of other denominations,
most of those erected during the period – simultaneously the era of great fortunes
and massive immigration – were in some version of the Gothic or Romanesque
modes. Unlike their Protestant and Anglican counterparts, though, Catholic
churches enriched the cityscape not just with the buildings themselves but also
with statuary, grottoes, and other ornament that could serve as the scene of organized or impromptu devotion. Weegee (born Arthur H. Fellig, the son of a
rabbi), best known for his flash images of lurid scenes of urban crime and other
low life, on one occasion captured an instance of such devotion to the Virgin
Mary, here on the grounds of Holy Name of Jesus Church in Manhattan (see
figure 31).

Some of the variety and character of Catholic building is discussed in greater
detail in other chapters, particularly that on the Old Northwest states; Chicago
has at least as compelling claims as New York to be the capital of American Catholicism. For Jews, however far-flung their American diaspora may have become,
there is only one "Jewish city" in this country, and that is New York. During the
colonial era, New York was one of a number of important sites for Sephardic
(Iberian) Jewish settlement along the Atlantic seaboard. Following a hostile reception in New Amsterdam by Peter Stuyvesant, a small colony began to devel-

op. The congregation Shearith Israel – also known as the Spanish and Portuguese Synagogue – was founded in 1654, and today occupies an 1897 Classical revival structure on Central Park West. Connected with it is a "Little Synagogue" that is a reproduction of its first real home, a 1730 Georgian building on Mill Street. The congregation's first and still extant burial ground, on St. James Place near Chinatown, was established in 1683 and utilized till 1828. Today it is the oldest surviving artifact of human construction in Manhattan; the congregation refuses to sell this sacred ground for secular use. Two other burial grounds are similarly maintained in Greenwich Village and Chelsea (White and Willensky 1978, 36, 75, 110, 200; Goldstone and Dalrymple 1974, 71–72; Fine and Wolfe 1978, 6–8).

A second and much larger wave of Jewish immigration, primarily of German-speaking Ashkenazim, took place during the early and middle decades of the nineteenth century. An Ashkenazic faction broke from the Sephardic-dominated Shearith Israel in 1825 to found Congregation B'nai Jeshurun in the African Presbyterian Mission Church on what is now Lafayette Street. This first home was an oddly eclectic combination of a Roman temple with a Gothic steeple, which was abandoned in 1851 for a Gothic revival structure designed for the congregation (Fine and Wolfe 1978, 11, 12).

As Jewish immigration continued, new synagogues began to come into being, often through fission from those already established arising out of cultural and, before long, religious differences. Some of the German-speaking Jewish newcomers brought with them the spirit of the Reform movement which had begun in eighteenth-century Germany as an attempt to bring the Jewish community into the modern era. Reform Jews used vernacular language rather than Hebrew in worship, ended separation of the sexes in the synagogue, and even abandoned the term "synagogue" in favor of "temple," an acknowledgment that they regarded the diaspora as permanent and normative and had no desire to see *the* Temple restored in Jerusalem.

One of the most successful split-offs from the stem that began with Shearith Israel was Emanu-El, founded in 1845 by Reform-minded German Jews. Designed by the Jewish architectural firm of Eidlitz and Fernbach in 1868, the congregation's first building of its own represented a new emphasis in Jewish design – the quest for a style that was not simply an appropriation of modes such as the Greek and Gothic revivals that had been popularized by a spectrum of Christian denominations but rather one that reflected an authentically Jewish past. Such a past was not easy to come by, since Diaspora Jews had for centuries adapted the architectural styles of host cultures. What emerged in mid-nineteenth-century America was a Romantic eclecticism that incorporated elements of Romanesque and Gothic but was distinguished by the use of Moorish motifs, reflecting the centuries-long symbiotic relationship between Sephardic Jews and Islamic culture in the lands around the Mediterranean basin.

The 1868 Temple Emanu-El was fundamentally a pre-Richardsonian Romanesque revival structure with two towers, a row of clerestory windows, and a transept. Both interior and exterior were colorful, reflecting the era's love of polychrome brickwork and mural painting. Most notable, though, were the bulbous domes of the towers, evocative of the Taj Mahal, south Asia's architectural monument to the Islamic religion. Perhaps the best description of the effect is "Jewish Victorian." Its austere, monumental Byzantine-Romanesque replacement on the same site, which dates from 1929, preserves the claim of its predecessor to be the largest Jewish house of worship in the world, seating 2500 (Fine and Wolfe 1978, 20–21; White and Willensky 1978, 222; Goldberger 1979, 230–31; Wischnitzer 1955, 74–77).

During the decades following the Civil War, yet another wave of Jews, this time from the "Pale of Settlement" in central and eastern Europe, began to arrive at Castle Garden and then at the new Ellis Island processing center for immigrants. These "New Immigration" Jews tended to be poor, Yiddish-speaking, and either religiously Orthodox or inclined toward radical secular politics. Many of the Reform Jews fled northwards in near-panic, emulating their Gentile neighbors who had already begun this progress uptown. The newcomers not only built synagogues – over five hundred were founded between 1880 and 1915 in the Lower East Side – but created entire communities, with slaughterhouses, ritual baths, kosher restaurants, yeshivas, and the other aspects of the built environment of the transplanted ghetto or shtetl. For a few decades, the vibrant Yiddish culture evoked in Irving Howe's *World of Our Fathers* blossomed, but it soon yielded to the by now traditional American Jewish penchant for social and geographical mobility (Fine and Wolfe 1978, 31).

The synagogues, great and small, of the Lower East Side and East Village reflected two basic architectural strategies. The first was borrowing, a tactic that would come full circle when later African American and Hispanic in-migrants in Manhattan and many other American cities would take over synagogues abandoned by Jews heading toward more prosperous urban neighborhoods or the suburbs. Many of the new immigration Jewish congregations bought either synagogues that had been left behind by their more established German counterparts, who were heading for Harlem or other neighborhoods farther uptown, or churches similarly left behind by Christian congregations. The result was, to say the least, an architectural variety, illustrated among surviving examples by the Congregation Beth Haknesseth Mogen Avraham, which acquired an 1845 Greek revival Methodist Protestant church on Attorney Street in 1884. Other congregations with more means were able to build their own houses of worship, usually in some adaptation of the *Rundbogenstil* Romanesque, the Gothic, or the Moorish styles, the latter featuring bulbous domes and keyhole-shaped doors and windows. More often than not the result, at times monumental in scale, combined features from two or more of these styles eclectically. A typical example was the Congregation Star of Jacob on Pitt Street, photographed in 1938 by Walter Rosenblum and later torn down for a housing project (see figure 32; Fine and Wolfe 1978, 80 and passim).

World War I and subsequent congressional acts cut off further large-scale immigration for some time. Later newcomers, such as the Hasidim fleeing the Holocaust, tended to gravitate to newer areas of settlement in Brooklyn and beyond, creating in such neighborhoods as Williamsburg and Crown Heights another, even more intense version of "total immersion" Jewish culture than had earlier flourished in the Lower East Side. Successful assimilated Jews worshiped at places such as the Park Avenue Synagogue on East Eighty-seventh Street, with the elaborate 1950s glass-facade Steinberg House adjoining it. A handful of the Lower East Side synagogues still survive, but most have fallen into disuse or underuse, or have been sold to still newer immigrant communities, usually Evangelical Protestant in persuasion (White and Willensky 1978, 236–37; Fine and Wolfe 1978, 34–36).

A final brief note on the religious architecture of Manhattan must here suffice. As has been the case in most other cities, few houses of worship have been built in Manhattan since World War II, though commercial structures have flourished. One interesting exception is Saint Peter's Lutheran Church, a congregation that sold its original building to the Citicorp Center with the proviso that it have new worship facilities made available in the new complex (see figure 33). The 1977 result is dramatic: at the foot of the giant aluminum-encased office tower on Lexington Avenue is a striking granite creation of triangular forms that opens directly onto street level. Inside is a worship space of stark wooden rectilinear shapes, adjoining a smaller chapel with sculpture designed by Louise Nevelson. Saint Peter's thus provides a small but elegant and visible presence of "new-time" religion in a city where the more ornate styles of most religious buildings contrast sharply with newer commercial structures. It invites comparison with Chicago's Loop Synagogue, described elsewhere, which similarly attempts to combine modern design with ritual space in the midst of urban busyness (Goldberger 1979, 158–59).

THE FEDERAL CITY

The District of Columbia is simultaneously anomalous and representative in American urban history. Until not very long ago, Washington was very much a southern city, embodying the lifestyles and social mores, including racial segregation, that had characterized regional life for many decades. As such, it could be perhaps better included in the chapter on the South. Recent decades have seen that older reality, for better or worse, yield to the same social logic that has been more typical of northern than southern cities, in which legal segregation has disappeared but de facto residential separation of the races has become the norm. As a consequence, two Washingtons have emerged. The first is that of its permanent residents, mainly African American, with its grim realities of poverty and the ever-present threat of crime and drug-related violence. Its religious artifacts are similar to those of most inner cities: storefront Pentecostal churches, older middle-class structures sold to poorer inner-city congregations, homes of new religions such as Islam in its traditional and black varieties, and a few "mainline" groups trying to hang on. These houses of worship are socially but not architecturally significant; little can be said of most of them that cannot be said of similar phenomena in Chicago, Detroit, New York, Philadelphia, and many other cities. This Washington is more significant in its typicality than in its distinctiveness.

The other Washington, familiar to visitors and the city's ever-changing population of politicians and bureaucrats, is unique in the nation. Georgetown, Connecticut Avenue, Kalorama Circle, Rock Creek Park, Dupont Circle, Lafayette Square, the Mall and Capitol Hill are familiar venues in this world, which is populated with the affluent and the powerful and examined daily by thousands of sightseers and political and business visitors from home and abroad. The city they behold is truly spectacular, and is based both on private and public wealth and on deliberate planning of a kind rare in American urban history. Philadelphia, perhaps, offers the most compelling parallel, and even that a partial one.

The federal city's history is coextensive with that of the Republic not only in terms of its central governmental activities but in its precise span of history. The District of Columbia was created out of the Maryland and Virginia towns of Georgetown and Alexandria and their surrounding countryside along the Potomac by Congress in 1790 as a home for the new federal government, which had previously found temporary quarters in Philadelphia and New York. Its primary designer, the French architect Pierre L'Enfant, was concerned not only with the practical realities of urban construction and the Baroque planning models popular in Europe but with the symbolic incorporation of the nature of the new republic into the infrastructure of the city itself.

The focus of L'Enfant's plan is the Mall, the center of the national government. From this axis radiate diagonally placed broad avenues named after the states in a manner that suggests their relative placement in macrocosmic geography, as well as their historical and political centrality. (New York and Pennsylvania Avenues, for example, occupy prominent places near the center.) These radial arteries intersect periodically at public squares. Rationality and symbolism thus combine to create a microcosm of the "First New Nation," one which, like its capital, had been "invented" rather than simply inherited through countless generations (Scott and Lee 1993, 16–18).

Throughout the history of the world, city planning has not been a purely secular phenomenon, especially for imperial capitals. For the Chinese, the Romans, the Aztecs, and many others, monumental structures for governmental and religious functions have stood together, and the very plans of the cities themselves have often been based on notions of cosmic orientation. L'Enfant's plan can be read this way; similarly, the District's Mall, though ostensibly civic, can also be interpreted as a religious phenomenon, at the core of what the sociologist Robert Bellah has described as America's "civil religion." Additive in character, its overall plan emerging in stages over two centuries, the Mall has come to include not only houses of government such as the Capitol but monuments to the nation's most revered leaders and myriad soldiers fallen in battle. In addition to Robert Mills's Washington Monument (1845–84), designed in the form of an Egyptian obelisk, and Henry Bacon's Greek-temple-like Lincoln Memorial (1912–22), the Mall has more recently been enhanced by Maya Lin's controversial Vietnam Veterans' Memorial (1982) and the still more recent sculptural evo-cation of American women of the Vietnam war. Although these various tributes exemplify the styles and ideologies of a number of historical eras, they blend with the vast expanse of grass and trees, shaped in part by the great landscape archi-tect Frederick Law Olmsted, into a cumulative whole of profound impact (Pamela Scott, "The Mall," in Scott and Lee 1993, 62–112).

The houses of government that line the Mall evoke a sense not only of bu-reaucratic functionality but, as exemplified in the Capitol (many architects, 1793–1865), a sense of symbolic monumentality deliberately evocative of the Roman Empire, in which government represents a sacred trust. Just as Manhattan's ar-chitecture, epitomized in its twentieth-century high-rise office buildings, be-speaks commerce as the city's raison d'être, so does Washington's focus on gov-ernment as its vital core. Zoning codes prohibit the high-rises that dominate most urban American skylines, and the Washington Monument defines the city's ver-tical limit.

Washington, like any American city, hosts a panoply of religious buildings, but even these take their cue from the broader theme of civil religion. Most promi-nent among them is the Cathedral Church of Saints Peter and Paul, better known as the National Cathedral (see figure 34). The cathedral was adumbrated at Washington's very beginnings by L'Enfant himself, who advocated "a great church for national purposes." Begun in 1906 under the aegis of Episcopal bish-op Henry Yates Satterlee as a house of prayer that would transcend denomina-tional distinctions, the cathedral's completion was delayed until 1990, when it was presided over by two prominent Anglicans, President George Bush and Queen Elizabeth II. Sited on Mount St. Alban's, it overlooks the entire city, symbolic of its conceivers' aspirations to build a spiritual *axis mundi* for the nation's capital and, implicitly, the nation itself (Spears 1990).

Designed by the English Gothic revivalist George Bodley, his Anglo-Ameri-can counterpart, Henry Vaughan, and their American successor, Philip Frohman, the cathedral is based on a fourteenth-century English scheme with a pair of fron-tal towers and a third at the crossing. Although the basic lines of the nave are forthright, the plan of the cathedral becomes more complex as one approaches the chancel, which is flanked by side chapels, including one for children. Still more chapels abound in the crypt, all elaborately decorated with stone and met-al carving, needlework and tapestries, and decorative arts of all sorts. The win-dows, like the sculpture and other artwork, reflect a variety of styles indicative of the lengthy (by American standards) span of its construction. Notable is the deep-hued Space Window, which includes a piece of rock from the moon. Here the architectonic sculptural programs of the medieval cathedrals are done yet one better (Scott and Lee 1993, 381–86).

One interesting and, in this country, unusual feature of the cathedral is its function as the repository of the remains of various notables, including Bishop Satterlee, the financier Andrew Mellon, and President Woodrow Wilson. Wil-son, who lies interred in the right aisle like a medieval knight, is notable here not only for his presence but also for the fact that he was a Presbyterian rather than

an Episcopalian. Similarly, the chapel at Princeton University, of which Wilson
served as president and which emerged from Presbyterian roots, was designed
in the Gothic mode by the arch-Anglican Ralph Adams Cram, who served as a
consulting architect to both the university and the cathedral. This ecumenism,
even if between elite denominations, underscores the intended role of the cathedral not simply as a denominational artifact – it serves not the local diocese but
rather as the seat of the presiding bishop – but as a national resource and symbol, a "house of prayer for all people."

Three of the houses of worship closest to the cathedral are two Eastern Orthodox churches – Saint Sophia and Saint Nicholas – and the Washington
Mosque (see figure 35), all of which blend in with the panoply of ambassadorial
residences that make this section of Washington so cosmopolitan. If the District's
houses of worship can be said to have a theme, two possibilities might be suggested: this very cosmopolitanism, counterbalanced by repeated invocations of
nationalism, or at least national identity. The National Cathedral incorporates
both of these motifs, as does the National Shrine of the Immaculate Conception,
located on the campus of Catholic University and designed by the prestigious
Catholic firm of Maginnis and Walsh beginning in 1919 (see figure 36). This giant
Byzantine-Romanesque domed church with its lofty adjoining stepped campanile expresses in its multiplicity of chapels, each dedicated to some avatar of the
Virgin Mary, the ethnic complexity of American Catholicism that is also at the
same time one. Although the Virgin has by tradition appeared in a variety of
places – Mexico's Guadalupe and Poland's Czestochowa being among the best
known – and as such has embodied the collective aspirations of very disparate
peoples, her national shrine here expresses simultaneously the oneness of both
the American people and the Catholic church.

The patriotic motif can also be found in many other Washington churches,
whether in explicit iconography or through historical association. Saint John's
Episcopal (1816), for example, which is located across Lafayette Square from the
White House, is interesting first as a fine example of the work of Benjamin Henry
Latrobe, the early nineteenth-century architect known for his creative manipu-
lation of geometrical spaces, as in his Baltimore Cathedral. Saint John's was originally designed in a Greek cross pattern (that is, with four equal arms) with a
shallow dome and cupola, but was later modified into a Latin cross with a Wren-
Gibbs style steeple and still later Victorianized with stained glass. Much of its
mystique, however, focuses on its identity as the "Church of the Presidents,"
derived from its proximity to the White House and the attendance both of Episcopalian presidents (such as James Madison, who selected what has become the
presidential pew) and of others who frequented it over the years. Many of the
kneeling cushions in the front pews have the presidential seal embroidered on
them, together with the names of the various chief executives who presumably
utilized them (Scott and Lee 1993, 162–63; Green 1970).

A walk up Sixteenth Street brings one to a pair of Protestant churches that
attained fame during the 1990s, when President and Hillary Clinton began to
attend the First Baptist (1954) and Foundry Methodist (1905) churches respec-

tively. First Baptist is a rather unusual example of post–World War II Gothic revival architecture, featuring stained glass windows evocative especially of Baptist themes. (Included are Roger Williams, the missionary Adoniram Judson, and "Mr. Average Baptist.") Foundry Methodist is a good example of the auditorium church in fashion during the late nineteenth and early twentieth centuries, also featuring the stained glass that had become common among Evangelical Protestant denominations by that time. Though neither church is architecturally distinguished, both share the aura generated by First Family patronage.

Other "mainline" Washington churches that reflect the city's preoccupation with political power and historic resonance include Saint Matthew's Catholic Cathedral (1893–). Designed by H. H. Richardson's protégés, Heins and LaFarge, this cathedral echoes the master's Trinity Church in Boston in the great open expanses and delicate tones of its interior. Its particular impact on the national consciousness derives from its central role in the funeral of John F. Kennedy, the nation's first Roman Catholic president. New York Avenue Presbyterian Church (1951), a Colonial revival structure with some Moderne touches, is interesting for its ministers Peter Marshall ("a man called Peter"), chaplain of the U.S. Senate, and George Docherty, the moving spirit behind the addition of the phrase "under God" to the Pledge of Allegiance. Its Lincoln Chapel and Parlor commemorate that president's association with the church, and its stained glass windows are another Protestant adaptation of a Catholic tradition, here also commemorating a panoply of national heroes. Metropolitan A.M.E. Church (1880–85), also known as "The Cathedral of African Methodism" and the "A.M.E. National Church," is an eclectic auditorium-style Victorian structure typical of urban middle-class black churches of its era. Featured during the Clinton inaugural activities in 1993, Metropolitan A.M.E. boasts of regular presidential visits since the time of William Howard Taft. Finally, National City Christian Church, designed by John Russell Pope of Jefferson Memorial fame in 1929–30, is the national church of the Disciples of Christ. Based on Gibbs's Saint Martin-in-the-Fields, it features stained glass windows commemorating the two presidents associated with the denomination, James Garfield and Lyndon Johnson (Cox 1974, 90; Scott and Lee 1993, 226 and 195–96; and individual church pamphlets).

REFLECTIONS

Although the mid-Atlantic states are deeply rooted in America's colonial past, the pluralistic sources of their foundings preclude any easy generalizations about their religious or cultural unity. More so than their neighboring regions in New England and the South, they anticipate the intense pluralism that would later characterize the new republic. Most particularly, their religious diversity – Anglican, Quaker, Presbyterian, Catholic, and various German groups – foreshadowed the still broader diversity that would be intensified with later waves of immigrants, and made clear early on that an American nation would have to be predicated on religious freedom in order to be viable.

The Quakers in the Delaware Valley gave the region its most intensely distinct religious character, expressed in architecture as well as in belief and social attitudes. Their presence and influence has lasted till the present day, even though their numerical strength has long since been eclipsed by Catholics, African Americans, and other, newer groups; even before the Revolution they had yielded political power to the forces represented by the sometimes Presbyterian, sometimes Anglican, always skeptical Ben Franklin. During the postcolonial decades, Philadelphia's religious architecture became characterized by a broad range of denominations and architects, often of note, who worked in the styles of the day. Distinguished among them were Benjamin Henry Latrobe, Roberts Mills, William Strickland, John Haviland, and Napoleon LeBrun. Unique to Philadelphia was its own Frank Furness, a flamboyantly eclectic Victorian architect whose designs included a number of local churches and synagogues. On the whole, however, the city's religious design history has been more cosmopolitan than idiosyncratic (O'Gorman 1983, 76–79).

The same might be said even more strongly about New York City, which emerged after independence as the cultural bellwether for the entire nation. Although its role as the center of American Jewish life has been undisputed, the built environment of its Jewish community has been characterized more by its intensity than its uniqueness. Similarly, the role of the region as a nurturer both of the Episcopal church and the Gothic revival with which it was for several decades so closely associated has been extremely significant. Here, again, we are talking not about a regionally restricted phenomenon but rather about one that rapidly spread well beyond regional boundaries. All of this points up the role of the region as a cosmopolitan center, one in which cultural trends emerge but from which they are rapidly emulated by the nation as a whole. In some senses, one might speak of this megalopolis as a national cultural hearth. The District of Columbia, similarly, is unique in its role as a monumental embodiment of iconography in its Mall, but iconography that by design is national rather than regional.

The most distinctive regional ambience of the mid-Atlantic states lies, perhaps unsurprisingly, in its hinterland rather than its metropolitan agglomerations. The "Pennsylvania Dutch" country of eastern Pennsylvania represents a unique concentration of colonial-era German culture, with a built environment ranging from that of the tradition-oriented Amish to the ethnically sectarian Ephrata community. Pockets of Polish and Ukrainian folk religion, such as the Our Lady of Czestochowa shrine in Doylestown, indicate the ethnic composition of the region. Similarly representative are the churches of the Welsh, another people skilled in the coal mining that was once a major economic mainstay. Like their urban Italian counterparts, however, none of these groups other than the German has been sufficiently dominant numerically to impart a unique flavor to the region.

The mid-Atlantic region is a study in an emergent national character. Although ethnic individuality persists, it has had to do so in an ethnically or at least religiously mixed environment. (Even the old German territory has recently been encroached upon significantly by Spanish-speaking immigrants.) Similarly, the monuments of the earliest dominant groups, such as the Anglicans and Quakers, still stand as historic shrines, but have been reduced to the sidelines in the actual religious life of subsequently more mixed populaces. The early Swedish and Dutch churches illustrate still more dramatically the submergence of their builders in a cosmopolitan culture. The mid-Atlantic states have been extremely important in their contribution to American religious architecture, but it is difficult to characterize that contribution as narrowly regional. Rather, it has been that of a region aspiring to lead a nation.

MID-ATLANTIC STATES: BIBLIOGRAPHY

Allen, Gerald. 1974. "The Fourth St. Thomas Church." *Architectural Record* 155, no. 4:118.

Baltzell, E. Digby. 1979. *Puritan Boston and Quaker Philadelphia.* Boston: Beacon Press.

Bilhartz, Terry D., ed. 1984. *Francis Asbury's America.* Grand Rapids, Mich.: Francis Asbury Press.

Brolin, Brent C. 1988. *The Battle of St. Bart's: A Tale of the Material and the Spiritual.* New York: William Morrow.

Cox, Warren J., et al. 1974. *A Guide to the Architecture of Washington, D.C.* New York: McGraw-Hill.

DeMille, George E. 1958. *Saint Thomas Church in the City of New York.* Austin, Tex.: Church Historical Society, 1958.

De Visser, John, and Harold Kalman. 1976. *Pioneer Churches.* New York: Norton.

Dorsey, John, and James D. Dilts. 1973. *A Guide to Baltimore Architecture.* Cambridge, Md.: Tidewater Publishers.

Faris, John T. 1926. *Old Churches and Meeting-Houses in and around Philadelphia.* Philadelphia: J. B. Lippincott.

Fine, Renée, and Gerard R. Wolfe. 1978. *The Synagogues of New York's Lower East Side.* New York: New York University Press.

Fischer, David Hackett. 1989. "North Midlands to the Delaware: The Friends' Migration, 1675–1725." In *Albion's Seed: Four British Folkways in America.* New York: Oxford University Press.

Friary, Donald Richard. 1971. "The Architecture of the Anglican Church in the Northern American Colonies: A Study of Religious, Social, and Cultural Expression." Ph.D. dissertation, University of Pennsylvania.

Garfinkel, Susan Laura. 1986. "Discipline, Discourse and Deviation: The Material Life of Philadelphia Quakers, 1762–1781." M.A. thesis, University of Delaware.

Goldberger, Paul. 1979. *The City Observed: New York, A Guide to the Architecture of Manhattan.* New York: Vintage.

Goldstone, Harmon H., and Martha Dalrymple. 1974. *History Preserved: A Guide to New York City Landmarks and Historic Districts.* New York: Simon and Schuster.

Gollin, Gillian Lindt. 1967. *Moravians in Two Worlds: A Study of Changing Communities.* New York: Columbia University Press.

Gowans, Alan. 1964. *Architecture in New Jersey.* Princeton, N.J.: D. Van Nostrand.

Green, Constance McLaughlin. 1970. *The Church on Lafayette Square: A History of St. John's Church, Washington, D.C., 1815–1970.* Washington, D.C.: Potomac Books.

Grove, Harold E. 1965. *St. Thomas Church.* New York: St. Thomas Church.

Howland, Richard H., and Eleanor P. Spencer. 1953. *The Architecture of Baltimore: A Pictorial History.* Baltimore: Johns Hopkins University Press.

James, Sydney V. 1963. *A People among Peoples: Quaker Benevolence in Eighteenth-Century America.* Cambridge, Mass.: Harvard University Press.

Kidley, Walter C. 1988. *Pittsburgh in Your Pocket: A Guide to Pittsburgh-Area Architecture.* Pittsburgh: Pittsburgh History and Landmarks Foundation.

Kowsky, Francis R., et al. 1981. *Buffalo Architecture: A Guide.* Cambridge, Mass.: MIT Press.

Malo, Paul. 1974. *Landmarks of Rochester and Monroe County: A Guide to Neighborhoods and Villages.* Syracuse: Syracuse University Press.

Maryland, A Guide to the Old Line State. 1940. New York: Oxford University Press.

Moulton, Elizabeth. 1964. *St. George's Church New York.* New York: St. George's Church.

Murtagh, William J. 1967. *Moravian Architecture and Town Planning: Bethlehem, Pennsylvania, and Other Eighteenth-Century American Settlements.* Chapel Hill: University of North Carolina Press.

O'Gorman, James F. 1983. *The Architecture of Frank Furness.* Philadelphia: Philadelphia Museum of Art.

Oliver, Richard. 1983. *Bertram Grosvenor Goodhue.* New York: Architectural History Foundation and the MIT Press.

Philadelphia Historic Preservation Corporation. 1994. *Sacred Sites of Center City: A Walking Tour.* Philadelphia: Philadelphia Historic Preservation Corporation.

Pierson, William H., Jr. 1970. *American Buildings and Their Architects: The Colonial and Neo-Classical Styles.* Garden City, N.Y.: Doubleday.

———. 1978. *American Buildings and Their Architects: Technology and the Picturesque, the Corporate and Early Gothic Styles.* Garden City, N.Y.: Doubleday, 1978.

Pittsburgh History and Landmarks Foundation. N.d. *An Ethnic Church Sampler.* Pittsburgh: n.p.

Rose, Harold Wickliffe. 1963. *The Colonial Houses of Worship in America.* New York: Hastings House.

Rothman, David J. 1971. *The Discovery of the Asylum: Social Order and Disorder in the New Republic.* Boston: Little, Brown.

Schmidt, Carl, and Ann Schmidt. 1959. *Architecture and Architects of Rochester, N.Y.* Rochester: Rochester Society of Architects.

Schuyler, Montgomery. 1910. "Architecture of American Colleges V." *Architectural Record* 28, no. 3:183–211.

Scott, Pamela, and Antoinette J. Lee. 1993. *Buildings of the District of Columbia.* New York: Oxford University Press.

Smith, Christine. 1988. *St. Bartholomew's Church in the City of New York.* New York: Oxford University Press.

Spears, George. 1990. "'Built for God and Man': National Cathedral Done after Eighty-three Years." *Dayton Daily News* Sept. 29:4C.

Stanton, Phoebe B. 1968. *The Gothic Revival and American Church Architecture: An Episode in Taste 1840–1856.* Baltimore: Johns Hopkins University Press.

Teitelman, Edward, and Richard W. Longstreth. 1974. *Architecture in Philadelphia: A Guide.* Cambridge, Mass.: MIT Press.

Toker, Franklin. 1994. *Pittsburgh: An Urban Portrait.* Pittsburgh: University of Pittsburgh Press.

Van Trump, James D. N.d. *"Our Eastern Domes, Fantastic, Bright . . .": Some Orthodox and Byzantine-Rite Churches in Allegheny County.* Pittsburgh: Pittsburgh History and Landmarks Foundation.

White, Norval, and Elliott Willensky. 1978. *AIA Guide to New York City*. New York: Collier.

Wilson, Robert H. 1976. *Freedom of Worship: Meeting Houses, Churches and Synagogues of Early Philadelphia*. Philadelphia: Old Philadelphia Churches Historical Association.

———. 1981. *Philadelphia Quakers 1681–1981*. Philadelphia: Philadelphia Yearly Meeting.

Wischnitzer, Rachel. 1955. *Synagogue Architecture in the United States: History and Interpretation*. Philadelphia: Jewish Publication Society of America.

Wurman, Richard Saul, and John Andrew Gallery. 1972. *Man-Made Philadelphia: A Guide to Its Physical and Cultural Environment*. Cambridge, Mass.: MIT Press.

Zepp, Ira G. 1981. *Sacred Spaces of Westminster*. Westminster, Md.: N.p.

17. Arch Street Meetinghouse, Philadelphia, Pennsylvania (exterior)

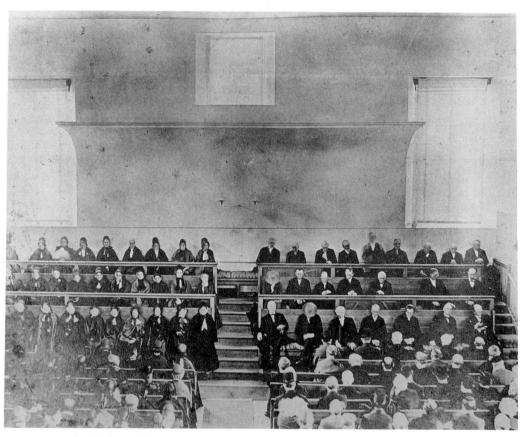

18. Arch Street Meetinghouse, interior

19. Mennonite Meetinghouse, Lancaster, Pennsylvania

20. Ephrata Cloister, Ephrata, Pennsylvania

21. *Old Swedes' (Gloria Dei) Church, Philadelphia, Pennsylvania*

22. St. George's Methodist Church, Philadelphia, Pennsylvania

23. Lovely Lane Methodist Church, Baltimore, Maryland

24. Basilica of the Assumption, Baltimore, Maryland

25. "Old Dutch Church — Tarrytown" (Dutch Reformed Church, Sleepy Hollow, New York), ca. 1910–25

26. St. James the Less Episcopal Church, Philadelphia, Pennsylvania

27. "Trinity Church and Wall Street Towers, New York, 1933"

29. St. Bartholomew's Episcopal Church, New York, New York

28. St. Thomas Episcopal Church, New York, New York

30. St. Patrick's Cathedral, New York, New York

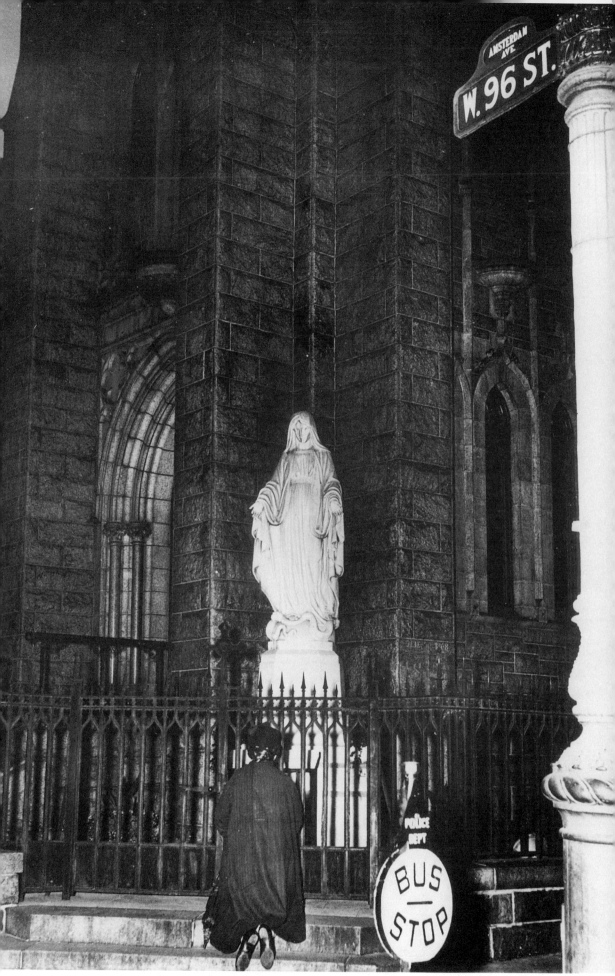

31. *"Untitled (One woman kneels at the still-closed church on the way to work)" (Holy Name of Jesus Church, New York, New York)*

33. *St. Peter's Lutheran Church, New York, New York*

32. *"Synagogue" (Pitt Street Synagogue, New York, New York), 1938*

34. National Cathedral, Washington, District of Columbia

35. *Washington Mosque, Washington, District of Columbia*

36. Shrine of the Immaculate Conception, Washington, District of Columbia

3 : The South

Of America's regions, the South is rivaled only by New England in its self-consciousness about being a special, separate place with a highly distinctive culture. From "Dixie" to grits and moon pies, the region that lies below the Mason-Dixon Line and (mostly) east of the Mississippi is still able to evoke a chain of associations, positive and negative but seldom neutral, among both native southerners and other Americans. Although race has traditionally been an important, if ambiguous, factor in defining southern particularity, other factors also surface when scholars try to pin down the components of regional identity: a sense of rootedness, the importance of family, the prestige of sports and the military, a subculture of violence, and, most particularly, the prevalence of religion, especially of the Evangelical Protestant variety.

Although its core can be defined by the eleven states that seceded from the nation to form the Confederacy in 1861 out of attachment to states rights and the "peculiar institution" of slavery, its periphery creates a transitional zone around the South. Four "border states" – Maryland, West Virginia, Kentucky, and Missouri – were never full members of the Confederacy, and the "southern-ness" of each was arguably less intense than that of their more militant neighbors. Conversely, the southern reaches of Ohio and Illinois as well as most of Indiana have been said to be "southern" in ethos and sympathies if not in geography. At the western boundary of the region, Texas especially illustrates the complexity of assessing regionalism in terms of geopolitical boundaries, since different sectors of the vast and populous Lone Star State can be variously regarded as southern, western, southwestern, or part of the Great Plains.

Even within the realm of the old Confederacy, regional culture varies according to historical and topographical factors. The original area of settlement lay along the Atlantic seaboard, and was colonized primarily by English settlers whose motivation was commercial. The society that emerged here was officially Anglican: the colonial South was the part of the thirteen colonies in which the Church of England was most thoroughly, though not always effectively, established. Its secular social structure was similarly hierarchical and rapidly became dominated by the great planters whose estates constituted the fundamental unit of settlement.

Other "sorts and conditions" of settlers contributed to the making of a regional society as well. The plantation economy was based on chattel slavery, and Africans began to be imported into Virginia even before the *Mayflower* had meandered to Plymouth in 1620. Indentured British servants and occasional unwilling Indians also provided labor for the tobacco fields. By the early eighteenth century, English and Africans were augmented by Scots-Irish, who began to settle the back country and transplanted their fiercely independent Presbyterian ways with them. Few of these newcomers became great plantation owners; rather, most were at the beginning frontiersmen who might eventually settle down into yeoman status, perhaps aided by a handful of black slaves.

The religious culture that emerged in the coastal Tidewater region and then the adjoining Piedmont closely followed class lines. The growth of Evangelicalism among poorer farmers began to challenge the early Anglican hegemony as independence encroached, and measures such as Thomas Jefferson's Bill for Establishing Religious Freedom, adopted by the Virginia legislature in 1786, helped bring a rapid end to religious establishment. Presbyterians, Methodists, and Baptists, who had been growing in importance since the pancolonial Great Awakening revivals of the 1740s, now proliferated openly and legally, although the Episcopal church persisted as a bastion of upper-class respectability. In later years, the Restorationist, Holiness, and Pentecostal movements would further swell the contours of Evangelicalism among white and African American alike. Mountain enclaves in the Appalachians and Ozarks developed their own distinctive culture among the poorer whites living there, providing still further elaborations on the Evangelical theme.

The "Bible Belt" that thus emerged throughout much of the South was reinforced by the limited ethnic composition of the region. Africa and the British Isles were the primary sources of population in much of the South, a result of limited economic opportunity and a closed, stratified social order not welcoming to newcomers. This isolation was affected profoundly by the great loss of the Civil War, which introduced alien northern elements into the political order and provoked massive resistance as intensive cultural myth-making glorified a romanticized antebellum past. Though this latter impulse led to a further closing of the social order, it was counterbalanced by "New South" promoters and entrepreneurs bent on modernizing the region through urbanization and industrialization. The results were brand new cities such as Birmingham, Alabama, and other cities rebuilt along new lines after massive wartime destruction, exemplified especially in Atlanta, Georgia.

From colonial times another, more cosmopolitan South also emerged along the Atlantic and Gulf coasts in particular. Peninsular Florida and southern Louisiana were both at times part of the Spanish borderlands, while the New Orleans and Mobile region was molded by French imperial designs as well. New Orleans's distinctive "Creole" culture also was shaped by a powerful Afro-Caribbean influence. Southern Florida was virtually invented by northerners eager

to exploit its climate and topographical amenities, and later overwhelmed by migration from Cuba, Haiti, and other parts of Latin America. Charleston, South
Carolina, was from its beginnings a fascinating combination of distinctively southern institutions and exotic pluralism. North Carolina has also from early times
been a mixture of "Deep South" extreme social conservatism, exemplified in
Senator Jesse Helms's remarkable durability, as well as religious and ethnic pluralism represented by the Quaker and Moravian presence from the early colonial era. More recently, the "Sun Belt" ethos of high tech industry and a rather
conservative sort of cosmopolitanism has taken root in enclaves such as Atlanta,
Charlotte, and the Chapel Hill-Durham-Raleigh "Triangle."

Religious architecture in the South, unsurprisingly, represents all of these
currents. In surveying it, we can start with Anglicanism in Virginia and other
Tidewater areas; move on to Charleston and New Orleans as examples of colonial and antebellum cosmopolitanism; follow up on the role of the Episcopal
church in the postcolonial period; survey the built environment of southern
Evangelicalism; and conclude with a brief look at recent developments throughout the region.

COLONIAL ANGLICANISM

Just as the meetinghouse expressed in material microcosm the ideological and
social underpinnings of Puritan society, so did the Anglican parish church in
colonial Virginia. Although parish structure and weekly worship closely resembled their English models, a number of circumstances converged to give Virginia
Anglicanism a distinct character. First, no Anglican bishop existed on the western side of the Atlantic prior to Independence. (Samuel Seabury was consecrated by Scottish bishops in 1784.) Therefore, episcopal supervision of colonial
religious life, nominally the duty of the bishop of London, was practically nonexistent, and the rituals of confirmation and priestly ordination could only be
received through a dangerous journey to the mother country.

Anglican clergy, whether native or, most usually, imported, were also in short
supply. Until the Society for the Propagation of the Gospel in Foreign Parts
began to take an active role in supporting missionaries after 1700, many of the
handful of ministers willing to work in the New World were of doubtful quality,
and often were motivated by a desire to escape from English discipline. The situation improved somewhat during the eighteenth century, but Virginia clergy
nevertheless labored under the disability of virtually total control by vestries, that
is, the groups of laymen responsible for the affairs of each parish. Without the
counterbalancing power of a bishop, these vestries, which were dominated by the
plantation-owning elite, frequently treated clergy as social inferiors and used the
power of the purse to ensure conformity to their wills.

The thirty-seven colonial Virginia Anglican churches that survive relatively
intact are, as architectural historian Dell Upton has demonstrated, remarkable
"texts" that can be read at a number of levels. Architecturally, they represent a

stage of building that has crossed the "vernacular threshold." Only a few examples of earlier generations of churches built from wood survive; the vast majority of those still extant are built from more durable brick. Brickwork, in fact,
provided the chief source of ornament; externally austere, most of these churches
derive whatever aesthetic appeal they have not from the lavish embellishment
associated with Gothic but rather from the use of rubbed brick and glazed "headers" – bricks with their glazed ends alternating with others placed lengthwise in
the pattern known as "Flemish bond." Most of the eighteenth-century churches
can generally be described as "Georgian" – symmetrical and deriving their inspiration from Renaissance classicism (Upton 1986, vii, 11, 39, 104).

At the liturgical level, Virginia colonial churches reflected a distinctly Low
Church understanding of the Anglican tradition. But Anglicanism even in its
Virginia version was never entirely Protestant. Canon law required that each
church have four liturgical "stations": pulpit, communion table, reading desk, and
font, somewhat more elaborate provisions than would have applied in the Reformed tradition. The basic ideal was that of Christopher Wren, the great architect responsible for the design of the ecclesiastical fabric of London following the Great Fire of 1666. Wren's work was, first, neoclassical, in the aesthetic
spirit of his time. Wren coined the phrase "auditory church" to describe his particular liturgical ideal, which was essentially Protestant. Wren's churches were
designed not to accommodate an elaborate ceremonial but rather to insure in-
telligibility of the preached Word that was central to a Calvinistic understanding of Christianity. His churches, and those in the colonies inspired by him, were
thus designed so that no participant in worship would be outside of easy hearing
distance of the preacher. Virginia churches thus were never expanded too far
horizontally; rather, when additional space was needed, wings were added in the
form of a transept. The result, such as Williamsburg's Bruton Parish Church, was
a cruciform shape, resorted to less for its symbolic associations than for its practical auditory qualities (Upton 1986, 56, 77–78, 81–83, 139; Friary 1971, 16–17).

Another way in which the Low Church character of Virginia churches of the
eighteenth century was manifested lay in the floor plan, in which no separation
occurred between the main body of the church and the chancel area that contained the altar. The result was a "room church," the nature of which becomes
especially apparent when contrasted with the ideals of the Ecclesiological movement of the mid-nineteenth century which emphasized the distinction between
chancel and nave. Instead of the rood (Old English for cross) screen characteristic of English medieval churches, which demarcated the most sacred part of the
church in which the Eucharist was celebrated, a simple rail and two steps were
all that separated the altar from the rest of the building. The term "table," in fact,
was preferred over the more Catholic "altar," and a simple wooden artifact was
used rather than one of marble. Clear rather than stained glass was indicative of
the values of the Enlightenment; clarity rather than mystery was the quality most
prized (Upton 1986, 50, 56–57, 72, 76, 150; Friary 1971, 37–57, 207).

The very names of these churches were indicative both of their Low Church
and what might be called their distinctively secular character. Bruton Parish,

Hickory Neck, Old Brick, Merchant's Hope, Saponey, Glebe, Hungars, Fork, and Slash – most of them bespoke locale, though some are obscure in origin. Others, like Old Saint Luke's in Isle of Wight County, received saints' names in the Catholic tradition in the nineteenth century. Beyond theological allegiance, these churches played a distinctive role in colonial Virginia society. For one thing, they played an important part in bringing a scattered populace together at regular intervals, thus promoting some sense of community. Also, as in the mother country, churches were not simply houses of worship, but symbols and agencies of the state. Their presence signified the transformation of chaos into order and the presence and majesty of the law, both civil and religious. Instead of depictions of Jesus and the saints, their walls were ornamented with the Decalogue and the king's arms, emblems of sacred and secular law working in tandem. Francis Marion Wigmore's photograph of the interior of Aquia Church in Stafford County, Virginia, illustrates some of these themes well (see figure 37; Rose 1963, 110–11; Upton 1986, vii, 55).

As Upton argues, the basic model for the colonial Virginia parish church was the house – most particularly, the house of a gentleman. Hospitality was the primary sign of a gentleman, and the church provided the same in the meal it ritually celebrated. And there was little question that it was the gentry that controlled the affairs of the church through their domination of the vestries. Gentlemen behaved differently in church from others, entering services as late as they cared to, and took places which, as in New England, represented their status in the broader community. The character and siting of pews reflected social rank, and the best pews – those closest to the pulpit – were the property of the most prestigious. Pew location sometimes verged on the eccentric, with some of the most prominent families having private pews in galleries, and others erecting "hanging" pews that emphasized their distinction while shielding them in part from common sight. Private entries, stairs, and windows were another sign of privilege, often at the cost of material symmetry. Slaves, however, had no clear place, as they would in the nineteenth century, and sometimes shared the pews of their masters. Until the intimate association between social role and responsibility vis-à-vis the church began to unravel as independence approached, the Virginia churches were both factors in and microcosms of the broader social order (Upton 1986, 205, 218, 222, 225, 227ff.).

Consideration of some specific colonial Virginia churches may illuminate their character and social roles further. The oldest surviving among these is Old Saint Luke's, or Newport, Church, near Smithfield in Isle of Wight County (see figure 38). Local pride based on inconclusive physical evidence long favored a 1632 dating, but recently scholars have placed it more probably at 1685. Saint Luke's is oriented toward the east, built of brick, and consists of a rectangular nave with a massive square tower. Inside, a screen separates the chancel area from that of the congregation. On the outside, many of its features, such as buttresses and paired lancet windows with Y-tracery, suggest a direct continuity with the Gothic tradition, which continued beyond the Renaissance both in England and its colonies in the West Indies. On the other hand, neoclassical features such as the

triangular pediment above the door and circular windows on the sides of the tower
indicate that this is not simply a transplanted medieval parish church. Saint Luke's
is thus a hybrid, its elements a transition between the high styles of two different eras, here bridged in a creative act of vernacular eclecticism (Upton 1986,
58–62; Rose 1963, 458–60; Pierson 1970, 34–45).

A somewhat later and more elaborate church that bears some structural resemblance to Old Saint Luke's is Saint Peter's Church, New Kent County (see
figure 39). Built originally in 1701–3 and thoroughly restored in 1953 after long
years of neglect, Saint Peter's is located between Richmond and Williamsburg
in a lovely wooded area. Its setting, however, was chosen not from considerations
of picturesqueness that influenced church siting during the Romantic era of the
Ecclesiological movement. Rather, in a society that was plantation-centered,
decentralized, and thoroughly nonurban, parish churches were sited along roads
or rivers at locations more or less convenient to the planters in a particular section of the colony. Arrival for worship on horseback was a sign of social status,
and horseblocks, hitching rails, and sometimes stables were provided in church-
yards. Architecturally, Saint Peter's most striking feature is its two-story square
tower, added in 1739–40, with a dormered pyramidal spire in the center and ball-
topped pinnacles at the corners. The first level was open on three sides, with
Norman arches, while the second story was used for a vestry room. A Flemish
"stepped gable" on either side adds a note of high-style embellishment. The
ornamental brickwork is in the "English bond" pattern, with rows of alternating
stretchers and headers. Saint Peter's was the parish church of Martha Dandridge
Custis, the widow who married George Washington there in 1759 (Rose 1963,
483–84; Upton 1986, 203–4).

Another church that represents a distinctive relationship between religion and
society is Christ Church in Lancaster County, built about 1732 in large measure
through the largesse of Robert "King" Carter, whose mansion "Corotoman"
stood in the midst of the vast family acreage nearby. Carter served at various times
as rector of the College of William and Mary, the speaker of the House of Burgesses, and acting governor of the Virginia colony. The church – the second one
on the site, both built by the family – served the local parish, but was clearly the
domain of a particular family.

Christ Church is built in the shape of a Greek cross, with the nave slightly
longer than the other three arms. It has a swag roof with four hips – that is, the
roof of each of the four segments has three faces, which break slightly as they
near the roofline. Each door is pedimented and flanked by brick pilasters. The
interior is also richly appointed, with a wine glass pulpit, a walnut communion
table, and marble font. Brass rods and damask curtains originally divided the box
pews. The most prominent pew, of course, was that of the Carter family, which
stood diagonally opposite the pulpit. The Carters in death remain close by as well;
the burial slabs of the donor's parents lie in the chancel, while Carter himself was
interred in a sarcophagus just outside the church in 1732 (Severens 1981, 51–
53; Rose 1963, 501–2).

Still another variation on the basic theme of church building reflecting social and political structure is illustrated in what is perhaps the best-known and most-visited of Virginia's colonial churches. Bruton Parish Church stands on Duke of Gloucester Street in Colonial Williamsburg, the capital of Virginia from 1699, when it was moved from Jamestown, till 1780, when Richmond acquired the honor (see figure 40). Williamsburg was large by the standards of colonial Virginia, where cities of any sort were scarce, but fell into a state of general neglect after independence until its restoration as a living historical museum and tourist attraction supported by Rockefeller family funds beginning in the 1930s. (Interestingly, it was Dr. W. A. R. Goodwin, then the church's rector, who persuaded John D. Rockefeller, Jr., of the desirability of such a restoration.) The city's general plan is linear, and its foci reflect the colonial centers of culture and power. At one end of Duke of Gloucester Street lies the (reconstructed) House of Burgesses; at its other sits the College of William and Mary. Not quite halfway between them lie Bruton Parish Church and, nearby on its own axis, the Royal Governor's Palace, an arrangement later reflected in the plan of Washington, D.C., with the branches of government spatially separated and the White House located off-axis from the Mall (Rose 1963, 454; Severens 1981, 17–20; Kammen 1991, 359ff.).

The current Bruton Parish Church is the third building to bear that name, a situation common enough in eighteenth-century Virginia. The church is cruciform – again, a common arrangement designed to increase access to the range of the pulpit. The governor had a pew of his own featuring a canopied chair just off the chancel. The Council of State and members of the House of Burgesses were seated in the transept, while William and Mary students were consigned to the west gallery. Architecturally, the church was inspired by the then-popular scheme of Christopher Wren, to whom is also attributed the central building of the college. Detail, such as the round-topped windows, is neoclassical, and the simple but graceful steeple ascends through two stages from the 1769 tower till it reaches its pyramidal spire. A brick fence encloses the churchyard, in which many parishioners lie buried (Rose 1963, 452–54; Pierson 1970, 94–95).

Much like their New England meetinghouse counterparts, the Anglican parish churches of colonial Virginia were far more than houses of worship. Like their English predecessors, which were entrusted with a wide variety of social functions, they represented the social and political orders as well as the religious. Indeed, in a new land, they were instrumental in helping establish that order. In their layouts, ornament, furnishings, and patterns of accommodating both the living and the dead, they became microcosms of the broader society. When that order changed, as it was doing at the time of the Revolution, the Anglican churches changed with it. Many fell into severe disrepair, some were taken over by newer denominations, and others vanished entirely, although some were resuscitated as bishops of the newly founded Protestant Episcopal church like Richard Channing Moore and William Meade fashioned a strong presence in Virginia. With the rise of historical consciousness and preservationist sentiment that began to develop in the 1930s, many were restored and now serve simultaneously as historical museums and, once again, flourishing parish churches.

A variation on the theme of Anglican establishment is illustrated in the Carolina colony. Chartered in 1663, its "Fundamental Constitution" was drawn up by John Locke, who was then serving as secretary to one of the colony's proprietors, Anthony Ashley Cooper. Although the Church of England was acknowledged as official, tolerance was simultaneously granted to those of other faiths. Religious tolerance was complemented by a general mood of Restoration England expansiveness, as well as a spirit of entrepreneurship that came with the "great port town's" being a social and commercial extension of the Barbados. As a result, the colony's capital, Charleston – named after the "Merry Monarch," Charles II – took from early on a cosmopolitan tone, and welcomed a religious and ethnic diversity unusual in most of the South (Severens 1981, 11; Rose 1963, 422; Rosen 1992, 9–12).

From its beginnings, Anglicanism played a significant role in shaping the material texture of the city and its environs. Charleston shared with Philadelphia the distinction of being a major city of the mid-colonial period that was deliberately platted rather than simply allowed to develop at random. The 1680 plan, most likely influenced by designs drawn up for the rebuilding of London after the Great Fire of 1666, provided for four main streets that converged at a central public square. At this juncture – the corner of what today are Broad and Meeting Streets – was reserved a place for a church, the original site of Saint Philip's and the present location of Saint Michael's. The spires of both – today and in centuries past – soared to dominate the skyline and proclaim the centrality of the Anglican faith in this, the most pluralistic of southern colonial cities (Severens 1981, 13; Rose 1963, 13).

Saint Philip's was the first of the city's monumental churches. The original 1681 black cypress building was replaced in 1710–11 by its second incarnation, the city's first high-style building in the Wren tradition, deliberately sited so as to close a street vista in the spirit of the new Baroque plan of London itself. Destroyed by fire in 1835, it was rebuilt largely as before on the exterior as a civic gesture acknowledging its historic importance after much public discussion. The interior, however, was refashioned in the spirit of Wren's successor as England's premier ecclesiastical architect, Sir James Gibbs, and the nearby colonial church based on his ideas, Saint Michael's (Rose 1963, 422; Severens 1988, 5, 84–87).

Although Saint Philip's still stands proudly a few blocks away, it is Saint Michael's that has become a virtual icon of the city's identity (see figure 41). The church originated in a 1751 act of the General Assembly that divided Charleston into two parishes. The new church, completed ten years later on the site of the original Saint Philip's in the city's center, was clearly Gibbsian in spirit, and may possibly have been designed by Peter Harrison, whose King's Chapel in Boston reflected the same neoclassical ideas. The building committee consisted of local dignitaries such as Charles Pinckney, who held many of the colony's highest offices, and Gabriel Manigault, possibly the richest man in all of the colonies.

Saint Michael's is divided into three principal volumes: the church itself; the
massive portico, which features brick columns; and the multilayered 185-foot steeple, which helps shape the city's distinctive skyline. The exterior is brick covered with stucco and painted white. The interior, remodeled in 1866 following devastation by the war and again in 1905 by the Tiffany Studios, features both the original carved native cedar as well as Victorian embellishments such as the stained glass windows in the shallow chancel. Memorial plaques abound, as they do in many of the churches of Charleston and other older southern cities. In the early 1990s, both Saint Michael's and Saint Philip's were undergoing extensive renovation yet again as a result of hurricane damage and long-deferred maintenance (Rose 1963, 422–24; Severens 1981, 53–56).

Before moving on to Charleston in the antebellum era, we should take note here of another significant colonial Anglican church in the Charleston area. Saint James Church, Goose Creek, was built between 1708 and 1719 following the Church Act of 1706, which had formally established the Church of England as official for the colony while allowing religious pluralism and set out nine parishes. Its parishioners, who had formed a congregation as early as 1685, were English Barbadians who came to be known as "Goose Creek men," a phrase eventually synonymous with hard-core support for establishment. The Goose Creek Church is a curious contrast with its urban counterparts. Stylistically, it is of West Indian origin, one-story high with a jerkin-head (that is, diagonally cut off) gable above the entrance. Like many southern churches, it is made of brick but covered over with pink-tinged stucco. Door and windows are surrounded with elaborate classical detail, including a pelican, an ancient Christian symbol for Christ adopted by the Society for the Propagation of the Gospel, sculpted into the pediment. The interior is even more elaborate; the visual focus is a central pulpit framed by a very Baroque altarpiece featuring the Commandments, the Creed, the Lord's Prayer, and the arms of King George I. Goose Creek, in short, is simultaneously very much a religious and political statement – indeed, of an ideology in which the two are virtually inseparable (Rose 1963, 425–26; Severens 1981, 53–54).

During the antebellum era, Charleston grew slowly, losing its place as one of the nation's premier cities; however, it simultaneously began to gather a reputation as a focus for radical southern thought with the nullification controversy and, eventually, secession. The falling-off of its role as a seaport was compensated by the coming of the railroads, and the 1830s especially saw a burst of prosperity that generated a broad spirit of civic improvement. As it had in colonial times, religious architecture continued to help shape and to be shaped by the broader civic ensemble, though now in a manner clearly reflective of the city's religious, if not its ideological, pluralism (Severens 1981, 136–37; Severens 1988, 23, 27, 58, 71).

Charleston's great contribution to the national architectural scene was Robert Mills (1781–1855), who later was appointed Architect of Public Buildings in Washington by President Jackson and went on to design the Treasury Building, the Washington Monument, and other governmental structures in the revival styles of the era. His Fireproof Building, built in the Greek revival style in 1822–27 and now home to the South Carolina Historical Society, was a major contribution both to the city's texture and the technology of construction. One of his most innovative contributions to religious design was abetted by Thomas Jefferson, who made available to Mills his extensive architectural holdings. The result was the Congregational Church (1804–6), whose facade greatly resembled Saint Michael's in overall contours if not in detail. The body, however, was circular, most likely influenced strongly by Palladio's drawings of the Roman Pantheon which Mills came across in Jefferson's library, as well as Sir James Gibbs's widely circulated *Book of Architecture*. The result, which was designed to hold up to 170 pews on the main level and another forty or fifty in the gallery, was destroyed by fire in 1861. It was later replaced by a newer church in the Richardsonian Romanesque mode in 1891, after even the ruins of Mills's creation had been destroyed by an earthquake (Severens 1981, 137; Liscombe 1985, 5–7; Swann n.d., 3–4).

A more lasting contribution by Mills is his First Baptist Church of 1822, which continues to house a congregation established by Baptist refugees from Maine that dates back to 1699 (see figure 42). Mills was commissioned to design this church by its minister, Richard Furman, a major figure in Southern Baptist history perpetuated in the name of a regional college. The church is basically Greek revival, though it incorporates a variety of Classical and neoclassical features. Mills designed a significant number of other churches as far north as Philadelphia during this period. Perhaps his best known creation is Richmond's Monumental Church (1812–17), built as an Episcopal church in memory of those killed in a disastrous theater fire in 1811 and now maintained by the Historic Richmond Foundation. Consisting of an octagonal body and a massive square porch with two Doric columns on each side, Monumental Church is an impressive exercise in reducing the geometry of the Classical vocabulary to its essentials (Liscombe 1985, 11–13, 14–15; Swann n.d., 10; Pierson 1970, 377–86).

During the following decades, Charleston's religiously diverse population began to express itself publicly through its members' various contributions to the cityscape. The Greek revival style was exemplified strikingly in Temple Beth Elohim, designed by the New York architect Cyrus Warner in 1840–41 (see figures 43 and 44). The congregation was originally founded by Portuguese Sephardim and was very likely the first in the United States to have adopted Reform principles. Featuring a Doric portico and a shallow dome on the interior, the foci of which are the Ark of the Covenant and the cantor's desk, the temple sits across Hasell Street from Saint Mary's Catholic Church (1839), also Greek revival in style. The original membership of Saint Mary's appears to have been primarily Irish, but it was later swelled by refugees from the 1793 slave revolt in Santo Domingo (Swann n.d., 16; Severens 1988, 120–21; Simmons n.d.).

Through the work of Mills especially, Charleston helped to popularize the Greek revival as the normative style for religious groups of all persuasions, in the North as well as the South. Even prior to the Civil War, however, the Gothic revival was beginning to make inroads – in the South, especially among Episcopalians in rural areas. Two of Charleston's churches, neither of them Episcopalian, illustrate this new stylistic enthusiasm wonderfully. The French Huguenot Church, founded in 1681 and still maintained as a prominent part of the city's history by this ethnic and religious group, was designed in 1845 by the local architect Edward Brickell White. White was familiar with the principles of the Ecclesiological Movement and had probably seen Upjohn's Trinity Church in New York City. Though thoroughly Gothic in inspiration, the Huguenot Church embodied structural compromises that would have horrified the Ecclesiologists, including cast iron moldings and pinnacles and vaults simulated with plaster (Severens 1988, 128–31; Swann n.d., 13).

Similarly but even more spectacularly *faux* Gothic is Charleston's Unitarian Church (see figure 45). The religious liberalism represented by Unitarianism was extremely rare in the antebellum South, given the dominance of Evangelical Protestantism. Here, however, a congregation primarily made up of displaced Yankees was presided over by Samuel Gilman, remembered today with his wife as a leading antebellum literary light and as the author of "Fair Harvard," written for that institution's bicentennial and still sung as its alma mater. The current church incorporates portions of the original building of 1774–87, and was expanded and thoroughly remodeled by the firm of Jones and Lee during Gilman's ministry in 1852–54. The interior, which features a dazzling array of fan and pendant vaults modeled on Henry VII's chapel at Westminster Abbey is, like that of the Huguenot Church, a confection of lath and plaster. The surrounding churchyard, with its picturesque tombs and Spanish moss, evokes an aura of Edgar Allen Poe or perhaps Tennessee Williams. Although the effect today is one of runaway romanticism, Gilman, who was influenced by that earnestly Protestant advocate of the Gothic John Ruskin, justified the ornament as indicative of the spirit of progress that resonated throughout the city during his time (Severens 1988, 201–5; Tillinghast 1993, 16; "Unitarian Church in Charleston," n.d.).

Although Charleston was pluralistic almost from its inception, there was never any question that its socially dominant stock was British and its religion of British Protestant origin. Louisiana, however, was another story. Originally including the entire Mississippi Valley, this broad enclave of French Catholic settlement was not notable for zeal in building houses of worship. According to one early French observer, "The Chevalier de la Salle . . . took possession of the country in the name of Louis XIV, called it Louisiana in honor of this prince, and constructed a fort there; the Spaniards would have built a church, the English a tavern" (S. Wilson 1973, 63 and n. 2).

The earliest French houses of worship in the southern reaches of the Mississippi Valley were either built by missionaries with native labor or else consisted of makeshift quarters in military outposts. The Jesuit Paul Du Ru, for example, worked among the native peoples further upriver, and discovered that these Mougoulachas and Bayogoulas were remarkably adept at building temples. In 1700, he put the latter to work at building a Christian church, for which he provided the gross dimensions and description – "In general appearance it is like a ship upside down" – and left the natives to supply the details, including local building techniques such as plaster made from moss and clay and mats woven from palmetto fronds used to cover the roof (S. Wilson 1973, 65–67).

Along the Gulf Coast, French settlement was more intense, but the vicissitudes of religious building were considerable. Mobile, for example, had a detailed plan along French Baroque lines drawn up for its development by 1711, the year of its founding. No specific provision was made in this plan for a church, however, and worship had to be conducted in a private home. Elaborate plans for an elegant church drawn up in 1724 came to naught. Similar neglect was characteristic of most other early French fortifications (S. Wilson 1973, 67, 68).

New Orleans is quite a different story from Mobile, where little evidence of the colonial French presence survives, especially in the religious realm. The first French colonists arrived at this Mississippi River city in 1718, and three years later platted it along the same lines as Mobile. This French penchant for planning, much on display in the mother country during the same era, is exemplified in New Orleans's Place d'Armes, now known as Jackson Square from the Clark Mills statue in honor of the hero of the Battle of New Orleans (Severens 1981, 128).

Although the Jackson statue is emblematic of the Americanization of New Orleans, the square's architecture reveals a more complicated story, one of layers of colonial development. Unlike in Mobile, a built religious presence was intended from nearly the beginning; the Baroque plan developed by Le Blond de La Tour in 1721 provided for a permanent church in the place of honor now occupied by Saint Louis Cathedral. The original, temporary church was a simple wooden affair that was destroyed by a hurricane in 1722. Its successor was built in 1727 in the more durable *colombage sur sol* mode – a kind of half-timbering technique, with heavy timbers on each side serving as buttresses against storms, and a Classical facade reflecting the French style of the day in simplified form (Severens 1981, 72–82).

The same social stratification exhibited in the colonial meetinghouses of New England and the Anglican churches of Virginia was reflected in this earliest Catholic church in French New Orleans. Disputes over precedence were rife in these early years, and in 1731 rules pertaining to rank and honor in churches which had earlier been promulgated for Canada were extended to Louisiana. In a letter to the French minister of Marine describing the new church, New Orleans officials noted that "Your Highness will see by the plan here attached, the arrangement of the pews that, at the time of the Company, were placed behind the two *prie dieu* seats for the Commandant and the First Director. The first one, on the epistle side, served for the Councillors and the one on the gospel side for the General Staff and the officers has not been changed." Pews for the various ranks of dignitaries and their families were variously located adjoining the sanctuary rail, opposite the pulpit, and in the transepts, reflecting their respective prestige. Interestingly, the church's tabernacle was taken from the Spanish during the capture of Pensacola in 1719, so that the interior arrangements reflected international as well as parochial politics (Severens 1981, 83; S. Wilson 1973, 83).

This intermediate version of the Saint Louis Cathedral gradually fell into decay

in the face of the city's punishing climate and finally disappeared in flames in 1788.
The current cathedral, which now stands on the same site, was financed by the
Spaniard Don Andrés Almonester y Roxas, and was erected in 1794. Together
with its flanking *cabildo*, which was the seat of the Spanish government, and the
presbytère, or rectory, it was designed by Don Gilberto Guillemard in a contemporary Spanish version of the Classical revival style. In 1820 and 1851, the
church – elevated to cathedral status in 1794 – was drastically remodeled. Benjamin Henry Latrobe, also known for his design of the Baltimore cathedral, contributed a central tower, belfry, and cupola during the first renovation. J. N. B.
de Pouilly was called upon for a thorough rebuilding of the then-decrepit cathedral in 1851, and changed its three bell-shaped cupolas to hexagonal spires. The
present-day cathedral, which contains only fragments of the original, is striking
but architecturally hard to classify; R. Warren Robison's description of it as "Romantic Classic Revival" may come as close as one can to accuracy. In any case, it
remains not only the focus of a striking urban space but a tangible reminder of
Louisiana's complex cultural history. This sense of history is evoked in Clarence
John Laughlin's 1938 photograph, "The Ram Looks Down on the Symbols of
the Past" (see figure 46; Severens 1981, 86–89; Cowan 1983, 184, 187; Robison
1984, 2–3, 16–18).

Not surprisingly, much of the other historic architecture of New Orleans is
that of the Catholic church. Saint Patrick's Church, for example, was designed
by James and Charles Dakin in 1840 on the lines of England's York Minster and
Exeter Cathedral for Irish settlers living in the "American" (as opposed to the
French) sector of the city. Saint Patrick's features a square tower rising in four
progressively diminishing stages; the Dakins' original plan for elaborate Gothic
ornamentation, however, disappeared in a dispute that left the completion of the
church in the hands of another architect, James Gallier. The Baroque twin-towered Saint Alphonsus was also built for the Irish in 1855–57, virtually across the
street from Saint Mary's Assumption Church, which was erected at the same time
by Redemptorist priests for a German Catholic congregation in a somewhat different rendering of the Baroque. Although French and Spanish Catholics gave
the city its original exotic flavor, the addition of German, Irish, Italian, and African American coreligionists expanded its cosmopolitanism in ways not always
recognized by outsiders (Severens 1981, 128; Ledner 1974, 36–37, 83–84; Robison 1984, 22–26).

Churches are not the totality of New Orleans's Catholic landscape. The only
building that can definitively be traced to the period of French ascendancy in the
city is the neoclassical Ursuline Convent on Chartres (pronounced "Charters")
Street, which was originally designed in 1745 and completed eight years later to
replace an earlier convent built in 1734. The original building, with a three-story elevation and striking cupola, bore a curious overall resemblance to the Wren
Building in Williamsburg, reflecting the pervasiveness of neoclassicism in the
colonial environment. The 1745 building has the same institutional profile with
a two-story elevation and a row of small dormers just above the roofline. Now
used as the rectory for nearby Saint Mary's Italian Church (1846), it has in its

long history variously served the Ursulines as a convent, school, and orphanage. After the sisters had moved elsewhere, it was briefly used as a meeting place for the state legislature, then later as the archiepiscopal residence. Ursuline educational and religious life, like that of many other religious orders, was conducted in the extensive institutional complex characteristic of heavily Catholic cities, although here the architecture reflected a distinctively French Colonial flavor (S. Wilson 1973, 91–97; Ledner 1974, 24–25; Federal Writers' Project 1938, 253).

A unique feature of the New Orleans religious cityscape is its cemeteries, which are built above ground because of the city's extremely high water table. Modeled perhaps on Spanish practice, these cemeteries are virtual necropolises, with the often elaborate crypts in a variety of architectural styles laid out on broad thoroughfares that can accommodate vehicles as well as pedestrians. Individual tombs are frequently surrounded by wrought iron fences, and the cemeteries are themselves enclosed. Although the earliest of these – Saint Louis Numbers 1 and 2, which date from 1789 and 1823 – were built for Catholic use, the subsequent diversification of the population during the American period led to others being founded for the broader community. Deaths from yellow fever epidemics and the Civil War expanded the need for burial space. The result is a city honeycombed with these unique deathscapes that blend with the distinctive architectural legacies of colonial and Victorian times to create a melange of visual images unique in this country (Cowan 1983, chap. 5).

Although New Orleans in its American phase rapidly acquired houses of worship in other traditions, such as the Gothic Episcopal Christ Church Cathedral (1886), Roman Catholicism has traditionally dominated the "churchscape" of New Orleans and the bayou country of southern Louisiana, the homeland of the "Cajuns" – French-speaking Acadians dispossessed by the British from their homes in Nova Scotia in *le grand dérangement* of 1755–57. Church construction came to a virtual halt during the era of the Civil War and Reconstruction, but began to increase later in the century and attained a sort of critical mass during the first three decades of the twentieth century, especially among Roman Catholics. This was the era of the "brick piles," grand constructs in the medieval styles that resulted from the collaboration of local clergy and lay leaders with architects or engineers imported from beyond the small, provincial cities of the bayou country. From the abundant examples one might select Saint Mary Pamela in Raceland (1867, 1934), in a highly simplified version of Gothic with *Rundbogenstil* corbeling; Saint Elizabeth in Paincourtville (1889), a much more elaborate two-towered version of Gothic; and Holy Trinity in downtown Shreveport (1896), a rather squat brick affair in the Richardsonian Romanesque mode, with a heavy transept and cone-topped twin towers. Although the regions naturally reflect the influences of the countries of their population's origin, an apt comparison for these monumental provincial churches in a land where the Catholic church literally dominates the landscape is the German Catholic domain of western Ohio, where a similar religious and cultural hegemony prevails with comparable visual results (Robison 1984, 29, 39, 40, 42).

Although the dominant strain of religiosity in the American South for some two centuries has been Evangelical Protestantism, significant diversity has always existed even beyond such atypical urban enclaves as Charleston and New Orleans. Anglicans, who during the colonial period constituted the religious establishment throughout the whole region, were reduced to an influential but disestablished minority after independence through loss of official status, through legislation such as the Virginia Statute for Religious Freedom, and through the mushrooming of the Evangelical denominations.

Southern Episcopalians, however, have always been a rather peculiar minority, especially if the term is equated with a sense of economic or political disinheritedness. This can hardly be said of the church that included Jefferson Davis, Robert E. Lee, and Leonidas Polk within its ranks. The church certainly languished during the decades following the Revolution, and many of the classic colonial churches of the Tidewater area fell into disrepair; some of these latter simply vanished, while others were taken over by various denominations. The church's resurgence under strong episcopal leadership beginning in the 1810s, however, restored some of these neglected landmarks, as did the historic preservation movement of the mid-twentieth century.

By the 1840s, the same High Church Ecclesiological movement that had such a dramatic impact on the religious landscape of New York, New Jersey, and Pennsylvania began to be felt below the Mason-Dixon Line as well. Among its leaders in the South was Levi Silliman Ives, Episcopal bishop of North Carolina, who confirmed the worst suspicions of Low Churchmen when he converted to Roman Catholicism in 1852, and Nicholas Hamner Cobbs, bishop of Alabama from 1844 to 1861. It was in these states and in Tennessee that High Church Episcopalianism and the Ecclesiological movement that usually accompanied it made a distinctive mark on the South, and created a visual image of Anglicanism more pervasive in that region than possibly in any other. The more secular southern appropriation of themes of medieval chivalry and social hierarchy, particularly as exemplified in the romantic novels of Sir Walter Scott, doubtless reinforced the appeal of the Gothic mode in the ecclesiastical realm as well (Patrick 1980, 121).

Although southern architects eventually took up the cause of Gothic themselves, much of the original wave of Ecclesiological design was the work of northerners such as the ubiquitous Richard Upjohn as well as others affiliated with the movement, including Frank Wills, Henry Dudley, and J. L. Priest. Some of their creations, such as Raleigh's Christ Church (Upjohn, 1846–61) and Mobile's Trinity Church (Wills and Dudley, 1853–55), were substantial urban churches with lofty towers and spires that became, with their Protestant imitators, an important part of the emergent southern cityscape. More abundant, however, though hardly unique to the South, were the board-and-batten wooden "Carpenter Gothic" churches that Upjohn had begun to popularize throughout the northern tier of states from Brunswick, Maine, to Delafield, Wisconsin. Churches designed specifically by Upjohn, those built according to designs he had provided, and many simply inspired by *Upjohn's Rural Architecture* of 1852 combined to produce a distinctive genre of church building so pervasive that it rapidly became a distinctive feature of the landscape. Examples are too numerous to permit more than a suggestive listing; a very tentative beginning might include the rustic Saint Luke's in Jacksonville, Alabama (1856–57) and the more ornate Christ Church in Holly Springs, Mississippi (1858). A more generic example of the application of the basic forms of the style to a simple boxlike structure is Zion Episcopal Church (ca. 1850) in Talbotton, Georgia, indicative of the transition of what had already become an easily replicated popular style into the vernacular vocabulary (Patrick 1980, 122, 123, 129–30; Crocker 1973, 155; Linley 1982, 127–28, 345).

During the Victorian era, Episcopal church architecture remained generally within the Gothic revival framework, but its variations could become fanciful, as in the free play of form exemplified in Peter J. Williamson's Saint Luke's Church (1887) in Cleveland, Tennessee. A number of Episcopal churches scattered throughout the region, however, give hints as to some of the ways in which that tradition has become entangled in the mesh of southern culture, often in a supportive role, at other times in a more oblique relationship. The very name of one such church boldly suggests cultural endorsement: the Robert E. Lee Memorial Church in Lexington, Virginia. Founded in staunch Presbyterian country in western Virginia near the Blue Ridge Mountains, what was originally known as Grace Church first met in 1844 in a Wren-Gibbs style building described by one member in provocative detail:

It was of brick, and the interior of the church was about sixty feet long, forty feet wide, and thirty-five feet high, with a gallery running around both sides and the front end. The end gallery accommodated a good-sized organ and choir seats for about twenty-five persons, and had a curtain in front of the choir. Each side gallery had three rows of pews, each row raised above the one in front of it, so that every one could see the preacher, and seated about fifty people each. The pulpit floor was about eight feet above the chancel floor, with the reading desk immediately in front of it, and about five feet lower, while the communion table and two hair cloth chairs stood on the chancel floor. The font was in the middle of the circular rail and directly in front of the middle aisle. Above the pulpit, on the end wall and near the top, was the sentence, in large capital letters MY HOUSE IS THE HOUSE OF PRAYER; and on the wall on either side of the pulpit was a large tablet, on one of which was written in gilt letters, large enough to be read from the floor of the church, The Lord's Prayer and the Creed; and on the other the Ten Commandments. The church was heated by two large cast-iron stoves, about two and one-half feet square and five feet long, with a sheet iron cylindrical drum over the top of each, through which the smoke passed into the smoke pipe, and thence into the chimneys in the rear wall of the building, on each side of the pulpit. The room, with its circular pillars supporting the galleries and their panelled walls, lent itself to evergreen decoration.

The picture evoked here is of a small country church which, though built in the middle of the nineteenth century, harked back to the eighteenth its appointments and the fundamental liturgical and theological principles which informed its decidedly Low Church design (Patrick 1981, 199; Mycoff 1974, 3–4).

After the Civil War, the parish acquired a distinguished new vestryman in the person of Robert E. Lee, who had come to Lexington as president of Washington College (later Washington and Lee.) After Lee's death in 1870, which took place shortly after his return home from a vestry meeting (a ritual thought by many Episcopalians to have at least a profoundly soporific effect), plans began to be drawn up for a new church in his memory. Grace (later R. E. Lee Memorial) Episcopal Church was begun in 1872 and completed eleven years later. Built of local limestone, it is a compact, almost squat Gothic revival church loosely in the Ecclesiological tradition. It has a single side tower with a tall, polygonal spire. Interestingly, the congregation at the time of its building was not notable for its Anglo-Catholic sentiments, but presumably adopted a style associated with American Anglicanism that by this time had lost its partisan connotations (Mycoff 1974, 7ff.; Brooke 1984, 31).

The Lee Memorial Church is one of a number of examples of how the Episcopal church became entwined in the southern post–Civil War culture of the "Lost Cause," celebrated in countless memorials throughout the region such as the series of large-scale statues of Lee and other Confederate leaders that dramatically punctuate Richmond's Monument Boulevard. A parallel example that is not specifically Episcopalian lies close by in the Lee Chapel of Washington and Lee University. Originally built in 1868 as a college chapel during Robert E. Lee's presidency of the institution in the years immediately following the Civil War, it was enlarged after Lee's death by the addition of an 1883 mausoleum in which Lee lies interred under a life-size effigy in the style of the sarcophagus of a medieval knight. (Another Virginian, Woodrow Wilson, lies similarly entombed in Washington's National Cathedral). The basement contains Lee's office, preserved in the exact state he left it at his death, and other Lee memorabilia in the manner of a saint's relics (C. Wilson 1980, 29; Eller 1994).

Another distinctly Anglican example is All Saints Chapel at the University of the South in Sewanee, Tennessee (see figure 47). Perched high atop a mountain in the Cumberlands near Chattanooga, "Sewanee," as the university has come to be known, exemplifies institutionally the quest for a distinctive southern intellectual culture over a century and a half. The university, which includes a theological seminary, was founded in 1857 by Leonidas Polk, Episcopal bishop of Louisiana, who later died as a Confederate major general during the Civil War. Polk had conceived of Sewanee as an authentically southern alternative where the scions of influential regional families could receive an elite education without exposure to the contaminating Yankee influences of Princeton or Yale. Sewanee's chapel was designed in 1910 by Gothic revivalist Ralph Adams Cram, who presumably identified with the religion-centered traditionalism that the university represented. All Saints resembles a miniature cathedral, with movable seating, a nave lined with the flags of the sponsoring southern dioceses, and a myriad of Civil War–era memorial plaques bedecking the walls. Embedded in the south wall is a fragment of the cornerstone of the original University Hall, destroyed by Union troops who made off with the remainder of the block as souvenirs; this scene of destruction is commemorated in one of the chapel's stained glass windows (Federal Writers' Project, Tennessee 1939, 483; Chitty 1979).

Other, very different examples of the relationship of the Episcopal church to the broader social order can be found throughout the region. A few miles off U.S. 27, not too far from Dayton, Tennessee, the scene of the 1925 Scopes Trial, can be found the restored remains of the Rugby colony. Founded in 1877 by Thomas Hughes, the British author of *Tom Brown's School Days*, Rugby was intended as a self-sustaining settlement in which respectable but not easily employable young Englishpeople might follow a virtuous way of life through manual labor and British customs, which included cricket and Anglicanism. Two structures stand out as central to Hughes's vision: the Public Library of 1882, which still contains a major collection of Victorian literature, and Christ Church. The latter, built in 1880 by the colonists themselves, is a simple white board-and-batten structure with double lancet windows, a small rose, and elaborate period furnishings including red and gold altar hangings, hand-carved wooden communion rails and bishop's seat, and walnut alms basins. The colony proved not to be successful; now maintained as a museum, its remains evoke the spirit of Brook Farm in Victorian Anglican guise (Federal Writers' Project, Tennessee 1939, 360–61; Egerton 1977, 36–37).

A final example of the Anglican presence in the South can be found in Anniston, Alabama, an industrial company town in the Appalachian foothills with a "New South" economy based on cast iron and textiles. In the midst of one of Anniston's residential areas is the spacious parklike campus of the Church of Saint Michael and All Angels, an imposing Norman Gothic assemblage of church, chapel, rectory, parish house, and 90-foot tower. Saint Michael's was built by John W. Noble "as a gift to his employees." How it was received by the latter is not recorded, but the church's plant is certainly a handsome addition to an otherwise dreary townscape (Walker 1975, 141).

EVANGELICAL PROTESTANTS

Although the South is in many places religiously and culturally diverse, especially along its coasts, it has for over a century and a half stood as one of the most religiously intense regions of the nation, with Evangelical Protestantism at its spiritual core. By the early nineteenth century what had once been a land divided between aristocratic elegance and frontier chaos was moving toward cultural homogeneity. Socially, this involved a biracial, hierarchical social order, a predominantly agricultural economy, and a pervasive loyalty to the norms of a core of Protestant churches. The latter have themselves reflected the social scale that has persisted well into the twentieth century. At its peak were Presbyterians and

Episcopalians; among the middling classes Methodists predominated; and a wide variety of Baptist churches flourished among the poorer folk. (This ordering should not be taken too absolutely, however, as the elegance of Robert Mills's Baptist Church in downtown Charleston illustrates.)

African American southerners developed their own rendering of folk Christianity during the era of slavery, and later established Baptist and Methodist networks of their own in an age when enforced segregation was the rule. After the turn of the twentieth century, Pentecostalism made heavy regional inroads among African American and white alike, and the Campbellite Churches of Christ flourished along the western rim of the region as well as in eastern Tennessee. Although Catholic churches could usually be found in the larger cities and along the areas of early French and Spanish settlement, inhospitality to the "new immigration" of the late nineteenth and early twentieth centuries worked against any large concentrations of Catholics, Jews, or Eastern Orthodox.

During the early decades of the nineteenth century, the South was not distinguished in the realm of religious building. The decentralized character of the plantation economy discouraged the growth of significant urban centers, and the Evangelical distrust of high culture and liturgical worship did not conduce toward architectural sophistication. The Christmas Conference of 1784, which established the Methodist Episcopal Church as an independent American denomination, counseled to "Let our chapels be built plain and decent: but not more expensively than is absolutely unavoidable. Otherwise the Necessity of raising money will make Rich Men Necessary to us. . . . But if so we must be dependent on them, yea, and be governed by them" (Patrick 1981, 105).

Visitors to Tennessee around 1800 commented on the absence of houses of worship; those that did exist before 1830 in this and other parts of the southern frontier were mainly log cabins such as the Buffalo Ridge Church in Washington County, built in 1793 of logs chinked with stones and mortar, a puncheon floor – made of logs laid side by side and planed flat on top – and one small, unglazed window, placed high to avoid Indian attack. Worshipers sat on split logs. This crude structure lasted until 1848, when local residents had achieved a considerable degree of prosperity. Housing was given priority over churches in a region which took religion but not its physical setting seriously (Patrick 1981, 103).

Gradually, however, the embourgeoisement of Evangelicalism, its growing prosperity, and its endorsement of the region's sociopolitical establishment and its values, led inevitably in the direction of the building of more substantial houses of worship. Presbyterians generally led the way, building in towns in part because their ministers frequently kept schools there. By the time that church building had become reasonably widespread, one style had emerged as normative for the entire South: the Greek revival. To be sure, this was an authentically national style that dominated public, religious, and domestic design as much in New England and its midwestern hinterlands as it did elsewhere. With respect to the Grecian mode, however, the South proved itself to be as American as any place, only perhaps more so. The antebellum plantation house, which after the Civil War emerged as a primary material expression of the "Myth of the Lost Cause," was in its classic form a Greek revival structure. Public buildings of the era such as the state capitols in Nashville (William Strickland, 1853) and Raleigh (Town and Davis, 1833–40) also frequently reflected this universal architectural vocabulary, as did in a later day Nashville's curious monument, the full-size replica of the Parthenon built in 1896–97 as the central building of the Tennessee Centennial Exposition (Patrick 1981, 106; Pierson 1970, 452ff.; Hamlin 1964, 197; Brumbaugh 1974, 2–9; Graham 1974, 160–61).

The Greek revival began as a "high style" design and was exemplified in its most sophisticated form in such monuments as Robert Mills's 1822 First Baptist Church in Charleston, one of six of that style in that city. It also appeared rapidly in smaller cities such as New Bern, North Carolina, where Uriah Sandy's First Presbyterian Church of 1819–22 features an Ionic portico and a five-stage square tower that culminates in an octagonal cupola. (Sandy, it might be noted, was very possibly of Connecticut origin, as were the partners Town and Davis cited in connection with the North Carolina capitol.) One of the most enduring of these structures is Mobile's Government Street Presbyterian Church (1836–37). Its designers, James Gallier and the Dakin brothers, were all from New Orleans but had been strongly influenced by Minard Lafever and his circle of New York architects who had helped elevate the style to a national enthusiasm. The overall effect is one of stylistic restraint, with an interior formally similar to a Wren-Gibbs church such as Saint Michael's in Charleston. The ornament, however, is authentically Greek. In the words of an English visitor shortly after its completion, "Its interior is unsurpassed in chasteness of style and elegance of decoration in the United States. There is a singular, but at the same time, a very happy union of the Egyptian and Greek in the elevated platform, answering the purposes of the pulpit, and the semi-Theban and semi-Corinthian [reredos], which seems to rise behind the platform, with the rich diagonally indented ceiling, and luxurious sofa-like pews, make this interior altogether the most strikingly beautiful I ever remember to have seen" (Severens 1981, 58).

Before long, however, the style had been assimilated into vernacular use, resulting in the widely scattered rural frame churches that so captured the photographic imagination of Walker Evans and others as the Farm Security Administration set out to document visually the simultaneous integrity and desperation of southern rural life during the depression era. One such church in New England has been evocatively described by architectural historian William H. Pierson, Jr., as "in its primitive unknowing way, it pleads to be Greek." The idiom was so universal by the 1830s, when this particular church was erected, that Pierson's phrase could be applied almost anywhere in the South as well – such as the church depicted in Walker Evans's 1936 "Wooden Church, Beaufort, South Carolina" (see figure 48). Although the general proportions are those of the Greek revival, the remainder of the design is strictly free-form vernacular, with the rough geometry of the door and window lines reflecting the creative sensibility of a folk artist (Pierson 1970, 440, 453–54; Hamlin 1964, 196; Federal Writers' Project, North Carolina 1939, 229; Severens 1981, 60).

Another photograph by Evans of the same year – entitled "Church Interior,
Alabama, 1936" – also enriches our understanding of the material culture of
southern Evangelicalism (see figure 49). The portable organ signifies both the
important role of group singing as well as sufficient middle-class status to afford
such a handsome Victorian instrument. (The contrast with the rough-hewn pews
is instructive.) The wall charts also bespeak middle-class preoccupation with
quantifiable achievement. The folding screen is probably a room divider, possibly used to partition space for instructional use. Taken as a whole, this church
seems to be poised on the cusp of two lives, that of primitive frontier evange-
lism and a more genteel faith born of material success.

Although Greek revival styles appealed primarily to urban white folk in antebellum days, the vernacular version was appropriated during the later nineteenth
century by rural African Americans as well. In his evocative pictorial study of the
Mississippi Delta, photographer Tom Rankin evokes vividly the texture of African American life in what traditionally has been one of the densest concentrations of rural black settlement in the nation (see figure 50). Here modest white
frame Missionary Baptist and other churches shape the landscape with their bell
towers and nearby burying grounds, some still with handmade gravestones. Interiors are correspondingly simple, usually featuring an enclosed sanctuary area
with a central wooden podium, a few tall-backed wooden chairs, and a communion table in front of the rail. River baptisms still abound here, and built and natural environment merge into one another as essential elements of a distinctive
traditional religious culture based very much on local and family identity. More
recent churches built of brick with simple geometrical spires placed directly on
the pitched roof presumably serve the same purposes well enough, but lack arresting visual properties (Rankin 1993, 18 and passim). The periodic waves of
church burning which have afflicted the South seem strategically aimed at the
material focus of black society.

The antebellum years were clearly defined by two styles – Gothic and Greek
revival – each of which carried an ideological burden, especially in the South. The
years of Civil War and Reconstruction saw little church building, with the attention of the region focused elsewhere and its material resources exhausted. Beginning around 1880, the South began to reemerge as something other than a con-
quered province, and a social system based on legally sanctioned segregation and
discrimination – "Jim Crow" – now replaced the institution of slavery that had been
permanently abandoned. Economic recovery was abetted by the "New South"
ideology, which promoted urban growth and industrialism; cities such as Atlanta,
destroyed by General Sherman during the war and subsequently rebuilt quite literally from the ground up, and Birmingham, Alabama, which did not even exist
prior to the war, exemplify this new turn toward a capitalist economy which had
previously been despised as "Yankee" in its cultural implications.

As the southern city began to emerge in its new configuration, houses of worship played prominent roles in delineating the emergent cityscapes. Organized
Protestantism, a bulwark of the values embodied in the new social order, was conspicuous in the monumental churches that are a part of virtually any southern

city today, most of which were built between 1880 and 1930. Although the overall pattern of this urban "churchscape" resembled that of its northern counterparts, the particulars differed in some interesting ways. Primary among these was the denominational grouping that predominated. Episcopalians were prominent here as elsewhere; their churches were almost invariably Gothic or some other variant of the medieval revival. Roman Catholics were usually represented architecturally in the larger cities, particularly with their monumental cathedrals, although not in the numbers characteristic of Boston, New York, Chicago, or other cities in which the impact of successive waves of European immigration had been heavy.

The other monumental churches that can be found in virtually any southern downtown of reasonable size are the Evangelical cluster: Baptist, Methodist, and Presbyterian – all in their southern forms that resulted from regional schisms over the slavery issue beginning in the 1840s. ("M.E. Church South" – Methodist Episcopal – can be found on many United Methodist churches of this vintage.) These older denominations were joined, particularly in the western fringe, by the Campbellite offshoots, Disciples and Churches of Christ. The styles of these churches are very similar for the most part to their northern counterparts – Victorian Gothic, Richardsonian Romanesque, and Ecole des Beaux Arts Classicism. Siting might be along a lengthy axis, such as Atlanta's Peachtree Street, or around a square, as is the case with the statehouse in Raleigh. Although talented architects occasionally executed churches in these styles with an individualistic flair, as a whole this generation of buildings reveals little of regional distinctiveness. A distinctive style of religiosity, in which individual redemption and social conservatism were the norms, prevailed across denominations throughout the region until the 1960s, but the South remained in architectural terms a cultural province of the North.

One way in which the South exhibited a certain degree of individuality in degree if not in kind was the prevalence of the auditorium church, in combination with any of the aforementioned popular styles. Baptist, Methodist, and Campbellite worship in particular stressed music (in the latter case, sometimes vocal only) and preaching over an elaborate and orchestrated formal liturgy. It therefore made sense that this type of internal arrangement, common enough in other regions, should be especially popular here. This design, in which a large stage with central pulpit, seating for an extensive choir, and, for more affluent congregations, individual "opera" seating arranged in curving tiers that rose as they extended toward the rear of the auditorium, proved just right for the kind of worship that still holds special favor throughout the region. One good example is Austin's First Methodist Church (1923), in the shadow of the state capitol. Modeled on the Roman Pantheon, it features a dome and two octastyle (eight-columned) facades perpendicular to one another, each facing a major avenue. Others include the First Baptist Church of Durham, North Carolina (Classical revival, 1927); First Christian Church on Fort Worth's Throckmorton Street (Van Slyke and Woodruff, 1912–14), also Classical in inspiration (see figure 51); and Dallas's enormous First Baptist, an 1890 polychromed brick Gothic revival structure that long played home to W. A. Criswell, a major leader of the Fundamentalist movement in Texas (Robinson 1985, 10, 1; Williamson 1973, 135).

All of the preceding examples have been churches built and used by primarily white congregations. After the Civil War, however, newly emancipated rural African Americans joined the smaller numbers of their already free urban counterparts to build houses of worship, primarily Baptist and Methodist, in similar styles. One such church which has taken on historic associations is Ebenezer Baptist Church in Atlanta, in which Martin Luther King, Sr., and his son and namesake both served as pastor. Designed in 1922 by an unknown architect, Ebenezer Baptist is a low-lying brick structure with twin, spireless towers built in a late, stripped-down version of Gothic revival, the last of a succession of buildings utilized by the congregation. Modest in size and roughly finished, the church has the usual apparatus of a Baptist church – central lectern on a dais with seating for the choir and, at the very rear, a baptistry, with an illuminated cross above. Stained glass windows commemorate Ebenezer's noted pastors. Today it constitutes part of a historic district maintained by the National Park Service in the black Atlanta neighborhood known as "Sweet Auburn"; nearby on Auburn Avenue are two other monumental black churches, Big Bethel A.M.E. (1891), notable for its prominent "Jesus Saves" sign, and the Wheat Street Baptist Church (Gournay 1993, 77–78 and 80–82; Franklin and O'Neal 1991, 3).

Another significant example of urban black church building is the Sixteenth Street Baptist Church in Birmingham, Alabama, a twin-towered brick Romanesque revival structure with an entrance arcade of three large round arches in the Richardsonian manner (see figure 52). The second church built by the congregation on the site, in a black commercial area a few blocks from the city's central business district, it was designed in 1911 by the local black architect Wallace A. Rayfield. (The original had been built in 1884.) Its September 1963 bombing, in which four children were killed, was a major turning point of the civil rights movement, and is commemorated in a recently added stained glass window by John Petts featuring an image of a crucified black Christ (*Alabama's Black Heritage* n.d., 4–5; White 1980, 115).

A final example of an auditorium church with distinctively southern resonances is Nashville's Ryman Auditorium of 1892 (see figure 53). Originally named the Union Gospel Tabernacle, it was later rechristened to honor its benefactor, a converted riverboat captain named Thomas Green Ryman. The auditorium, which in its eclectically red brick Gothic elements resembles other period civic buildings such as Cincinnati's Music Hall, was conceived by Ryman as a tabernacle for Sam Jones, who at the time of its completion in 1890 was one of the most popular and influential revivalists in the South. Although the building was used by Jones, B. Fay Mills, Dwight L. Moody, Billy Sunday, and other evangelists on many occasions, it also from early on was the setting for a wide variety of cultural and civic events, especially after the addition of a gallery made it the largest such building in the entire South. These included Lyceum and Chautauqua program series; Anti-Saloon League and Confederate veterans' rallies; lectures by prominent public figures such as William Jennings Bryan, General

William Booth, Booker T. Washington, and Frances Willard; and musical performances by the Fisk Jubilee Singers, Ignace Jan Paderewski, and Marian Anderson. This intermingling of Evangelical Protestantism with the political and "middle-brow" cultural life of the era is an interesting glimpse into the role of religion in southern urban society.

The subsequent metamorphoses of Ryman Auditorium are also revelatory of the role that Nashville has played as a hub of a distinctively regional culture, in which religious and secular motifs are hard to disentangle. The Grand Ole Opry, which originated at a local radio station in 1925, found a permanent home at the Ryman around 1941, and remained there till its permanent relocation at suburban Opryland in 1974. The devotion of its fans to the Opry, which celebrated its final night at the Ryman with a gospel sing led by Johnny Cash and June Carter, has led to its acquiring the nickname of the "Mother Church" of country music – a designation reminiscent of the shrinelike status acquired by Memphis's Graceland, to which untold thousands of Elvis Presley fans have made pilgrimages. The Ryman, which for many years was maintained as something of a shrine and used only occasionally for special events, was renovated and reopened for regular public performances with a June 1994 live broadcast led by Garrison Keillor, the Minnesota storyteller known for his celebration of the role of religion and music in American regional cultures (Graham 1974, 90–91; Henderson 1968; Eiland 1992; "Special Ryman Centennial Edition" 1992, 1993, 1994).

Southern church building during the middle and later decades of the twentieth century has been influenced considerably by the growth and expansion of the Evangelical tradition, first regionally and, more recently, far beyond the boundaries of the South. The favorable publicity that Evangelicalism began to receive during the 1970s, symbolized in Jimmy Carter's election to the presidency, rapidly turned it and other aspects of southern culture such as country music and conservative politics, into "export commodities." Two hallmarks of southern Protestant architecture are *style* and *scale*. With regard to the first, the Gothic revival persisted well into the twentieth century as an appropriate idiom for middle-class southern urban churches: the Highland Park Methodist Church (1927) and Highland Park Presbyterian Church (1941), both designed by local architect Mark Lemmon, in the well-to-do Dallas neighborhood which includes the Southern Methodist University campus, are a good case in point (Sumner 1978, 77).

Scale is nicely illustrated by Bellevue Baptist Church in the suburbs of Memphis, Tennessee, named one of the nation's "great churches" by the *Christian Century* in 1950. At that time housed in an urban complex in what is now inner-city Memphis, the congregation decided in 1983 to relocate in the expanding suburb of Cordova and completed its new plant there in 1989. In scale, Bellevue Baptist qualifies for the title of "megachurch." Its roof line is low, and its facade is lined with twenty-one columns over which is superimposed a pedimented porte cochere with seven slightly taller columns. Although the scale of church is expressed in its horizontal sweep rather than by verticality, its overall design motifs evoke the neocolonial style favored by hundreds of other Southern Baptist churches and those of many other denominations throughout the region. (Here the importance of *style* emerges again.) The "mega" character of the plant is revealed in the "worship center's" seating capacity of 7000, plus an addition 310 seats for the choir and 100 more for an orchestra. Thirty-one acres of asphalt-paved parking lot provide spaces for 3500 cars in the midst of a campus that totals 376 acres (Balmer 1993).

Bellevue Baptist is simply a giant version of countless such newer churches, many of them fundamentalist or Pentecostal, that have mushroomed throughout the suburbs of the South and its environs, including much of southwestern Ohio. Although Bellevue Baptist continues to call itself a "church," many of its counterparts, particularly of the Pentecostal variety, choose less traditional names, such as "Christian Life Center" or "Family Ministries," in preference to such older, more biblically rooted Free Church designations as "temple" or "tabernacle." Like Bellevue Baptist, these buildings sometimes are designed to evoke historical resonances, especially of the Wren-Gibbs style, with the cluster of religious and cultural associations discussed in the context of the World War II–era *Time* covers in the earlier chapter on New England. Baptists seem especially attached to this patriotic resonance; Pentecostal and Holiness congregations, however, seem more attracted to modern designs devoid of historical references. As a consequence, their houses of worship are not readily identifiable as such, and might be easily mistaken for conference hotels or corporate centers sited for easy access from the interstate rings that encircle most good-sized cities.

Not all newer churches are so grand in scale. Those built by congregations of more modest size and means, however, are similar in their avoidance of all but rudimentary evidences of "churchliness." Some are drastically simplified mini-versions of the Wren-Gibbs plan, with a modest plastic steeple perched on the angle of the pitched roof. Others resemble ranch-style houses, with an entrance on the long side and little to announce their identity beyond a sign, sometimes mounted on wheels, with changeable plastic letters to proclaim catchy evangelical slogans. Built of brick or of inexpensive framing, they dot the landscape of the rural South and dominate the Appalachian region, aligning themselves with the Free Church tradition that from its beginnings had espoused simplicity and the rejection of any attempt to create a space that could be regarded as sacred. (See illustrations in Dorgan for some good examples.)

Before concluding this survey of the built environment of southern Evangelical Protestantism, we should also consider that not all religious activity takes place in churches (or tabernacles, temples, and other Evangelical equivalent terms.) Our discussion of Nashville's Ryman Auditorium provided an example of a building of mixed religious and other cultural uses, including Chautauqua programs. The Chautauqua movement began in upstate New York in the 1870s under Methodist auspices, as a training program for Sunday school teachers. Before long, the original Chautauqua had expanded into a summer settlement of permanent private residences and public facilities, focusing more on educational and cultural than overtly religious activity. The general environment strongly resembled that of the Methodist Holiness camp meeting described in the New England chapter, such as Wesleyan Grove on Martha's Vineyard. These were in turn based on earlier camp meetings, primarily in the South, which had originated in crude, unstructured frontier revivals such as that at Cane Ridge, Kentucky, in 1801, and later become routinized by the Methodists in particular into highly structured ritual events with permanent physical facilities (T. Morrison 1974; Bruce 1974).

The Chautauqua movement that flourished in the South around the turn of the twentieth century had its roots in all of the above. Although it existed under various auspices, one surviving example gives a good illustration of what the phenomenon was about. The Monteagle Sunday School Assembly was founded by Tennessee's interdenominational Sunday school convention in 1882. The winning site to host this activity was Monteagle, a small mountain town located close to the University of the South at Sewanee. The ethos at Monteagle was shaped by the progressive wing of southern religion and society, which fostered both a "modernistic" approach to theological issues such as biblical criticism and a commitment to contemporary Evangelical social causes such as temperance. The programs offered there focused on education, including that for Sunday school teachers, with other cultural events similar to those held at Ryman Auditorium regularly scheduled as well.

The physical environment at Monteagle was spacious and relaxed but also controlled. The site was originally chosen because of its pleasant rustic setting, the cool mountain air in the summer, and accessibility by rail. Soon hundreds of people were in residence during the summer months, with lodging facilities such as a hotel and a summer teachers' home. Tents and, later, individual dwellings were used to provide housing as well. A chapel and an auditorium were both completed in 1901, the latter a twenty-sided polygon 140 feet in diameter with seating for 3600. Other buildings included a Children's Temple for evening prayer service and a Hall of Philosophy, which included a gymnasium, presumably following the idea of *mens sana in corpore sano*.

From its beginnings, the Monteagle Chautauqua was a genteel affair, catering to middle-class southerners within the Evangelical consensus but intolerant of its less-disciplined fringes. Illustrative is the story of the visit of the revivalist Sam Jones, for whom the Ryman Auditorium had been built. When over 2000 folk arrived to hear him, Jones demanded that the gates be opened to all, including those who had not paid the admission charge, in keeping with revival meeting practice. Monteagle, however, was not a revival camp meeting; the gates remained closed, and Jones refused to preach. In other ways, a decorous gentility asserted itself; though smoking and drinking were strongly discouraged, for example, they were not absolutely forbidden. No fanaticism was to be displayed here.

The Monteagle Chautauqua began to lose ground as the twentieth century progressed, with other recreational allures and alternative educational programs competing for its once burgeoning clientele. Public buildings diminished in number through attrition, and private residences, like those in Wesleyan Grove, became more elaborate, though never palatial. The Monteagle Assembly is very much alive today, but its life is that of a summer community of like-minded fam-

ilies rather than a corporate effort. Its award-winning Warren Chapel, designed
by E. A. Keeble in 1950, is one of the few modern public buildings; it is rustic in appearance, with a broad nave, gently pitched roof, and one wall composed entirely of glass to provide a sense of unity with the environment. Some 163 Victorian "gingerbread" cottages, similar to those in other such colonies such as Wesleyan Grove or Methodist-sponsored Lakeside on the Ohio shore of Lake Erie, provide the pleasantly anachronistic core of what is now a secular family vacation setting. Nor is Monteagle alone; a number of other communities, such as North Carolina's Methodist-affiliated Lake Junaluska, still have substantial residential populations as well as a full array of summer activities (Porter 1963; Wood 1983; Charles H. Lippy, personal communication).

The idea of parklike recreational areas with religious overtones by no means died with Chautauqua, but continued in parts of the South to reinvent itself in accordance with prevailing cultural themes. Religious theme parks, though not restricted to the South, seem particularly at home in that region, given the prestige enjoyed by religion in southern culture. One example is Christus Gardens in Gatlinburg, Tennessee, where tableaux of biblical scenes are presented with what a promotional brochure describes as "gripping realism." Da Vinci's *Last Supper* is similarly evoked in various media throughout the region, for example, in gourd seeds at the Gourd Museum in Angier, North Carolina, and in butterfly wings at the Christ Only Art Gallery in Eureka Springs, Arkansas. The latter complex, founded by "Old Christian Right" spokesman Gerald L. K. Smith, also features a Bible Museum and the Christ of the Ozarks statue. Holy Land USA in Bedford, Virginia, is a farm with biblical references scattered throughout – for example, passages alluding to swine above the pigpen – and re-creations of biblical scenes. A workshop on the farm enables visitors to purchase a crown of thorns or nails "similar to the ones used to crucify our Lord" (Barth 1986, 147, 150, 155–56).

Perhaps the best known of such tourist attractions is Heritage USA near Charlotte, North Carolina, an enterprise of the later discredited and imprisoned televangelist Jim Bakker and his former wife Tammy Faye. Described by *Newsweek* religion editor Kenneth Woodward as a "Disneyland for the Devout," Heritage in its heyday offered patrons – mostly Evangelicals, some of whom had purchased life memberships which proved to be of dubious worth – lodging in its Grand Hotel "a 491-unit, four-diamond rated atrium hotel with concierge service, bell service and doorman service," among other accommodation options. A sign in gold Gothic letters at the Grand Hotel proclaimed that "Jesus Christ is Lord," and wake-up calls informed their recipients that "This is the day the Lord has made." Other amenities included counseling in an "upper room"; baptisms in the hotel's swimming pool; a Passion play in an amphitheater (a popular feature at other southern locales as well); and a carousel, petting zoo, 200-foot-tall water slide, miniature golf course, and other solidly middle-class, sometimes nostalgic, always edifying amusements.

Jim Bakker's inspiration for Heritage USA lay in his memories of Pentecostal summer camps, with swimming holes and other rustic pleasures conducted under careful moralistic supervision. In a *Newsweek* interview in 1986, Bakker declared that "Many of our campgrounds were built during the tourist cabin era, and that's where they stayed. But society went to the Holiday Inn, and our campgrounds didn't keep up. My dream was to bring the Christian campground up to the 20th century." The result was an Evangelical haven. Its centerpiece, the Grand Hotel, has been described by one not-entirely-friendly observer in the following language:

> The Heritage Grand Hotel, four stories of brick and glass and stone unable to make up its mind between Renaissance and Georgian colonial. Jim Bakker's meretricious monument to American bad taste. You could enter the hotel past platoons of majordomos uniformed in white silk and tassels. Or you could go around the other way, through the Heritage Village retail mall, a cobbled arcade lined with "shoppes" and stores all done up in Walt Disney Victorian, pastel tints and fake facades, like a giant confection waiting to be gobbled. . . . A world of sensuous Christian pleasure. A seductive fun house adorned with elaborate mahogany panelling and crystal chandeliers and gold sconces and phony gilt-laden Queen Anne furnishings.

Whatever one may think of enterprises such as Heritage, it is clear that it manifested profusely the symbiotic relationship that latter-day American Evangelicalism has frequently demonstrated with a capitalistic culture of consumption. After the fall of the Bakkers, the future of Heritage was uncertain; at one point in the early 1990s it had been taken over by a Malaysian consortium (Woodward 1986; Alderson 1988; James 1993, 6–7, 193).

DIVERSITY

Although Evangelical Protestantism has clearly dominated the southern religious scene for the past two centuries, and variations on the Classical and medieval revival styles have shaped much of its architectural expression, Charleston and New Orleans have already illustrated that the religious culture of the South has not been monolithic. To conclude our survey of the region, we might consider two ways in which diversity has manifested itself in the South: religious and stylistic pluralism. The Catholic presence has already been noticed, but the Jewish community in the South has only been touched upon, in the case of Temple Beth Elohim in Charleston – the city which at one point had the largest Jewish community in the nation. Jews have been since at least the early nineteenth century a small but significant element in the regional ethnic mix, exemplified most clearly in the role Judah Benjamin played in the cabinet of the Confederate government. From their regional beginnings, Jewish merchants, mainly of German background, played the same role in the South that they did in other parts of the nation, namely, that of peddlers and shopkeepers.

With the establishment of a Jewish commercial and social presence came Jewish temples and synagogues, of which Beth Elohim was an early and architec-

turally dramatic example. Southern Jewish architecture and the residential patterns around which it has grown have generally not differed dramatically from
the national pattern. In Birmingham, Alabama, for example, Jewish immigrants –
in this New South city, from eastern Europe – originally lived in a neighborhood
known as Northside from about 1880 till 1920. Here were founded one Orthodox and two Reform congregations, together with other institutions such as a
YMHA, kosher butchers, and a Jewish club. The original Temple Emanu-El, built
in 1886, was very much in the "Jewish Victorian" mode, with the onion domes
and Gothic and ogee arches common to the style. All the congregations eventually abandoned the neighborhood, which became African American; Emanu-El
built a new domed Classical revival home in 1912–13 in the Highland Avenue
and Southside area, where it remains today. Another congregation, the Orthodox Knesseth Israel, abandoned its original home that featured twin Tuscan towers and relocated in a farther suburb in a low-lying modern structure (*Century of
Reverence* n.d.; White 1980, 116–17).

The situation of Jews in mid-sized cities is illustrated visually in Greensboro,
North Carolina, where the Cone family became a major presence in the textile
industry late in the nineteenth century. (The legacy of the Cones is memorial-
ized in a variety of local institutions, including a hospital and the handsome art
gallery at the University of North Carolina at Greensboro.) By 1908 a Reform
congregation had been founded, and by 1924 the small but handsome octastyle
Classical revival Temple Emanuel designed by Richard Upjohn's son Hobart had
been completed not far from the downtown area. Five years later the First Presbyterian Church erected its new quarters across the street in a line perpendicular to Emanuel. Known locally as the "Mighty Fortress," First Presbyterian, also
designed by Hobart Upjohn, is modeled on the Cathedral of Saint Cecelia at Albi
in France. Its twin round thick brick towers capped with diminutive spires indeed give a militant appearance to this style, sometimes known as "Fortress
Gothic." The small-scale elegance of Emanuel contrasts interestingly with the
imposing presence of its Gentile neighbor. Both traditions play a major role in
the local civic establishment, but their relative numerical importance is indicated materially here in unmistakable terms (Arnett 1955, 171ff.; *Temple Emanuel*
1982, 9; materials provided by First Presbyterian Church, Greensboro; I would
also like to express appreciation to Prof. Henry Levenson of UNCG for information on the local Jewish community).

In smaller cities Jews also established a small but significant presence during
the mid-nineteenth century, frequently building small brick synagogues that
resembled lodge halls, distinguished only if at all by some telltale Moorish detail. These can still be found in towns like Anniston, Alabama, or Port Gibson,
Mississippi, where Temple Gemulith Chessed, which dates from the 1890s, is said
to be the only example of Moorish architecture in the entire state. As younger
Jews flee such towns for larger cities like Atlanta and Charlotte, where Jewish
life focuses on the suburbs and their modern houses of worship, many of the small
town temples are falling into disrepair, and the local Jewish cemeteries are abandoned to similar neglect (Chafets 1988, 24; Postal and Koppman 1979, 172).

In addition to the Jewish community, sectarian groups at one time or another have established themselves in the South, particularly North Carolina. Here the Quakers were a major presence during the colonial era, where they dominated the Assembly by 1703. They fell from power, however, after refusing to swear allegiance to Queen Anne, and many migrated northward, especially to Indiana, after it became clear that they could not make peace with a society based on slavery. The center for those who remained became Guilford County, where Guilford College in Greensboro, a campus built in simplified Georgian lines, remains an institutional focus. Older meetinghouses follow the Pennsylvania model of adapting popular architectural modes in stylized form; that in Jamestown, for example, is a simple gable-end brick domestic structure with twin chimneys, while the New Friends Church in High Point is of Greek revival design. Most of the more than 150 meetings that remain in the state today are "programmed," that is, on the Protestant model of structured services. Modern meetinghouses usually follow the southern pattern of neo-Colonial revival (Russell and Megivern 1986, 22–31).

North Carolina, like its southern namesake, was receptive, especially during the colonial era, to a broader pattern of settlement than that of simply British stock. Place-names like New Bern are indicative of a German-speaking presence in particular, and a handful of stone gable-end colonial Lutheran and Reformed churches – some of which shared the same facilities during their early years – remain as a testimony of their presence. The most notable group of Central European origin, however, were the Moravians, whose settlement in the vicinity of what is now Winston-Salem was a parallel endeavor to their presence in Pennsylvania (Russell and Megivern 1986, 96–113).

This general area was originally called Wachovia, an Anglicized version of the name of their founder, Count Ludwig von Zinzendorf's, estate in Moravia. An original settlement, Bethabara, is still maintained north of Winston-Salem. The main focus of the North Carolina Moravians, however, was in what is preserved as Old Salem Village, for many years now a part of the city formed by the merger of the Moravians' Salem with the manufacturing town of Winston. This settlement, restored in the 1950s after threats of further destruction prompted the organization of a highly effective preservation movement, demonstrates two architectural phases. The first, characterized by *Fachwerk* (half-timbering) construction, shows the original medieval Germanic tradition of folk building; many of the pre-Revolutionary buildings in which it is evident have been extensively restored or rebuilt. A major shift in cultural influence is illustrated in the Home Moravian Church, originally built in 1800 and remodeled many times subsequently. It is a large brick gable-end building with round arched windows and a bell-shaped cupola, which reflects the Wren-Gibbs influence more than the old *Fachwerk* tradition. Although its original interior featured simple benches and lacked a pulpit, its current shape is not notably different from that of many mainline Protestant churches. A central square and an extensive cemetery known as "God's Acre," in which row after row of identical gravemarkers bespeak a vision of social equality, are also distinctive features of Old Salem Village (James 1993, 17–20 and passim).

Diversity in twentieth-century southern religious architecture has been the
exception rather than the rule in much of the South, except for major metropolitan areas such as Miami, where Jewish retirees from New York and Catholics from Cuba constitute major segments of the population, and "New South" centers such as Atlanta and Charlotte, where Hindu temples and Islamic centers have begun to make themselves evident. (This may be changing, though, as illustrated in the recent opening of a Zen Buddhist retreat center near Asheville, North Carolina, and two Hindu temples in Columbia, South Carolina.) A few examples of architectural diversity should be noted, although they tend to be much scarcer than in the northeastern quadrant or along the Pacific coast. Frank Lloyd Wright, for example, designed one of his eighteen religious buildings as the Pfeiffer Chapel for Florida Southern College in Lakeland in 1938. Based on a diamond plan, it consists of a horizontal auditorium with numerous intersecting geometrical forms and textures, and a vertical lantern tower, also of concrete, projecting upward. No views of the surrounding area are possible from the chapel itself; rather, light comes from above, and its entire thrust is skyward (Charles H. Lippy, personal communication; Storer 1974, no. 251; Pfeiffer 1976).

Florida Southern College is sited on a citrus grove, and Wright designed his chapel and other buildings around that siting. What is perhaps the most acclaimed of more recent southern religious architecture similarly adapts itself to its physical setting. E. Fay Jones was called to design Thorncrown Chapel near Eureka Springs, Arkansas, when local residents complained of the litter and confusion caused by tourists attracted to the town's Passion Play. Jones, an Arkansas designer who has described himself as "a frustrated cathedral builder born 500 years too late," completed his masterwork in 1980; in 1990, he received the Gold Medal of the American Institute of Architects, partially in recognition of this work.

Thorncrown Chapel, sited in the midst of a stand of hardwood trees, measures only 60 by 24 feet. Although it contains no ornamental features, it evokes a sense of a Gothic cathedral through its verticality, its pointed arches, and the extraordinary overall effect of lightness that its openwork crossed timber construction makes possible. The result evokes the belief of the Romantic era that Gothic architecture took its distinctive forms in imitation of the primeval forests that still abounded in Europe during the Middle Ages. Though Jones is an avowed follower of Frank Lloyd Wright, whose principles of simplicity and organic relationship with the natural environment are clear here, he might also be viewed as a more remote descendant of Richard Upjohn, whose pairing of Gothic principles with indigenous American wooden construction created a distinctive idiom that the entire nation, and the South especially, adopted as its own. In any case, Thorncrown Chapel has proven enormously popular as a tourist destination, attracting some 40,000 visitors annually. Many weddings are also performed in this nondenominational setting, which functions strictly as a chapel with no permanent congregation or programming. It is also a resonant expression of the Ozarks as a distinctive natural and cultural subregion within the South as a whole (Dean 1991).

The story of the built environment of southern Evangelicalism is in a way a microcosm of the broader regional social and religious experience: a strongly cohesive and homogeneous society defined against a more powerful national order perceived as hostile, but upon which the South was still dependent in many ways; a biracial society in which the races were deeply intertwined, especially in religious matters; a traditional society brought abruptly into the industrial age, with a lingering ambivalence about its metamorphosis but a deep attraction to its newfound values and lifestyles. All of these characteristics are clearly manifest in the South's religious and architectural history, which has focused on a small number of styles shared by the two races and a small cluster of denominations, deeply indebted to the broader national culture but appropriating and exaggerating certain particular features of that culture. Ventures such as the Bellevue Baptist Church and Heritage USA represent the culmination of certain of these trends, not universally perceived as lovely.

On the other hand, the South has encompassed within itself at least pockets of pluralism and even playfulness. New Orleans, Charleston, and Miami (which will be dealt with in the chapter on the Spanish borderlands) remain as enclaves of dramatic ethnic mixture and religious and architectural expressiveness. North Carolina has hosted a fascinating mixture of religious cultures, and Atlanta, Birmingham, and Charlotte have demonstrated that commercial and industrial urban life can generate its own social and religious scenes. And, though architectural innovation has not always been prized, Charleston's Gothic extravaganzas, Nashville's remarkable Egyptian revival Downtown Presbyterian Church (William Strickland, 1849–51; see figure 54), and Thorncrown Chapel punctuate the region's Evangelical revivalism in often delightful ways.

THE SOUTH: BIBLIOGRAPHY

Alabama's Black Heritage: A Tour of Historic Sites. N.d. Montgomery, Ala.: Bureau of Tourism
    and Travel.

Alderson, Jeremy Weir. 1988. "Beyond the Bakkers: Religious Meetings." *Meetings and
    Conventions* 23 (Jan.): 85–89.

Arnett, Ethel Stephens. 1955. *Greensboro, North Carolina: The County Seat of Guilford.*
    Chapel Hill: University of North Carolina Press.

Balmer, Randall. 1993. "Churchgoing: Bellevue Baptist Church near Memphis." *Christian
    Century* 110, no. 15: 484–88.

Barth, Jack, et al. 1986. *Roadside America.* New York: Simon and Schuster.

Binney, Marcus. 1978 "Virginia's Country Churches." *Country Life* 163, no. 4216: 1138–40.

Brock, Henry Irving. 1930. *Colonial Churches in Virginia.* Richmond: Dale Press.

Brooke, George M., Jr. 1984. "General Lee's Church: The History of the Protestant
    Episcopal Church in Lexington, Virginia, 1840–1975." Lexington: News-Gazette.

Bruce, Dickson D., Jr. 1974. *And They All Sang Hallelujah: Plain-Folk Camp-Meeting Religion,
    1800–1845.* Knoxville: University of Tennessee Press.

Brumbaugh, Thomas B., et al., eds. 1974. *Architecture of Middle Tennessee: The Historic
    American Buildings Survey.* Nashville: Vanderbilt University Press.

The Buildings of Biloxi: An Architectural Survey. 1976. Biloxi: City of Biloxi.

A Century of Reverence 1882–1982: Temple Emanu-El, Birmingham, Alabama. N.d. Privately printed.

Chafets, Ze'ev. 1988. *Members of the Tribe: On the Road in Jewish America.* New York: Bantam Books.

Chambers, S. Allen, Jr. 1981. *Lynchburg, An Architectural History.* Charlottesville: University Press of Virginia.

Chitty, Arthur Ben. 1979. "Sewanee: Then and Now." *Tennessee Historical Quarterly* 38, no. 4: 383–400.

Cowan, Walter G., et al. 1983. *New Orleans Yesterday and Today: A Guide to the City.* Baton Rouge: Louisiana State University Press.

Crocker, Mary Wallace. 1973. *Historic Architecture in Mississippi.* Jackson: University and College Press of Mississippi.

[Daughters of the American Revolution]. 1976. *The Pioneer Churches of Florida.* Chuluota, Fla.: Mickler House.

Davis, Margaret. 1936. "Tidewater Churches." *South Atlantic Quarterly* 35, no. 1: 86–97.

Dawe, Louise Belote. 1973. "Christ Church, Lancaster County." *Virginia Cavalcade* 23 (Autumn): 20–33.

Dean, Andrea Oppenheimer. 1991. "The Cathedral Builder Born 500 Years Too Late." *Smithsonian* 22, no. 5: 102–11. (On E. Fay Jones.)

DeBolt, Margaret Wayt. 1976. *Savannah: A Historical Portrait.* Virginia Beach, Va.: Donning Co.

Dorgan, Howard. 1987. *Giving Glory to God in Appalachia: Worship Practices of Six Baptist Subdenominations.* Knoxville: University of Tennessee Press, 1987.

Dorsey, Stephen P. 1952. *Early English Churches in America.* New York: Oxford University Press.

Dulaney, Paul S. 1976. *The Architecture of Historic Richmond.* 2d ed. Charlottesville: University Press of Virginia.

Egerton, John. 1977. *Visions of Utopia: Nashoba, Rugby, Ruskin, and the "New Communities" in Tennessee's Past.* Knoxville: University of Tennessee Press.

Eiland, William U. 1992. *Nashville's Mother Church: The History of the Ryman Auditorium.* Nashville: Opryland USA.

Eller, John. 1994. "'Lee Surrendered and They Didn't': Lost Cause Devotees and the Sacrality of the Washington College Chapel." Miami University seminar paper.

Federal Writers' Project of the Works Project Administration for the City of New Orleans. 1938. *New Orleans City Guide.* Boston: Houghton Mifflin.

Federal Writers' Project of the Federal Works Administration for the State of North Carolina. 1939. *North Carolina, A Guide to the Old North State.* Chapel Hill: University of North Carolina Press.

Federal Writers' Project of the Work Projects Administration for the State of Tennessee. 1939. *Tennessee: A Guide to the State.* New York: Viking.

Forman, Henry Chandlee. 1948. *The Architecture of the Old South: The Mediaeval Style, 1585–1850.* Cambridge, Mass.: Harvard University Press.

Franklin, Gordon T., and Malinda K. O'Neal. 1991. *Ebenezer Centennial Publication: A Pictorial History of Ebenezer Baptist Church.* Atlanta: Ebenezer Baptist Church.

Fraser, Charles. 1940. *A Charleston Sketchbook—1796–1806.* Charleston: Carolina Art Association.

Friary, Donald Richard. 1971. "The Architecture of the Anglican Church in the Northern

American Colonies: A Study in Religious, Social, and Cultural Expression." Ph.D. dissertation, University of Pennsylvania.

Futagawa, Yukio, ed. and photog. 1973. *Paul M. Rudolph, Interdenominational Chapel, Tuskegee Institute, Tuskegee, Alabama, 1960–69 . . .* Tokyo: A.D.A. EDITA.

Gamble, Robert. 1987. *The Alabama Catalog: Historic American Buildings Survey, A Guide to the Early Architecture of the State.* University: University of Alabama Press.

Gournay, Isabelle. 1993. *AIA Guide to the Architecture of Atlanta.* Athens: University of Georgia Press.

Graham, Eleanor, ed. 1974. *Nashville: A Short History and Selected Buildings.* Nashville: Historical Commission of Metropolitan Nashville-Davidson County.

Grigg, Milton L. 1963. "The Colonial Churches of Virginia." *Stained Glass* 58 (Summer): 30–37.

Hamlin, Talbot. 1964 (1944). *Greek Revival Architecture in America.* New York: Dover.

Heck, Robert W. 1995. *Religious Architecture in Louisiana.* Baton Rouge: Louisiana State University Press.

Henderson, Jerry. 1968. "Nashville's Ryman Auditorium." *Tennessee Historical Quarterly* 27, no. 4: 305–28.

Hollis, Daniel W. 1961. *Look to the Rock: One Hundred Ante-bellum Presbyterian Churches of the South.* Richmond, Va.: John Knox Press.

Jacoby, Mary Moore, ed. 1994. *The Churches of Charleston and the Lowcountry.* Charleston, N.C.: Preservation Society of Charleston.

James, Hunter. 1993. *Old Salem: Official Guidebook.* Winston-Salem, N.C.: Old Salem, Inc.

———. 1993. *Smile Pretty and Say Jesus: The Last Great Days of PTL.* Athens: University of Georgia Press.

Johnson, Eugene J. 1990. *Memphis, An Architectural Guide.* Knoxville: University of Tennessee Press.

Johnson, Mayme Hart. 1986. *A Treasury of Tennessee Churches.* Brentwood, Tenn.: JM Productions.

Kammen, Michael. 1991. *Mystic Chords of Memory: The Transformation of Tradition in American Culture.* New York: Knopf.

Kocher, A. Lawrence, and Howard Dearstyne. 1949. *Colonial Williamsburg: Its Buildings and Grounds.* Williamsburg: Colonial Williamsburg Inc.

Lancaster, Clay. 1991. *Antebellum Architecture of Kentucky.* Lexington: University Press of Kentucky.

Lanning, John Tate. 1935. *The Spanish Missions of Georgia.* Chapel Hill: University of North Carolina Press.

Ledner, Albert C., et al. 1974. *A Guide to New Orleans Architecture.* New Orleans: New Orleans Chapter of the American Institute of Architects.

Lilly, Edward G., ed., and Clifford L. Legerton, comp. 1966. *Historic Churches of Charleston, South Carolina.* Charleston, N.C.: Legerton and Co.

Linley, John. 1982. *The Georgia Catalog: Historic American Buildings Survey, a Guide to the Architecture of the State.* Athens: University of Georgia Press.

Liscombe, Rhodori W. 1985. *The Church Architecture of Robert Mills.* Easley, S.C.: Southern History Press.

Lyle, Royster, Jr., and Pamela Hemenway Simpson. 1977. *The Architecture of Historic Lexington.* Charlottesville: Historic Lexington Foundation/University Press of Virginia.

Martin, Thomas L. 1957. *Churches of Davie County, North Carolina: A Photographic Study.* Charlotte, N.C.: n.p.

Mason, George Carrington. 1945. *Colonial Churches of Tidewater Virginia*. Richmond, Va.: Whittet and Shepperson.

McClure, Harlan, and Vernon Hodges. 1970. *South Carolina Architecture 1670–1970*. N.p.: South Carolina Tricentennial Commission.

McKee, Harley J., comp. 1965. *Records of Buildings in Charleston and the South Carolina Low Country*. Philadelphia: HABS, National Park Service, U.S. Dept. of the Interior, Eastern Office.

[Mobile City Planning Commission]. 1974. *Nineteenth Century Mobile Architecture, An Inventory of Existing Buildings*. Mobile, Ala.: Mobile City Planning Commission/City of Mobile.

Morgan, William. 1979. *Louisville: Architecture and the Urban Environment*. Dublin, N.H.: William L. Bauhan.

Morrison, Mary L., ed. 1979. *Historic Savannah: Survey of Significant Buildings in the Historic and Victorian Districts of Savannah, Georgia*. Savannah, Ga.: Historic Savannah Foundation and the Junior League of Savannah.

Morrison, Theodore. 1974. *Chautauqua: A Center for Education, Religion, and the Arts in America*. Chicago: University of Chicago Press.

Mycoff, David. 1974. "An Architectural History of R. E. Lee Memorial Episcopal Church." Unpublished paper, Washington and Lee College.

Newcomb, Rexford. 1953. *Architecture in Old Kentucky*. Urbana: University of Illinois Press.

Nichols, Frederick Doveton. 1976. *The Architecture of Georgia*. Savannah, Ga.: Beehive Press.

O'Neal, William B. 1968. *Architecture in Virginia*. New York: Virginia Museum/Walker & Co.

Patrick, James. 1980. "Ecclesiological Gothic in the Antebellum South." *Winterthur Portfolio* 15, no. 2: 117–38.

———. 1981. *Architecture in Tennessee 1768–1897*. Knoxville: University of Tennessee Press.

Pfeiffer, Bruce Brooks (text), and Yukio Futagawa (photography). 1976. *Pfeiffer Chapel, Florida Southern College . . .* Tokyo: A.D.A. Edita.

Pierson, William H., Jr. 1970. *American Buildings and Their Architects: The Colonial and Neo-Classical Styles*. Garden City, N.Y.: Doubleday.

Porter, Curt. 1963 "Chautauqua and Tennessee: Monteagle and the Independent Assemblies." *Tennessee Historical Quarterly* 22, no. 4: 347–60.

Postal, Bernard, and Lionel Koppman. 1979. *American Jewish Landmarks: A Travel Guide and History*. Vol. 2: *The South and Southwest*. New York: Fleet Press.

Rankin, Tom. 1993. *Sacred Space: Photographs from the Mississippi Delta*. Jackson: University Press of Mississippi.

Rawlings, James Scott. 1963. *Virginia's Colonial Churches, An Architectural Guide: Together with Their Surviving Books, Silver and Furnishings*. Richmond, Va.: Garrett and Massie.

Robinson, Willard B. 1985. "Texas Baptist Architecture," *Journal of Texas Baptist History* 5: 1–31.

Robison, R. Warren. 1984. *Louisiana Church Architecture*. USL Architecture Series, no. 2. Lafayette, La.: Center for Louisiana Studies, University of Southwestern Louisiana.

Rose, Harold Wickliffe. 1963. *The Colonial Houses of Worship in America*. New York: Hastings House.

Rosen, Robert. 1992. *A Short History of Charleston*. Charleston, S.C.: Peninsula Press.

Rouse, Jordan K. 1961. *Some Interesting Colonial Churches in North Carolina*. Kannapolis, N.C.

Russell, Anne, and Marjorie Megivern. 1986. *North Carolina Portraits of Faith, A Pictorial History of Religions.* Norfolk, Va.: Donning Co.

Sampson, Gloria. 1987. *Historic Churches and Temples of Georgia.* Macon, Ga.: Mercer University Press.

Scully, Arthur, Jr. 1973. *James Dakin, Architect, His Career in New York and the South.* Baton Rouge: Louisiana State University Press.

Sellers, Hazel Crowson. 1941. *Old South Carolina Churches.* Columbia, S.C.: Crowson Ptg. Co.

Severens, Kenneth. 1981. *Southern Architecture: 350 Years of Distinctive American Buildings.* New York: E. P. Dutton.

———. 1988. *Charleston: Architecture and Civic Destiny.* Knoxville: University of Tennessee Press.

Simmons, Agatha Agar. N.d. "A Brief History of St. Mary's Catholic Church." Pamphlet. N.p.

Simons, Albert, and Samuel Lapham, eds. 1927, 1970. *The Early Architecture of Charleston.* 2d ed. Columbia S.C.: University of South Carolina Press.

"Special Ryman Centennial Edition." 1992, 1993, 1994. *Opry Observer* 5, 5 (June 1992); 6, 3 (Spring 1993); and 7, 3 (Apr. 1994).

Storer, William Allin. 1974. *The Architecture of Frank Lloyd Wright.* Cambridge, Mass.: MIT Press.

Sumner, Alan R., ed. 1978. *Dallasights: An Anthology of Architecture and Open Spaces.* Dallas: American Institute of Architects, Dallas Chapter.

Swann, Nita. N.d. "Complete Walking Tour of Historic Charleston." Charleston, S.C.: Charleston Pub. Co.

Temple Emanuel, Greensboro, North Carolina. 1982. [Greensboro?]: privately printed.

Thomas, Samuel W., and William Morgan. 1975. *Old Louisville: The Victorian Era.* Louisville: *The Courier Journal, The Louisville Times,* Dan Courier, Inc.

Tillinghast, Richard. 1993. "Admiring Charleston's Pews and Spires." *New York Sunday Times* travel section, May 23: 13.

Trotter, An [sic] R. 1991. "Paradise Lost: Religious Theme Parks in the Southern United States." M.A. thesis, New York University.

"The Unitarian Church in Charleston, South Carolina." N.d. Pamphlet

Upton, Dell. 1986. *Holy Things and Profane: Anglican Parish Churches in Colonial Virginia.* New York: Architectural History Foundation and MIT Press.

Walker, Alice Billings, ed. 1975 (1941). *Alabama, a Guide to the Deep South.* Rev. ed. New York: Hastings House.

Weissbach, Lee Shai. 1995. *The Synagogues of Kentucky: Architecture and History.* Lexington: University Press of Kentucky.

Whiffen, Marcus. 1958. *The Public Buildings of Williamsburg, Colonial Capital of Virginia: An Architectural Survey.* Williamsburg, Va.: Colonial Williamsburg.

White, Marjorie Longnecker. 1980. *Downtown Birmingham: Architectural and Historical Walking Tour Guide.* Birmingham, Ala.: Birmingham Historical Society.

Wigmore, Francis Marion. 1929. *The Old Parish Churches of Virginia.* Washington D.C.: U.S. Government Printing Office.

Williamson, Roxanne Kuter. 1973. *Austin, Texas, an American Architectural History.* San Antonio, Tex.: Trinity University Press.

Willimon, William H. (text), and Richard Cheek (photography). 1986. *The Chapel, Duke University.* Durham, N.C.: Duke University Stores.

Wilson, Charles Reagan. 1980. *Baptized in Blood: The Religion of the Lost Cause, 1865–1920.* Athens: University of Georgia Press.

Wilson, Samuel, Jr. 1973. "Religious Architecture in French Colonial Louisiana." *Winterthur Portfolio* 8: 63–106. Charlottesville: University of Virginia Press.

Winston Salem Section of the North Carolina Chapter of the American Institute of Architects. 1978. *Architectural Guide Winston-Salem Forsyth County.* Winston-Salem, N.C.: Winston Salem Section, NCAIA.

Wood, Ernest. 1983. "Chautauqua in the Cumberlands." *Southern Living* 18, no. 7: 102–5.

Woodward, Kenneth L. 1986. "A Disneyland for the Devout." *Newsweek* Aug. 11: 48–49.

37. Aquia Church, Stafford County, Virginia

38. Old St. Luke's, Isle of Wight County, Virginia

39. St. Peter's Episcopal Church, New Kent County, Virginia

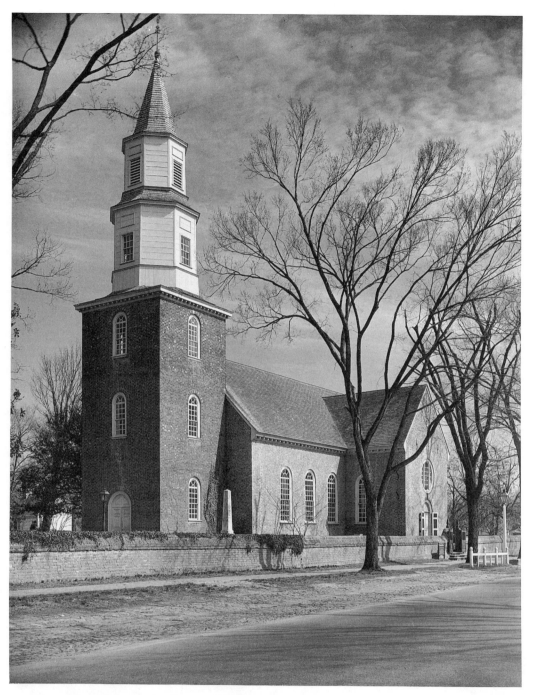

40. Bruton Parish Church, Williamsburg, Virginia

41. *St. Michael's Episcopal Church, Charleston, South Carolina*

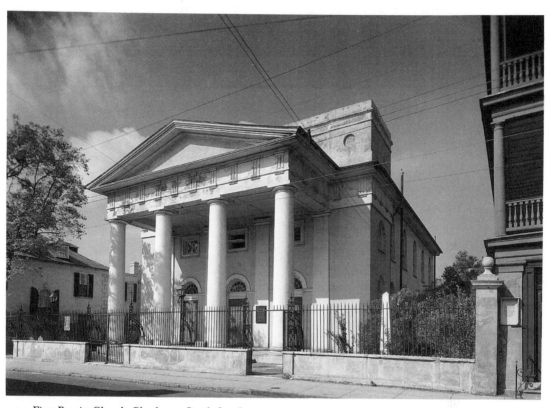

42. First Baptist Church, Charleston, South Carolina

43. Temple Beth Elohim, Charleston, South Carolina (exterior)

44. *Temple Beth Elohim, interior*

45. *Unitarian Church, Charleston, South Carolina*

46. *"Ram Looks Down on the Symbols of the Past"* (St. Louis Cathedral, New Orleans, Louisiana)

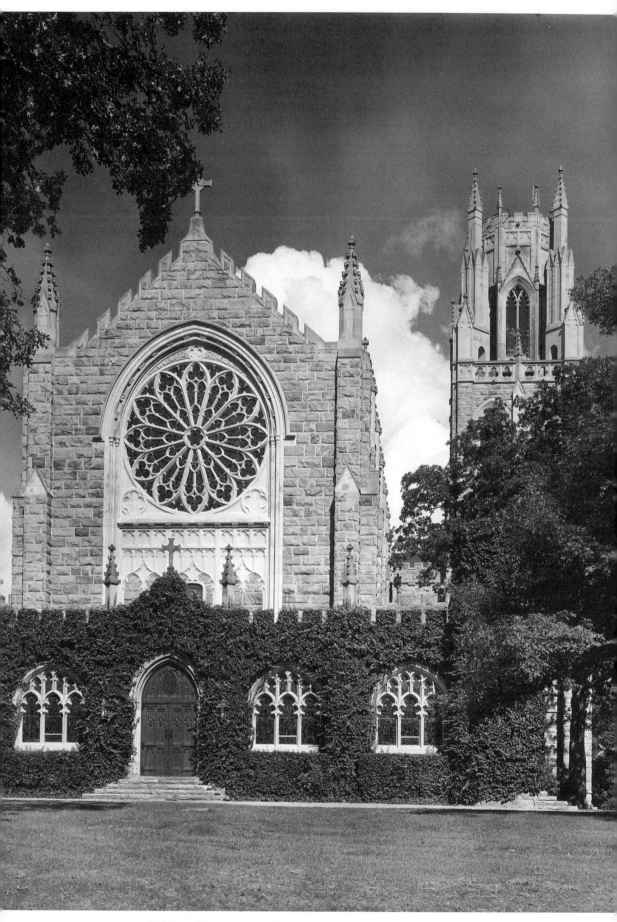

47. *All Saints' Chapel, Sewanee, Tennessee*

48. Wooden Church, Beaufort, South Carolina, 1936

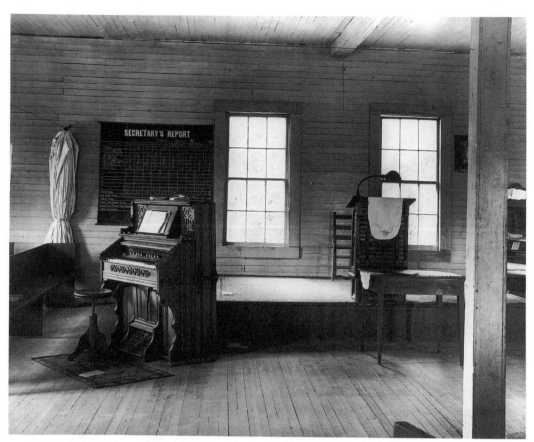

49. Church Interior, Alabama, 1936

50. Bethlehem No. 2 M.B. Church, Mississippi

51. "Throckmorton Street, Fort Worth, Texas, 1976" (First Christian Church)

52. Sixteenth Street Baptist Church, Birmingham, Alabama

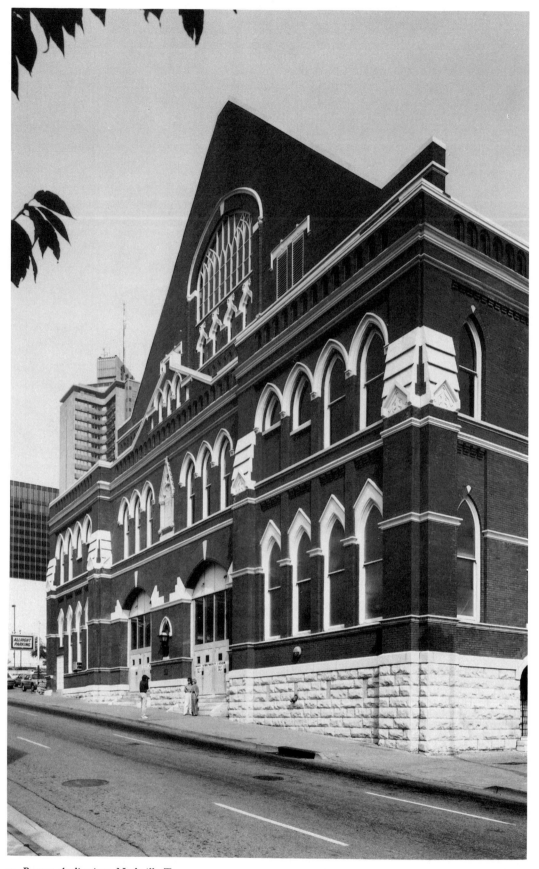

53. Ryman Auditorium, Nashville, Tennessee

54. Downtown Presbyterian Church, Nashville, Tennessee

4 : The Old Northwest

The idea of the Midwest – or, occasionally, Middle West – is one of the least digested in the American vocabulary of mental images. A major part of the "flyover country" experienced only at a considerable vertical distance by image-shapers who haunt either coast, the states that lie between the Appalachians and the Rockies constitute for many an undifferentiated agricultural collectivity relieved occasionally by decaying industrial cities. The reality, of course, is far more complicated and somewhat more cheerful than this dismal mental aggregate implies.

Geographers differ over exactly how to divide up this cultural region and frequently slice it into several smaller zones. For our purposes, it seems best to separate it into two, with the Mississippi River as our point of demarcation. The area lying between the Mississippi, the Appalachians, the Mason-Dixon line, and the Canadian border coincides roughly with that territory set apart by Congress in 1785 as the Old Northwest. It also, less conventionally, includes the western parts of New York and Pennsylvania, which have more in common socioeconomically and culturally with their western than their eastern neighbors. The Plains states lying to the west will be dealt with elsewhere.

Within the territory covered by this chapter, some further internal distinctions need to be made in order to clarify the emergence of distinctive cultural patterns within the region. Each of the Old Northwest's subregions overlaps a cultural zone in neighboring states. In the far northern belt, the thinly dispersed population shares with southern Canada an economy based on extractive industries such as iron and copper mining, lumbering, fishing, and, more

recently, recreation. The next belt, running through central Wisconsin and Michigan into Ontario and upstate New York, is primarily agricultural, exemplified
in Wisconsin's widely known dairy industry. ("Eat cheese or die" has been pro-
posed as a state motto.) The southern Great Lakes region – the economic and
demographic core of the Old Northwest – subsists in the "rust belt" industrial
cities of Milwaukee, Chicago, Toledo, Detroit, Cleveland, Akron, Youngstown,
Buffalo, and Pittsburgh. The southeastern counties of Ohio are part of Appalachia, and they share with West Virginia and Kentucky a thin economic base of
agriculture and coal mining. Southwestern Ohio, much of Indiana, and southern Illinois were all originally social extensions of the South, though nineteenth-
century immigration gave the region a more polyglot ethnic character than most
of the slave-holding region. Finally, the agricultural zone of central Indiana and
Illinois extends westward, with prairies changing into plains.

Although the lake and river systems of the region gave it a certain strategic
importance for the British and French during the colonial period, the main in-
ducement to midwestern settlement has not been military, political, or religious.
Traditionally, people have come to mid-America for two closely related reasons:
land and work. Exceptions can be easily adduced, such as the utopian colonists
in New Harmony, Indiana, or the German Forty-Eighters in Cincinnati. The
main lures for British, Germans, Irish, Poles, Finns, and the many other ethnic
groups who populated the postcolonial Old Northwest states, however, have been
the abundance of cheap land facilitated by the Northwest Ordinance and the
subsequent creation of thousands upon thousands of jobs for unskilled or semi-
skilled workers in the railroads and canals, the Chicago stockyards, the Detroit
auto factories, and the steel mills of Pittsburgh. Land, water, and natural resources
made wealth possible. European immigrants, Euro-American in-migrants from
the Northeast, and African American refugees from the South created the economic wealth and, in their coming and settling, brought with them a human
wealth of cultural and religious traditions that blended more or less harmoniously into this "virgin land" after its aboriginal inhabitants had been driven off.

Unlike the various regions of the East, West, and South, the Midwest cannot
easily be treated as a culture hearth except in a limited and complex sense. Un-
doubtedly one could argue that Polish Catholicism was introduced into the
United States through the Great Lakes industrial cities. However, the impact of
this introduction simply cannot be compared with that of the Puritans in New
England, the Quakers in Philadelphia, the Scotch-Irish Presbyterians in Virginia,
or even the Spanish Catholics in the Southwest. Instead of being the first and
formative cultural group, they were one among many latecomers who carved out
a significant but largely self-contained niche for themselves in urban enclaves such
as Detroit's Hamtramck and Chicago's Milwaukee Avenue. And, like their mul-
tiplex ethnic counterparts, many in later generations abandoned these core areas of settlements for the suburbs, intermarrying and leaving a steadily diminishing population with any visible cultural distinctiveness. In short, no single
cultural group, whether Connecticut Yankee or Slavic Catholic, can claim any
special preeminence in the region as a whole.

Another reason that the Old Northwest zone is hard to characterize culturally has been suggested by historians Andrew Cayton and Peter Onuf. Given the
predominantly commercial motivations for settling the region, the early shapers
of the Old Northwest's ethos consciously articulated a self-interpretation stressing
universality rather than particularity. Ethnic enclaves apart, midwesterners in the
culturally and economically mixed region east of the Mississippi have fancied
themselves not as guardians of a cherished heritage but as harbingers of a national
culture free from the divisive and inhibiting regionalism they saw weighing down
New England and the South. Midwesterners were first American, and only midwestern as an afterthought. Although a certain romanticization of an agricultural past has shaped subsequent regional self-interpretation, the reality of ethnic
mixture and overwhelming urbanization – 80 percent of Ohio was classified as
urban or suburban in the 1990 census – has beclouded such a mythos save perhaps in isolated parts of Hoosierdom (Cayton and Onuf 1990).

EARLY SETTLEMENT PATTERNS

The earliest inhabitants of the region were Native Americans of various
groups – among them Delawares, Shawnee, and Miamis in the south, and Otta-
was, Winnebagos, and Chippewa in the north. These were seminomadic peoples for the most part, and no permanent structures of theirs remain. The only
fixed physical reminders of their cultures actually predate the natives whom the
first European-descended settlers encountered. These are earthen mounds, often of gigantic scale, the purpose of which is not clearly known but most likely
related to ritual. Prominent among these are forty mounds at Cahokia Mounds
State Park near East St. Louis, Illinois, and the Great Serpent Mound near Chil-
licothe, Ohio, which follows along the edge of a hill in snakelike curved form
for 1330 feet. Today, a few reminders of the continuance of a native presence can
be found in scattered places, such as the modest shingled gable-end American
Indian Gospel Church in Dunningville, Michigan (Writers' Program [Ohio]
1940, 509; Vuilleumier and Vuilleumier 1976, 133).

The French presence in the colonial period, preserved vibrantly at the mouth
of the Mississippi in New Orleans, today exists only vestigially in the Old Northwest, primarily in place names such as Vincennes, Detroit, and Sault Ste. Marie.
(Many of Detroit's streets, such as Gratiot and Beaubien, also echo this early and
now largely vanished influence and are invariably mispronounced by proper
Gallic standards.) Although French missionaries were active in the early evangelization of parts of the region and played a role in such important events as
the founding of the University of Notre Dame and the state of Michigan, they
were not the advance guard of any significant group of settlers. The material
culture of the French can be found in a few small Mississippi River communities such as Prairie de Rocher in Illinois. Their churches were mainly humble
chapels; among the few surviving is the Church of the Holy Family, built in 1799
out of vertically placed walnut logs near Cahokia, Illinois, in the palisade style

of construction utilized in French Canada. Another, built in the contrasting *pièce*
sur pièce manner of horizontal log placement, is the 1743 Church of Ste. Anne at
Colonial Michilimacinac near Mackinaw City at the northernmost tip of Michigan's lower peninsula (Eckert 1993, 416–17; Vuilleumier and Vuilleumier 1976,
127, 133).

Other examples of folk architecture demonstrating the adaptation of Old
World techniques to the New World environment can be found today particularly in Wisconsin, much of which was first settled primarily by Germans and
Scandinavians. Log construction, of which only a few scattered examples survive
throughout the region, is illustrated in the Hauge Norwegian Evangelical Lutheran Church in Dane County (see figure 55). Built originally in 1852, it is now
preserved as a museum. Its interior fortunately preserves distinctive techniques
now largely lost, such as the application of lime plaster directly to the logs themselves and a combined altar-pulpit reflecting a distinctively Norwegian liturgical tradition. A Roman Catholic counterpart is Saint Wenceslaus Church, built
around 1850 by German-speaking Bohemian Catholics in similar fashion. As was
common with many vernacular churches, the original appearance gave way to
"improvements" following latter-day fashions – in this case, the covering of the
original logs with a board-and-batten frame treatment to evoke a dim echo of
the popular Victorian "Carpenter Gothic" mode (Perrin 1981, 14–15).

Another traditional pattern of construction, more sophisticated than the temporary log church, is *Fachwerk*, better known in English as the "half-timbering"
characteristic of the Tudor revival style that became popular in this country in
fashionable neighborhoods during the 1920s. Although much of the characteristic picturesque zigzag effect of this technique has been achieved only superficially in recent years through simulated painting, the original method involved
the conservation of timber though the use of horizontal and diagonal wooden
beams to create a framework that could then be filled in with less expensive
masonry or a mixture of clay and straw or other abundant materials.

Although some Episcopal churches were later built in this fashion during the
heyday of the medieval *revival*, only a few genuine *survivals* of this style as a technique of folk building remain – for example, the Lutheran Kripplein Christi
Church in Dodge County and Saint Paul's at Woodland, both built by German-
speaking immigrant congregations around 1860. According to Richard Perrin,
the historian of Wisconsin's vernacular building, the first has suffered from in-
sensitive renovation, while the latter was demolished in 1891 because of structural collapse. Open-timber framing, a less-sturdy version of *Fachwerk*, was employed later in the century to provide structural shells for churches in the Greek
and Gothic revival styles as well, taking advantage of the then-plentiful softwood
coming from the state's emergent timber industry. Most of these structures were
architecturally quite simple, sometimes employing eclectic stylistic mixes, and
were adapted by a wide range of denominations (Perrin 1981, 40).

An interesting example of this design process is illustrated in Saint Peter Catholic Church in Lafayette County, which has subsequently been preserved in the
Old World Wisconsin museum complex. Designed by the missionary priest Sam-

uel Mazzuchelli in 1841, it is a simple rectangular frame building with a Greek revival profile, pointed-arch Gothic revival windows, and wooden siding cut to imitate rusticated stonework. Here is real eclecticism, brought to the midwestern frontier by a sophisticated European clergyman making do with the limited resources available, and blending in skillfully with the fashions of the dominant national culture (Perrin 1981, 40, 42, 54).

THE ENGLISH PRESENCE

A predictable sequence of building stages had developed by the latter part of the nineteenth century in Wisconsin as elsewhere. The first, provisional stage was illustrated in the log and *Fachwerk* churches that were erected in the techniques of the homeland, using native materials. These were often regarded as make-do structures intended to fill a void temporarily. The second stage involved more solidly built but still modest churches, now reflecting building techniques and styles widespread in the new country. A third stage was characteristic of well-settled towns and emergent cities, populated by second- or later generation Americans who had acquired the communal stability, wealth, and sophistication to build in a more monumental mode. Brick churches were characteristic of this phase in the Midwest, as exemplified in the Gothic revival Saint Luke's Episcopal (late 1860s) and Greek revival First Presbyterian churches of Racine.

Two particularly interesting regional examples of provincial high style design were based on plans by Richard Upjohn, the Anglican popularizer of a sophisticated version of "Carpenter Gothic." Both are associated with the Ecclesiological movement influential in some circles of the Episcopal church during the mid-nineteenth century, which stressed the particular appropriateness of the Gothic style for use in sacramental, liturgical worship. Parts of the upper Midwest in which this High Church sentiment still runs strong have been given the nickname "the Biretta Belt," after the Roman Catholic–style headgear affected by some Anglican clergy. Historically, many of these clergy – who would insist on being referred to as "priests" rather than "ministers" – have been trained at Nashotah House in the Wisconsin town of the same name. Nashotah House's Chapel of Saint Mary the Virgin, which bears a distinctly High Church name, was designed by Upjohn and built in 1859–60 (see figure 56). Based on Saint James the Less, the prototypical American Ecclesiological church in the Philadelphia area built a few years earlier, the Nashotah chapel is an English Gothic parish church distinguished by an octagonal chancel at its eastern (altar) end and a dramatic bell cote – that is, a flat, slender tower attached to the nave with a succession of pointed-arch openings carved within its stone frame (Pierson 1978, 192–94).

Another example of High Anglicanism on the western prairie is Saint John Chrysostom's Episcopal church (1851) in nearby Delafield, Wisconsin. This parish church stands on a hilltop with a freestanding bell tower. Built of vertical boards and alternating battens, its distinctive ornamental effects derive both from

this skillful use of wood and from its barge (or verge) boards, that is, boards attached perpendicularly to the projecting gable ends which are pierced in an ornamental geometric pattern (Pierson 1978, 56).

The initial Anglo-American presence in the region often represented an earlier, more lasting, and more architecturally sophisticated expression than that of
many of the continental newcomers. Much of the northeastern section of Ohio
was initially controlled by Connecticut as that state's "Western Reserve," part of
which was designated "Firelands" and awarded to emigrants as compensation for
property lost through British malice during the Revolution. In 1807 the Congregationalist missionary David Bacon organized a short-lived attempt to promote a religiously based colony in the area of Tallmadge, including Presbyterians who in 1801 had become allied with his fellow latter-day Puritans through
the "Plan of Union" devised to minimize denominational competition in frontier lands. It was not until the 1820s that Connecticut-born Lemuel Porter designed the splendid church on Tallmadge's New England-style green that in 1944
adorned the *Life* magazine cover as an emblem of America's common spiritual
values. (See figure 1.)

The Tallmadge church was a late, provincial (though very handsome) expression of a style that was already yielding in New England to the appeal of the simpler Greek revival, construed by many as an invocation of the ideals of Greek
democracy. Regionally, this style found what was perhaps its most monumental
ecclesiastical expression in Cincinnati's Saint Peter in Chains Roman Catholic
Cathedral at the diametrically opposite end of the state (see figure 57). Saint
Peter's, later extended and completely remodeled in its interior in a 1950s interpretation of Hellenic decor, was based on an actual Greek temple – the
Horologium, or Temple of the Winds – and capped with the usual Wren-Gibbs
style tower in stone. Its architect, Henry Walter, also won the design competition for the Ohio state capitol in Columbus, in the ubiquitous Greek style.

The participants in the "Yankee Exodus" who settled the Western Reserve
were generally not too quick to build churches; David Bacon's quirky experiment
to the contrary, their motivation was primarily economic, fleeing New England's
exhausted soil. The Congregationalists, however, with other denominations primarily from New England, soon began to dot the landscape not only with Greek
revival houses but also with churches, many of them humble in scale. In some
cases, several groups would initially collaborate – as did the Methodists, Presbyterians, and Universalists in North Olmsted, Ohio – in erecting a union meetinghouse, a practice hardly unknown in northern New England.

By the 1830s, denominations of all sorts were erecting small Greek temples,
usually fashioned from wood and capped with a steeple and sometimes a spire as
well. Many of these departed from the purity of the ideal by adding, initially or
later, Gothic features, such as the pointed-arch window over the door of the
Universalist church in North Olmsted (1847) and the full program of such windows on the Episcopal church in Peninsula (1835). One of the first Roman Catholic churches in the area, Our Lady of the Lake, was built in 1840 in what is now
Cleveland. Known popularly as "Saint Mary's on the Flats," it was a good-sized

frame structure in the Greek revival mode. However, the four Doric columns of the porch formed by an extension of the roofline were complemented not only by pointed-arch windows but a pyramidally steepled tower with pinnacles at each corner (Butler 1963, 45–60).

Subsequent churches and synagogues in the greater Cleveland area fell in with the succession of nationally popular styles, beginning with the Greek and progressing through the Gothic and the *Rundbogenstil*, with greater or lesser degrees of sophistication. The elite Episcopalians generally commanded the better architects here and elsewhere, as illustrated in the handsome Saint John's Historic Episcopal Church on Cleveland's Church Avenue. Built of stone beginning in 1836, it has a square central tower with four pinnacles flanked by two small, graceful minaret-like pinnacle-capped towers at either end of the facade. An interesting variant on the theme and a striking example of vernacular design is the Mormon Temple at Kirtland, just east of Cleveland, where that nascent group erected its first, short-lived community during the 1830s (see figure 58). Although this, the first of the Latter-day Saints' temples, is a novelty in its interior details, it is also, in its overall configuration, very much a product of its place and time (the Kirtland Temple is discussed at greater length in chap. 5).

THE WELSH IN OHIO

Another British outpost in eastern Ohio, beginning in 1818, was established by the arrival of Welsh immigrants in Gallia and Jackson counties near what is today the West Virginia border. This was one of the earliest significant Welsh settlements in the region; while Welsh Quakers had settled in the Philadelphia area in the previous century, later migrants to the mining regions of Pennsylvania and Wisconsin did not begin to gather in large numbers till mid-century. Although Anglicanism had some small clerical representation among these Celts, the large majority were Non-Conformist by persuasion. This rejection of religious establishment is reflected in the denominational array of the early Welsh in southeastern Ohio: Congregational, Baptist, and Calvinistic Methodist (a distinctive Welsh movement which merged with the Northern Presbyterians in 1920.)

The earliest extant chapel among these transplanted dissenters, a log cabin built in 1841, was called Tyn Rhos – "house on the moor." A number of other structures from the mid-nineteenth century in the immediate area are almost universally built in some vernacular variant of the Greek revival, a style appropriate to the spirit of British Non-Conformity, which deliberately espoused classical forms in reaction against the popularity of the Gothic revival in fashionable Anglican circles. Many of these early churches also had two symmetrically placed front doors, indicating another British tradition of avoidance of mixed seating. This pattern can be found in churches of this period throughout much of southern Ohio among a variety of denominations, ranging from Presbyterians to Shakers to German Brethren ("Dunkers"). Many of these chapels were

abandoned as subsequent generations left the farms for Columbus, and are now
preserved as sentimental reminders of a rural ethnic past; sometimes they are the sites of *gymanfa ganus* (gih-MAHN-fah GAH-nees), the traditional Welsh massive communal hymn-sing. The Oak Hill Congregational Church, a small brick two-doored Greek revival structure, now serves as a museum.

A distinctive feature of the Welsh chapels of southwestern Ohio is the addition of a small outbuilding known as a *ty capel* or "house chapel." Since the early ministers were itinerants and often rode considerable distances between preaching assignments, these structures were invented locally to provide places for ministerial rest and refreshment. They were also utilized as multipurpose buildings, both for church functions and for secular schooling before communities provided separate facilities for education (Struble 1989; Lloyd 1995).

THE GERMANS

After the French, who left behind few substantial settlements, the major Roman Catholic presence in the Old Northwest in general and Ohio in particular was that of the Irish and the Germans. The former, though numerous, were generally quite poor, working their way west through jobs on the canals and the railroads. They brought with them little in the way of a distinctive architectural tradition, since the poverty of their lives in the old country and the political and cultural domination of their land by the English allowed little opportunity for much beyond a folk architecture. Their churches in the Old Northwest, as elsewhere, tended to follow broader Catholic trends, particularly the French Gothic mode already seen among the Irish of New England.

German-speaking Catholics, together with their Protestant and Jewish counterparts, brought with them not great wealth but at least a modicum of money and skills. This enabled them to settle on Ohio's rich farmlands as well as in urban areas, such as the three cities said to define the "German Triangle" – Cincinnati, Milwaukee, and St. Louis. In city and town alike, German Catholics erected a plethora of churches by the middle to latter decades of the century, usually on a grand scale and almost invariably of the red brick that abounded in Ohio. Most of their churches were adaptations in this new material idiom of styles familiar in the old country: the Gothic, the Renaissance, and the *Rundbogenstil*, the German variety of Romanesque revival that reflected a northern Italian influence and anticipated the more distinctively American Richardsonian version that would sweep the nation in the century's later decades. A drive from Cincinnati in the southwestern corner of Ohio to Fremont in the north central region of the state provides a tour of this re-creation of *Deutschtum* in mid-America. The core of the "Queen City's" nineteenth-century German settlement is located just north of the downtown grid and is still known as "Over-the-Rhine" – after the "Rhine" (actually, the Miami and Erie) canal that formed its southern border. Today an inner-city neighborhood peopled mainly by African Americans and Appalachians and the subject of endless debates about gentrification, the district still abounds in the Italianate style favored by German immigrants of an earlier century. Many of the storefronts of these typically three-story structures once housed saloons; Vine Street alone, one of the area's north-south thoroughfares, once boasted 113 in a two-mile segment. Although the city's reputation as a brewing center did not survive Prohibition, the attachment of local German Catholics to the *Biergarten* prompted Archbishop Purcell to divide his administration between two vice-chancellors; only the one supervising Irish parishes dared to advocate temperance (Clubbe 1992, 205).

The earliest neighborhood Catholic church still bears the inscription "St. Marien's Kirche" and the date 1841 on the medallion on its triangular brick pediment, indicative of the adaptation of the Greek revival style even by these early German settlers. Old Saint Mary's, as it is better known today, boasts an enormous reliquary reflective of the piety of pre–Vatican II Catholicism, and still regularly offers German masses for an elderly clientele. Nearby St. Paulus Kirche (Saint Paul's Church), begun in 1848 as the seventh Cincinnati church for German Catholics and the second in the Over-the-Rhine neighborhood, is eclectic in character, having undergone a major remodeling by the notable local architect Samuel Hannaford after a disastrous 1899 fire. In the 1990s, having been desacralized, it was serving as headquarters for the Verdin Company, the world's largest manufacturer of bells, carillons, and clocks.

German Protestant churches in Over-the-Rhine, such as Salem United Church of Christ (1867; formerly Deutsch evangelish reformirte [*sic*] Salem's Kirche) and Philippus Church (1890), with its gold finger pointing heavenward from the spire tip, tend to follow the red-brick version of the Gothic that had replaced classical themes among German congregations of all sorts by the latter half of the century. Other of the city's German Catholic churches, such as Saint George's, an 1873 twin-towered adaptation of the *Rundbogenstil* also designed by Samuel Hannaford, illustrate the same tendency toward medievalism. (Saint George's was closed by the archdiocese in 1993 and its congregation merged with that of nearby Saint Monica's, once the cathedral, in a neighborhood now uneasily shared by the University of Cincinnati and its socioeconomically marginal neighbors; it has since been turned into an interdenominational campus ministry center [Clubbe 1992, 213, 234, 279].)

The same patterns prevail as one moves north to Hamilton, the seat of adjoining Butler County. St. Johannes Kirche, a rather simple 1867 Romanesque structure, was built by the German Reformed faction of a congregation originally merged on the Prussian model. The Lutheran component had withdrawn to form the Zion Evangelical Lutheran Church and erected a Gothic revival building in 1865, also of brick. The Americanized descendants of the Reformed group eventually reorganized as Saint John's United Church of Christ, the denomination that unites northern Ohio Congregationalists and the German Reformed of the southern part of the state. In the early 1990s, the building was acquired by an Evangelical group. Saint Stephen's (1836, remodeled frequently) and Saint Joseph's (1866) Catholic churches, respectively Gothic and Romanesque in style, were located only a few blocks from one another, but were

both needed to serve a growing throng of German and some Irish immigrants
to the city. Saint Stephen's is now renamed Saint Julie Billiart, a concession to another parish closed in the kind of merger that had become painfully frequent by the 1980s, necessitated by changing demographic patterns and an acute shortage of clergy (Schwartz 1986, 100ff.).

North of Butler lie Darke, Green, Auglaize, and especially Mercer counties, the core of the densely German Catholic settlement of west central Ohio expressed in toponyms such as Minster, Saint Mary, Saint Henry, and Maria Stein – "the land of the cross-tipped churches," which now constitutes a historic district. Mercer and its adjoining counties offer a striking landscape of rich, flat farmland punctuated by gleaming aluminum-capped silos and the spires and domes of these German churches. John Baskin evoked them well in *Ohio* magazine: "The villages [the German immigrants] established then are similar now: two dozen houses, a grocery, a hardware store, maybe a small branch bank and a library, all huddled against an amazing Catholic church of Gothic or Romanesque design with a towering steeple, some of them over a hundred feet high and visible for miles across the flatness. In some places, a half-dozen of them can be seen at once. There are dozens of them, strung magnificently across the prairie, something like an ecclesiastical version of the modern landscape's utility tower, transmitting the ethereal." The role of these churches for these German towns is roughly analogous to that of the meetinghouse on the New England green: they simultaneously define and dominate the landscape (Baskin 1992, 116).

Many of these parishes had humble church beginnings among the immigrant priests, congregants, and builders of the mid-nineteenth century, most of them new arrivals from heavily Catholic German-speaking states such as Oldenburg (the name of a town in neighboring Indiana) and Hannover. The early buildings were usually modest log structures with small steeples superimposed. A second, brief stage would frequently consist of a vernacular adaptation of the Greek revival mode that constituted something of a national church style in the 1830s and 1840s. Toward the end of the century, local parishioners had grown sufficiently numerous and prosperous to remodel dramatically the earlier, more modest brick structures or build anew in the styles characteristic of their homelands, employing local master builders or architects in nearby small cities such as Lima. Immaculate Conception Church (1901–3) in Celina (population 9137 in 1980) is a giant Renaissance revival church of red brick with two frontal towers and a great central green-tinged metal dome. Saint Augustine's in Minster (1849, enlarged and remodeled frequently) is a twin-towered mixture of styles. Another Immaculate Conception church, this one in tiny Ottoville (population 833), about thirty miles to the northeast, is similarly massive and of red brick, but in the Gothic style with two towers. (See Hoying 1982 for a good discussion of this area's history.)

Emblematic of the region's religious trajectory is the spacious campus of Saint Charles Seminary, starkly sited in the middle of spacious farmland on State Road 127 near Cartagena. Now a retirement home for the order's aging members, the seminary once trained priests of the Congregation of the Precious Blood, a German-founded religious community entrusted with the spiritual care of the German-speaking Catholics of the region. The conversion of such grand-scale buildings as seminaries and motherhouses for orders of religious women to newer functions such as retirement homes echoes a broader national trend. This phenomenon of retrenchment is also exemplified in the pattern of parish consolidation already noted as well as in the closing of the imposing classical revival Saint Mary's Seminary in Cincinnati and the moving of its numerically diminished students and faculty to the gentler suburban campus of the defunct Saint Gregory's minor (that is, high school level) seminary.

Another aspect of a distinctively Catholic presence is the Shrine of the Holy Relics at Maria Stein. Its reliquary chapel, which contains hundreds of bodily parts and other objects associated with saints, is housed in portions of the former motherhouse of the Sisters of the Precious Blood, a German order that accompanied the industrious priests who developed such an ambitious network of churches for their Teutonic charges. The change in this spacious facility's function (it is now a retreat center) is another indication of dramatic changes in religious life even in this enclave of dense and traditional Catholic population (*Guide . . . to the Shrine* 1989).

Traveling northeast from Ottoville along State Road 224, one comes in a half-hour or so to Fremont, a regional agricultural center of some 17,000 people southeast of Toledo. Its still-gracious tree-lined avenues of opulent Victorian-era homes contrast painfully with its forlorn business district. Fremont's most striking feature, though, is its churches. Within a few blocks can be found eight of them, monumental in scale, clustered around the park and neighboring courthouse, and flanked by two modest memorials to the dead of recent and more remote conflicts.

Though Catholic churches were frequently the most dramatic structures in German-American communities, other varieties of Christianity were not lacking. As already illustrated in Cincinnati, the material expression of Lutheran and Reformed congregations differed more in scale and, particularly in the latter case, in interior arrangements and decoration than in style. At the extremes, many Catholic churches had elaborate Gothic altars and vivid stations of the cross; Reformed churches, echoing their Calvinist heritage, would have simpler, pulpit-centered interiors, though often featuring dark wooden Gothic-style furnishings.

A more striking contrast lies in the building patterns of the latter-day Anabaptists, the Amish and Mennonites who settled much of central Ohio and Indiana after their earlier colonies in southeastern Pennsylvania could no longer support their growing population. The more traditional Amish eschewed distinctive houses for worship altogether, and gathered instead in houses for communal prayer. One might interpret their entire landscape as sacred, since they communally endeavored to perpetuate the daily living patterns of the Reformation-era Swiss-German ancestors as a kind of "strong time." An Indiana guidebook describes this landscape well in discussing the so-called Amish Turnpike near Berne, "where numerous Amish farms may be seen and are conspicuous by their windmills, the absence of power lines, and Amish working in the fields. Be alert for horse-drawn traffic." Their less rigid and more assimilated Mennonite coreligionists, like their Indiana Quaker counterparts, did erect buildings identifiable as churches or meetinghouses; the First Mennonite Church (1912) in the same, evocatively named Berne, Indiana, is a vast, rather plain brick adaptation of Gothic, known locally as "The Big M" (Taylor 1989, 39).

SECTARIANS AND UTOPIANS

Although Quakers, or the Society of Friends, settled in Ohio locales such as Wilmington, their midwestern focus has from early times been Richmond, Indiana, an industrial city now located on I-70 near the Ohio border. Quakers from North Carolina began to settle early in the nineteenth century in Richmond, where land was abundant and slavery outlawed. Their continuing presence in the region is still perpetuated in Richmond's Earlham College and the nearby School of Theology. Earlham's meetinghouse dates only from 1952, but the county's museum is housed in the 1865 Hicksite Meetinghouse. This latter is a long, eclectic red brick structure near downtown Richmond; its entrance is constituted by a gable placed in the center of one of the long sides. This adaptation of Quaker "plain style" to the norms of the Victorian Midwest is indicative of the transformation of much of regional Friendly life during the nineteenth century, when the influence of the Holiness movement, especially strong in Indiana, was inclining the course of Quaker practice toward that of Evangelical Protestantism. Similarly, many of the smaller Quaker meetinghouses of the region and period resemble Methodist churches much more than they evoke their Philadelphia antecedents.

If the Ohio border of Indiana is dotted with physical reminders of the sectarian – Anabaptist and Quaker – strains of midwestern settlement, the state's western boundary boasts at least one conspicuous manifestation of its utopian past. New Harmony, at the juncture of the Wabash and the Ohio Rivers, was the site in the early nineteenth century of two successive, short-lived communities. The original settlement was the work of a German Lutheran-derived group of communitarians from Württemberg led by George Rapp, and known as the Harmonists. This industrious people rapidly erected substantial brick dormitories in a style that resembled Georgian in its symmetry but was distinctively German in such features as double-pitch roofs with dormers. The skilled artisans the community attracted also graced these dwellings with some remarkable innovations such as mass production of building components and a primitive sort of air conditioning. Rapp soon decided, however, that the group's economic future lay in a removal back to the more populous Pennsylvania country in which they had first settled in America.

The Rappites sold their entire community in 1825 to Robert Owen, a Welsh secular utopian businessman and philanthropist. Owen's experiment lasted only two years, but his son Robert Dale and others remained in the region for some time and maintained New Harmony's reputation as a center for advanced social thought. In the 1970s a latter-day Owen, Kenneth, set to work with his wife's family trust to restore the community not as a museum but as part of a revital-ized social unit. A major addition to New Harmony's built environment was "The Roofless Church," designed by Philip Johnson, better known as the architect of California's Crystal Cathedral. Built of red brick with a floor of limestone, it culminates in a canopy of pine shingles around which a variety of trees converge. Another feature of the restored community is the grave of the theologian Paul Tillich, who chose to be buried there for the ideals associated with the place (Bongartz 1978; Taylor 1989, 249).

Two other religious communities in the region that have also been restored during the twentieth century are located near one another south of Canton in eastern Ohio, near the area of densest Amish settlement in that state. Schoen-brunn was founded by the Moravian missionary David Zeisberger as a settlement for Christian Indians from a variety of tribes. Its log church was destroyed with the rest of the settlement, as were many of the Indians who returned following the Revolution to claim the possessions they had abandoned for the duration of that conflict. Nearby Zoar was founded in 1817 by the mystically inclined Jo-seph Baumeler and a group of disenchanted Lutheran followers who held all property in common, a characteristic of many of the religious and secular utopi-an experiments of the time. A meetinghouse and Baumeler's home, both of brick, have been restored since the community's disbanding in 1898, together with a two-and-a-half-acre garden based on a description of the New Jerusalem in Revelation 21 and 22 (Writers' Program [Ohio] 1940, 471–72; Vuilleumier and Vuilleumier 1976, 149).

ETHNIC DIVERSITY

The ethnic checkerboard of the Old Northwest states could be described at much greater length, though at the risk of the settling in of the law of diminish-ing returns. As its name implies, Holland, Michigan, was along with Grand Rapids a focus of a heavily Dutch settlement dating from religious turmoil in the Neth-erlands during the mid-nineteenth century. Though tulip festivals and bumper stickers reading "If You're Not Dutch, You're Not Much" still remind the visi-tor of that group's continuing regional hegemony, it would be hard to deduce their presence from their churches. Hope College, the Reformed Church's edu-cational outpost in Holland, features the stepped gables and polychrome brick-work characteristic of the mother country's building style, as does Holland's Hope Church (1874). On the whole, however, Holland's churches tend toward the neoclassical or Gothic revival, placing them in the mainstream of the Reformed building tradition in this country.

Michigan's northern peninsula, settled by a variety of peoples, including many Finns, attracted by job opportunities in the mining, lumber, and other extrac-tive industries, is similarly characterized in its churches not by a great deal of stylistic distinctiveness but rather by the extensive utilization of the varieties of handsome sandstone indigenous to the region. By the later nineteenth century, in short, the Midwest had developed, or embraced, the set of styles characteristic more broadly of Victorian American church design, and simply added a few regional twists. Ethnicity was still a powerful factor in religious practice, but not in its outward and visible manifestations.

A final look at the interaction of religion, region, and ethnicity as expressed in church architecture emerges from the valuable study of southern Illinois vernacular building patterns published in 1988 by John M. Coggeshall and Jo Anne Nast. This region's towns were settled during the middle to later decades of the nineteenth century by a wide variety of ethnic groups, including African Americans, English, French, Germans, Italians, Poles, and Slovaks. Many of the churches, here as elsewhere throughout the region, were small brick or stone gable-end buildings with towers in some version of the Classical or medieval revival styles of the era. Examples include Saint Boniface's 1856 Greek revival church built by the Low German settlers of Germantown in 1856, and the low, broad-fronted twin-towered *Rundbogenstil* Saint Charles Borromeo church, built in DuBois in 1908; despite its patron's name, the congregation was primarily Polish. Italian Catholics, on the other hand, erected an ethnically recognizable house of worship, Our Lady of Mt. Carmel, in Herrin in the late nineteenth century, as revealed in its red tiled roof and striking campanile; the stained glass window dedicated to Saint Patrick donated by another group in town reveal that southern European dominance of the region was not complete. Inscriptions over the doorway, themes of stained glass windows, styles of carvings such as stations of the cross, and the languages in which tombstones are inscribed are in these towns frequently more reliable guides to ethnic origins than church architecture itself (Coggeshall and Nast 1988, 94, 120, 145–47).

Though Roman Catholics of varying backgrounds were dominant in many of these and similar towns throughout the entire region, another form of non-Protestant Christianity also manifests itself here and at the other geographical extreme of the Great Lakes states. In Royalton, Illinois, for example, the Protection of the Virgin Mary Orthodox Church reveals to more western European sensibilities its Eastern Orthodox identity in both its exotic name and form. The main body of the frame church, built by its Slovak parishioners in the World War I era, is a gable-end rectangle with entry through a substantial square tower joined to the nave at its front. Atop the louvered polygonal steeple, however, rests a revelatory onion dome topped by a distinctively Slavic cross. This eastern European variant of the traditional symbol of Christianity features a diagonal rectangular stroke through the lower vertical element and a smaller crossbar near that element's top, representing in greater detail the supposed configuration of its original than do western versions. On the interior, the church was furnished with benches only for the elderly for many decades, following the Orthodox custom of standing during lengthy services; pews were not added until 1964. Similar modest churches, erected by Russians, Ukrainians, and other Slavic groups during the era of the New Immigration, dot the factory and mining towns of northeastern Ohio and western Pennsylvania as well (Coggeshall and Nast 1988, 165).

The one state of the Old Northwest so far dealt with only peripherally has been Indiana. This has not been entirely accidental, since the Hoosier State's demographics differ markedly from those of its neighbors. The other four states in the region were settled first by in-migration from the northeastern United States, then later primarily by out-migration from northern Europe and in-migration of African Americans from the South (with significant pockets of Italian, Greek, Mexican, and Middle Eastern settlement as well.) Indiana was bypassed for the most part by these currents; with the exceptions of its major urban centers, Indianapolis and Gary, it has remained a heavily rural state strongly molded by its original colonization by southerners moving up from the Carolinas especially. Though some of these migrants, such as Richmond's Quakers, left the region to escape the baleful influence of its "Peculiar Institution" of slavery, many others brought southern values with them, as demonstrated by the political hegemony exercised by the Ku Klux Klan during much of the decade of the 1920s. African Americans, as a result, are not plentiful except in such metropolitan areas as Gary, itself more an adjunct to Chicago than part of Indiana proper.

The distinctive culture of Indiana is visible at a variety of levels in its built environment. Its agricultural background is evidenced in the proliferation of small barnlike storage sheds found ubiquitously on suburban tracts, and in the bounteous farm-style cooking purveyed at the Laughners and MCL chains of cafeterias. At another level the cityscape of Richmond, mentioned earlier in conjunction with its Quaker presence, reveals an interesting configuration of artifacts. Churches of the "mainline" denominations – Catholic, Disciples, Episcopal, Presbyterian – join the old Hicksite Friends Meetinghouse (now a museum) on major arteries flanking the central business district, built in the familiar styles of the Victorian Midwest. Also off-center is the Wayne County courthouse, an imposing Richardsonian Romanesque structure on the lawn of which is displayed a World War II–era tank and a stone tablet on which is engraved the Decalogue – the latter the gift of a local service organization. This juxtaposition of governmental presence, military power, and religious law is a graphic reminder of the core values of this southern-derived populace. The nearby Indiana football hall of fame, housed in what appears to be a former bank, completes the picture.

The downtown area of Indianapolis, the state's metropolis and capital, also makes a startling visual statement of the region's ethos. Although Edwin May's 1880-era neoclassical domed capitol building is striking enough, it does not occupy the city's visual center. On one side, it is flanked by the giant 1984 Hoosier Dome, a large but not architecturally memorable modern sports arena that seats 61,000 spectators. (The Indianapolis Motor Speedway that features the annual 500 race lies further from the city's core.) The most "imageable" feature of the central city, however, is Bruno Schmitz's 1902 Indiana Soldiers' and Sailors' Monument, an obelisk bedecked and surrounded with large-scale sculptural ornament on military themes and encircled with a roadway lined with many of the

city's most important commercial structures. Tucked among these is the Irish
architect William Tinsley's jewellike Christ Church Episcopal cathedral of the 1850s, a small-scale Gothic revival church later patronized by the pharmaceutical magnate and philanthropist Eli Lilly.

Although a few other houses of worship, such as the twin-towered French Gothic Saint Mary's Catholic church of 1910–12, add to the cityscape, Indianapolis is shaped visually by other forces. In addition to the Soldiers' and Sailors' Memorial, one also finds nearby the mausoleum-like Indiana World War Memorial of 1927, which occupies a block of downtown space. Across the street lies Obelisk Square; this 1923 100-foot shaft of black granite features bronze sculptures on the themes of law, science, religion, and education. Even more dramatic is the Scottish Rite Cathedral, a 1927–29 Perpendicular Gothic Masonic hall that occupies another entire city block. With Notre Dame's Golden Dome, it can be read as one of two major foci of Hoosier religious culture. Nearby is the Murat Shrine Temple, a sizable auditorium dating from 1910 that hosts stage entertainments and is elaborately decorated with Middle Eastern architectural motifs, murals, and other expressive devices reminiscent of some of the more lavish Art Deco movie palaces of the 1920s. Masonic temples are visible features of many smaller Indiana cities, and are major parts of many southern urban scenes as well (Taylor 1989, 391ff.).

The overall effect of this series of monumental buildings on the flat prairieland of central Indiana is striking. Instead of the usual spread of commercial buildings, vital or abandoned, that characterize most central business districts, downtown Indianapolis resembles the District of Columbia more than its midwestern counterparts of Cleveland, Chicago, or Detroit. These memorials stand stark in their monumental horizontality and isolation. Their message seems to be that the core values of the state are civic, military, athletic, and fraternal, with religion and commerce playing muted, subordinate roles. The idea of a central city in the modern sense, as the core of commercial and artistic activity, seems absent here; Indianapolis is rather a monumental urban space, rich in religious-like iconography but curiously lacking in powerful evidences of the organized religion that plays such an important role in the state's culture.

The distinctive culture of Indiana manifests itself in other, sometimes unexpected urban settings. South Bend in the state's north central sector would be yet another grim rustbelt city that had seen better days save for its one distinctive feature: the University of Notre Dame, America's archetypal Catholic college that came to its greatest eminence in the media during the heyday of the anti-Catholic Ku Klux Klan's domination of state politics. That Notre Dame came to this eminence through athletics, one of the primary icons of Hoosier self-expression, is an interesting indication of the symbiotic relationship that American Catholicism had entered into with both national and regional culture. (To be sure, Notre Dame later, during the lengthy administration of Theodore Hesburgh, began to distinguish itself academically as well – as did its secular counterpart in Bloomington, which has balanced its Nobel Prize winners with basketball coach Bobby Knight.)

While most of the myriad of religiously founded colleges in the region follow similar lines of Victorian campus planning and architectural fashion, Notre Dame stands apart from most in its distinctive imageability. A log chapel near picturesque St. Mary's Lake is a 1906 re-creation of the original 1831 structure built by French missionary Stephen Badin. Nearby is a one-seventh-scale re-creation of the grotto of Our Lady of Lourdes, the site of the mid-nineteenth-century apparition of the Virgin Mary to Saint Bernadette Soubirous. Such grottoes, which range from the domestic to the monumental, can be found on Catholic lands throughout much of the region, and reflect the association of the supernatural with distinctive natural features such as groves, caves, and lakes in the syncretistic popular Catholic piety that has emerged over the centuries (McDannell 1995, 154–62).

A more conspicuous feature of the campus is the Golden Dome that crowns the 1879 Administration Building; together with the neighboring 1870 Gothic Sacred Heart Church, this cluster forms one major focus of the campus (see figure 59). The other is the massive elliptical 1930 stadium which seats nearly sixty thousand fans, built at the height of Notre Dame's fame in the sports-crazed media of the 1920s when Knute Rockne, George "The Gipper" Gipp, and the Four Horsemen of the backfield had captured the national imagination. Next to the stadium is the 1963 fourteen-story Memorial Library, which features "The Word of Life" mural by Millard Sheets. Easily visible from the stadium, this artwork features a giant portrait of Jesus with his hands raised in the sign fans recognize as that employed by referees to indicate a six-point score. Though this juxtaposition is presumably accidental, "Touchdown Jesus" has entered the university's extensive lore as another symbol of the opening that sports has provided for the recognition of minority communities by the broader public, even in nativist Indiana (Taylor 1989, 534–36).

THE GREAT LAKES CITIES

The great cities of the Old Northwest are diverse enough, as rapidly growing Indianapolis illustrates. Their religious landscapes not only contain many fine and distinctive buildings but also collectively illustrate some important principles of the relationship between the American city and the built environments of its religious communities. Among these principles are the symbiotic growth of cities and houses of worship during the nineteenth century in the context of a commonly shared polis; the emergence of more specialized forms of religious building during the twentieth, as residence and commercial zones began to differentiate from one another sharply; and the importance of ethnicity in shaping urban worship patterns. Three cities offer themselves as particularly relevant: Cincinnati, the earliest to flourish and the most southern in geographical and cultural setting; Detroit, which became synonymous first with the immigrant-manned automobile industry and then with a distinctive inner-city musical sound; and Chicago, Carl Sandburg's "city of the big shoulders," which literally had to reinvent itself after the devastating fire of 1871 that destroyed all but one of the city's churches.

During much of the nineteenth century, the fabric of the developing American city revealed a dynamic interaction between the increasingly pluralistic religious sphere and the broader civic realm. Illustrations of this development have already been seen in New England, on the New Haven Green of the 1810s and in Boston's Copley Square during the 1870s and 1880s. In these and other cases, churches of a variety of denominations, mainly elite and Protestant, informally collaborated in shaping central urban spaces; here monumental churches interplayed with park space and civic buildings, such as Boston's Public Library, to create a sphere of calm and stately urban elegance in the midst of commercial bustle.

Cincinnati provides an instructive midwestern counterpart to this phenomenon. As the city expanded and moved northward from its original locus along the Ohio River, and as immigration from the German states in particular swelled its population and increased its religious diversity, a distinctive urban center began to develop at the corner of Eighth and Plum Street, a few blocks west and north of the city's present center at Fountain Square. The first component was Saint Peter in Chains Roman Catholic Cathedral, built under the aegis of Bishop (later Archbishop) John Purcell. Purcell was no shrinking violet, and attracted considerable attention through his public debates with such figures as Alexander Campbell, a founder of the Restorationist movement in frontier Protestantism that eventually split into the Disciples of Christ and the Churches of Christ. The cathedral's architect, Henry Walter, took as his model the Greek Horologium, or Temple of the Winds, and capped it with a steeple in the Wren-Gibbs tradition. Saint Peter's presumably made a significant public statement about the importance of the Catholic presence in the community when completed in 1845.

By the 1930s, however, the cathedral's section of downtown had deteriorated badly, and Archbishop John McNicholas abandoned it for his favored architect Henry Schulte's elegant Byzantine-Romanesque Saint Monica's in Clifton. In the 1950s yet another archbishop decided to restore Saint Peter's in part as a vote of confidence in reclaiming the central city from chaos. Its interior was remodeled into its present configuration, with elaborate Corinthian columns and other ornamental detail reflecting an attempt to bring it into conformity with its Hellenic exterior. Its massive freestanding altar is also an interesting anticipation of the liturgical theology of Vatican II (Giglierano and Overmyer 1988, 73; Clubbe 1992, 49–51).

The second element of this distinctive urban configuration is the Plum Street Temple, the house of worship built for the Reform-minded B'nai Yeshurun congregation under the aegis of its nationally influential leader, Isaac Mayer Wise (see figure 60). Designed in 1865 by James Keyes Wilson, the temple remains a stunning example of what might best be described as the "Jewish Victorian" style. Basically Byzantine in inspiration, it incorporates Moorish elements such as two slender minaret-like towers, perhaps reflecting the Sephardic strain in the congregation's origins, as well as Gothic features.

Although the congregation flourished under the leadership of Wise who, among other things, founded Cincinnati's Hebrew Union College as the first rabbinical seminary in the United States, the city's Jewish population later demonstrated a restlessness typical of similar communities in many American cities. Plum Street was actually the congregation's second home; an earlier downtown structure passed into the hands of a black church. By the 1920s, many of Cincinnati's Jews started to move to Avondale, a nearby suburb where synagogues and temples began to line Reading Road, its main thoroughfare. By the 1950s, another set of demographic changes precipitated a communal move to Amberly Village in the farther suburbs; relocations of B'nai Yeshurun accompanied each move, culminating in the modern Isaac Wise Center used by the congregation for worship today. Although the splendid temple on Plum Street is still opened for High Holy Days and other special occasions, all but one of the other Jewish houses of worship in the downtown and Avondale areas had closed by the 1980s, with many of them taken over by black and white southern congregations for very different sorts of worship. On the other hand, synagogues and temples abound in Amberly Village, where one can also find two country clubs – one for German and the other for "Russian" (that is, eastern European) Jews or their descendants (Giglierano and Overmyer 1988, 72–73; Clubbe 1992, 51–53).

Saint Peter in Chains and the Plum Street Temple face one another on the southern side of the Eighth Street intersection. On the northwest corner stood the domed First Congregational Church-Unitarian, whose pulpit in an earlier building had once been served by William Henry Channing. Built in 1870, the church was demolished in 1945 as population shifts led its congregation to the suburbs, along with those of many other urban churches. Another liberal congregation, the Saint John German Protestant Church, was housed during the same era a few blocks north in Over-the-Rhine, just down Elm Street from the city's splendid Victorian Gothic Music Hall of 1878. In 1948, the congregation, now formally Unitarian in affiliation, moved northward to the affluent Clifton area, and its 1868 red brick church was taken over by a black congregation (Giglierano and Overmyer 1988, 71, 98).

Covenant–First Presbyterian, which stands back-to-back against the Plum Street Temple, is the amalgamated lineal descendant of an even more influential branch of the Reformed tradition in the Queen City. During the 1830s, Presbyterianism found in Cincinnati its major western redoubt, exemplified in the city's Lane Theological Seminary and its eminent revivalist president, Lyman Beecher. Just as Lane moved long ago to merge with Chicago's McCormack Seminary, and its site on Gilbert Avenue is now occupied by a Cadillac dealership, so has Beecher's Second Presbyterian Church become absorbed into the multiple merger that eventually resulted in today's Covenant–First Presbyterian. The 1875 Gothic revival church on Elm Street is interesting primarily for its interior arrangements. Its auditorium-style plan is turned ninety degrees to the building's main axis, on the model, its literature informs us, of Scottish tithing barns of an earlier era. The large platform features dark wood Victorian Gothic pulpit furniture designed by the local woodcarvers William and Henry Fry. Despite the

building's elegant design and the craftsmanship of its furnishings, Covenant–First
Presbyterian's future is endangered by an aging, dwindling congregation as it faces the twenty-first century. Presbyterianism, like Reform Judaism, is still strong in the Cincinnati area, but its bastions are now found in the suburbs rather than the downtown (Giglierano and Overmyer 1988, 81; Clubbe 1992, 46; Covenant–First Presbyterian n.d.).

In addition to the downtown cluster, with houses of worship occupying two or more corner sites at a major intersection, the linear arterial pattern was another common feature of Victorian-era urban church siting in the Midwest and elsewhere during the later nineteenth century. One good example is Cleveland's Euclid Avenue; an even better one is Detroit's Woodward Avenue, one of the major boulevards radiating out from the city's downtown core. Although its splendor has become tarnished since the city's rapid decline in prosperity after its 1967 riots, Woodward still is the site of Detroit's fine Institute of Arts and Cass Gilbert's monumental Public Library of 1921. Although the owners of many churches have since changed, Woodward has since the 1820s been the site of several of the city's most prestigious houses of worship. This clustering earned the nickname "Piety Hill," for the section by the 1840s featured First Presbyterian, First Methodist, and Saint Paul's Episcopal, each designed in a different revival style, in the same close-packed block. During the Victorian era, these were joined or replaced by Saint John Episcopal (1861), Central Methodist (1867), Woodward Avenue Baptist (1887), First Unitarian (1890), and First Congregational (1891), all in one variety or another of the medieval revival styles ubiquitous during the century's later decades. Mason and Rice's First Presbyterian of 1889, which replaced the congregation's earlier Wren-Gibbs style church, is particularly notable for its heavy reliance on H. H. Richardson's Trinity Church in Boston (Quaife 1951, 53, 120, 134; Eckert 1993; Meyer 1971, 68).

By the early decades of the twentieth century, a panoply of ecclesiastical power began to appear on Woodward. Ralph Adams Cram, the nation's most influential Gothicist, designed the Episcopal Cathedral Church of Saint Paul (1908–11). Saint Paul's features a tile floor made by Pewabic Pottery, Detroit's major contribution to the Arts and Crafts movement. Also on Woodward stands Henry Walsh's 1915 Blessed Sacrament Cathedral, the seat of the powerful archbishop who presided over the city's multitudinous, multiethnic Catholic populace. Plans for an even grander cathedral had been drawn up at Bishop Michael Gallagher's request by Maginnis and Walsh, the nation's most prominent Catholic architectural firm, but construction was delayed by the Great Depression and eventually abandoned. Despite this failure, Gallagher ranked with Cincinnati's John McNicholas and Chicago's George Mundelein among the "Builder Bishops" of mid-twentieth-century American Catholicism, who lived and built in the grand style of Renaissance princes. Maginnis and Walsh did design for him an elaborate neo-Tudor residence in then-fashionable Palmer Woods, which was later sold to John Salley of the Detroit Pistons. Its Cincinnati counterpart was similarly acquired by pizza magnate "Buddy" LaRosa after the princely episcopal lifestyle had been eclipsed by the problems of the declining inner city and Vatican II had called Catholic triumphalism into serious theological question (Tentler 1990, 310; Meyer 1971, 119; Eckert 1993, 101).

Finally, Woodward Avenue was for a time the site of Temple Beth El, Michigan's first Jewish congregation, which dated to 1860. Modeled on the Roman Pantheon and erected in 1903, Beth El was designed by Albert Kahn, Detroit's premier architect in its great age of automobile-manufacturing-based prosperity. (Kahn also designed the Fisher and General Motors Buildings, two of Detroit's great Art Deco era office towers; Henry Ford's monumental Highland Park and River Rouge plants; and many auto magnates' palatial residences in nearby Grosse Pointe.) Beth El's second home, also on Woodward, was also designed by Kahn in 1927; it is an octastyle Ionic-order temple reminiscent of the Lincoln Memorial in Washington. Jewish residential patterns, however, followed those of other cities, with a massive outflux into the northwestern suburbs culminating with the urban riots of 1967. The second Beth El metamorphosed into the Lighthouse Cathedral. Beth El's congregation relocated in affluent Bloomfield Hills in 1973 in a new structure designed by Minoru Yamasaki, also known for civic and commercial design in the Detroit area, and inspired by the ancient Hebrew Tent of Meeting motif. Nearby Southfield, a major site of Jewish suburban resettlement, boasts a number of modern synagogues and temples, most notably Shaarey Zedek. Designed by Albert Kahn Associates and Percival Goodman in 1962, it is distinguished by a dramatically soaring pyramidal sanctuary as well as distinguished contemporary sculpture and stained glass (Meyer 1971, 71, figs. 13 and 135; Ferry 1970, 10; Eckert 1993, 99, 170, 174).

Another example of one major artery on which a variety of houses of worship were located is Chicago's LaSalle Drive. Michigan Avenue, the city's most fashionable street, is known mainly for Fourth Presbyterian, one of Ralph Adams Cram's ventures into design for the Reformed tradition, and typically in Cram's Gothic style (1914; see figure 61). This elegant and massive complex is similar in style, conception, and social import to another of Cram's works, East Liberty Presbyterian Church (1931–35) in Pittsburgh, a monument to the largesse of the Mellon family. Fourth Presbyterian stands in splendid isolation among its commercial neighbors on the city's "Magnificent Mile"; like Boston's Trinity, it is dwarfed by a later secular creation, the 1969 John Hancock Center (Lane and Kezys 1981, 130–31; Toker 1986, 209–10).

The two cathedrals lie between Michigan and LaSalle, an avenue with a remarkable diversity of religious structures. Two related buildings are the Moody Bible Institute (1937–39) and the auditorium-style Moody Memorial Church (1924–25), both named in honor of the city's great revivalist preacher and organizer, Dwight L. Moody. In between the two lie a number of churches illustrating not power and prestige but rather the extraordinary mixture of ethnic and theological communities that had come to characterize the nation's "Second City" by the early twentieth century. Among them are the Anglo-Catholic Church of the Ascension (French Gothic, 1882–87); LaSalle Street Church, originally Evangelical Lutheran and later independent Evangelical (Gothic, 1882–86); the Greek Orthodox Annunciation Cathedral (1910), characterized by the dome associated with that tradition; and First Saint Paul's Evangelical Lutheran Church (1969–70), a windowless brick structure of superimposed rectangles rounded at the chancel end and sited in the midst of the Carl Sandburg Village development (see figure 62). Chicago as much as any city had by the early twentieth century come to symbolize the cultural pluralism that the New Immigration had imposed upon the nation, and a few blocks of LaSalle Drive are sufficient to give it good illustration (Lane and Kezys 1981).

A final example of the urban boulevard on which houses of worship have arrayed themselves longitudinally is Indianapolis's Meridian Street, which bisects the city as its north-south axis. Traveling north from the city center, one passes a dazzling array of monumental buildings – the various war memorials and the Scottish Rite Temple described earlier, the *Turnverein*, and Saints Peter and Paul Catholic Cathedral (1905, 1936), an imposing Classical revival structure sadly sandwiched between lesser buildings that block any good vantage. A primarily commercial area follows, dotted with splendidly imaginative 1920s-era apartment buildings, and one rather new house of worship, modeled on an English parish church – Trinity Episcopal (1952). The neighborhood changes rather for the worse before opening onto the street's "historic district" – like Dallas's Swiss Avenue, an imposing array of grand homes in the varied revival styles popular during the 1920s. Guarding the corner of Meridian and Thirty-eighth Streets like a sentinel at the boundary between elegance and urban sprawl is the giant North United Methodist Church, a grand Gothic plant completed in 1931. Farther north lie the Georgian revival Meridian Street United Methodist Church (1952) and neo-Norman Saint Paul's Episcopal (1941). Past the northern boundary of the historic district are the Indianapolis Hebrew Congregation (1957–88) and the massive Second Presbyterian Church (1957–88), a latter-day Gothic revival tribute to the Reformation in its statuary. Still newer churches – Southern Baptist, United Methodist, Evangelical Covenant – can be found on intersecting Eighty-sixth Street not far from Meridian's terminus at the interstate ramp (Ball 1975, 98, 104, 105, 108).

Meridian Street can thus be read as a study in the city's suburban expansion as well as in the denominations that served the northward-moving elite. The Episcopalian and Presbyterian presence is hardly surprising, and Catholics and Jews are significantly located terminally rather than centrally. What is interesting here is the regional prominence of Methodism, which is also represented in three imposing downtown structures, Lockerbie Square (1882), Roberts Park (1876), and Fletcher Place (1872–80) United Methodist Churches (Ball 1975, 74; Riley-Lockerbie Ministerial Association n.d.).

MIDWESTERN ETHNIC PLURALISM

By the beginning of the twentieth century, the major cities of the Great Lakes region boasted religious structures in sufficient number and variety to reflect their changing social composition. Many of the most elegant houses of worship were maintained by denominations – Congregational, Episcopal, Presbyterian, Unitarian – whose British colonial origins correlated with the enhanced status of their latter-day followers. German Jews, financially and culturally successful but not universally accepted socially, erected "separate but equal" facilities, following their pattern of not entirely voluntary residential segregation. These Jews formed a sort of transitional category between the old-line religious and social establishment on the one hand and the newer immigrants on the other; among these were substantial numbers of Jews of eastern European origin who would gradually penetrate into the Midwest after their initiation in the tenements of New York's Lower East Side. On the other side of the social dividing line were masses of Roman Catholics, primarily from southern and eastern Europe, whose leadership came from the ranks of the already established but socially marginal Irish. Although overwhelmingly found among the working classes who manned Detroit's factories and Chicago's stockyards, they could nevertheless collectively muster the resources to produce churches on at least as monumental a scale as their more established neighbors.

We have already mentioned the cathedrals of Cincinnati and Detroit among the religious buildings that helped define the contours of the Great Lakes cityscape at the major nodes and avenues of the nineteenth-century downtown. Parish churches, though frequently of more modest scale, could also be physically and aesthetically imposing, even though the resources for their design and erection came not from vast individual fortunes but rather from thousands of small, painfully earned contributions. The first generation of major Catholic churches in the northeastern quadrant of the nation was typically of Irish or, regionally, French or German provenance. Patrick Keeley, already encountered in New England, was the ubiquitous architect of many of these structures, working often in an adaptation of the French Gothic mode. Keeley, for example, designed Most Holy Trinity Church for Detroit's Irish, which was built during the 1850s and 1860s, and also planned four of Chicago's Catholic churches, including the rebuilding of its Holy Name Cathedral (1874–75) after the 1871 fire (Lane and Kezys 1981, 36–37).

By the end of the nineteenth century, the New Immigration was affecting all aspects of American life, especially its cities. The Great Lakes cities were affected by this deluge of newcomers more than any except, perhaps, for New York itself. Orthodox Jews were slow to build monumentally, given their poverty and lack of a firm tradition of synagogue architecture, which had been developed in this country till now primarily by their better-off German Reform counterparts. The round domes of Orthodox churches began to appear in the Greektowns of Detroit and Chicago, while the onion domes of the churches of their Slavic coreligionists abounded especially in the eastern segment of the region, in cities such as Pittsburgh, Cleveland, and Akron. An interesting representative of Eastern Orthodox church architecture is Cleveland's Saint Theodosius Russian Orthodox Cathedral, where the wedding scenes from the 1978 film *The Deer Hunter* were shot. Built in 1911, possibly with financial assistance from Czar Nicholas II, Saint Theodosius overlooks a vast valley filled with enormous steel plants. The

exterior is visually enriched by its thirteen onion domes, the central one for Jesus,
and the other smaller domes for each of the Apostles. The interior is a typically Eastern Orthodox panoply of visual images, with iconic representations of the heavenly realm filling walls, windows, and icon screens in mural painting, stained glass, and the icons themselves. Stepping into it from the rather grim surrounding neighborhood achieves the desired effect of translating the worshiper into the heavenly realm while remaining here on earth (Armstrong 1992, 238–39).

Another interesting example of a midwestern Orthodox church is Chicago's Holy Trinity Cathedral of 1899–1903 (see figure 63). Holy Trinity sits unostentatiously on a side street in a heavily Slavic neighborhood across from the almost uncannily modern Saint Mary of Nazareth Hospital, which evokes the surrealist film *Brazil.* The cathedral is unusual among Orthodox churches in having been designed by a prominent architect – in this case, Louis Sullivan, best known for his Chicago and other midwestern commercial buildings. (Holy Trinity is one of but two churches Sullivan ever designed.) Small and jewellike in its elegance, it features an octagonal dome over a square central space and a single frontal tower, both capped with traditional onion domes (Lane and Kezys 1981, 106–7; Sinkevitch 1993, 250).

Numerically and politically, however, it was Roman and Uniate Catholics from what were or would become Italy, Croatia, Slovenia, the Czech Republic, Slovakia, Hungary, Poland, and Lithuania, as well as later migrants from Mexico, who dominated immigration into this region. Nearly homogeneous ethnic neighborhoods began to abound, and their churches gave them identity and status. In Detroit, for example, Saint Albertus parish, founded in 1871, rapidly grew to be the city's largest, reflecting in its growth both the concentration of Polish immigrants and the stormy history of that group's relationship with non-Polish bishops. (One of its pastors, Dominic Kolasinski, was guarded in his rectory for months by parishioners after refusing to accept dismissal by his bishop.) Polish separatism was also expressed politically in the emergence of the independent municipality of Hamtramck, entirely surrounded by the city of Detroit and demographically almost purely Polish. By 1925, the Polish Catholic community had grown sufficiently established to engage the services of the Anglican architect Ralph Adams Cram to design its Gothic Saint Florian Church, which dominates the town's modest, tidy working-class homes from a hilltop like a medieval cathedral (Darden 1984, 197–98; Tentler 1990, 31; Eckert 1993, 113; *St. Florian Parish* 1983?).

In Detroit and Chicago especially, a distinctive genre of church building emerged among Polish communities, the "Polish cathedral." Where most Catholic churches were built in grander or humbler variations on the Gothic and Romanesque themes popular across the country, the ambitious prelates and their loyal congregations in the Great Lakes Polonias often chose instead to make monumental statements in the Renaissance style of the mother country. The scale of these structures was often enormous, reflecting both the great size of these parishes and the episcopal ambitions of their clerical leaders. Still visible from the freeways, many of these "cathedrals," such as Chicago's Saint Stanislaus

Kostka (Patrick Keeley, 1877–81; see figure 64), now often serve African American or Latino constituencies, while others have been closed by their archbishops as no longer economically viable (Lane and Kezys 1981, 42–43; Kantowicz 1985, 14–15).

World War I marked the end of the great era of the New Immigration, and the ensuing decades saw increased centralization of archdiocesan planning and a diminishing of the importance of ethnicity in parish identity. Another manifestation of this growing isolation from Europe was the indigenization of the American Catholic clergy, accomplished through a vast seminary building program designed to socialize native-born young men into a clerical culture at once English-speaking, episcopally dominated, and intensely Catholic. Old Mount Saint Mary's, Cincinnati's now-abandoned and collapsing Classical complex, is a good example of the monumental vision of ecclesiastical leaders such as that city's Archbishop McNicholas. His Chicago counterpart, George Mundelein, expressed his desire that such institutions should be distinctly American by ordering his "court" architect, Joseph McCarthy, to design the chapel for Saint Mary of the Lake Seminary on the model of the First Congregational Church in Old Lyme, Connecticut (see figure 65). Following Vatican II, many such institutions – especially "minor" seminaries for high-school-age students – either closed their doors or opened them to a much wider constituency, including the women from whom young seminarians had once been rigorously shielded (Giglierano and Overmyer 1988, 410; Kantowicz 1985, 24–25).

EXPERIMENTS WITH MODERNITY

Perhaps because of its lack of colonial roots, the Old Northwest has been singularly hospitable to modern trends in religious design. One of the Detroit area's most distinctive buildings, for example, is Royal Oak's Shrine of the Little Flower (see figure 66). The shrine was designed by Henry J. McGill and built in 1929–31 by Father Charles Coughlin, the "radio priest" who began his media career vigorously supporting Franklin Roosevelt's New Deal and later retreated into a populism bordering on endorsement of the Third Reich. Designed as a testimony to the Catholic presence after the then-powerful Ku Klux Klan had attempted to intimidate Coughlin, the octagonal shrine and its dramatic Charity Crucifixion Tower is one of only a handful of significant American churches built in the Moderne or Art Deco style usually associated with banks, movie theaters, and skyscrapers (Eckert 1993, 171–72).

Two other interesting attempts to adapt religious design to changing urban patterns can be found in Chicago's downtown Loop district. In 1922–24 what is now the First United Methodist Church, the city's oldest congregation, erected an eighteen-floor office tower; the cross on its Gothic spire is 568 feet above ground level, giving it the distinction of being the tallest church in the world (see figure 67). The main worship space is on the ground level, decorated in the Arts and Crafts–influenced Gothic popular among mainline Protestant churches of the 1920s; another chapel, featuring a wood panel of Jesus surveying the city – reminiscent of the Social Gospel novel, *If Christ Came to Chicago* – is situated in the tower. A copy of Warner Sallman's 1924 "Head of Christ" in the lobby completes this testimonial to urban Protestant taste in the burgeoning era of urbanization (Lane and Kezys 1981, 163).

Around the corner from the Chicago Temple on Clark Street is the Chicago Loop Synagogue (1957–58; see figure 68). Wedged in between a fast food restaurant and an office tower, this externally inconspicuous structure houses a subtly dramatic interior space. A ramp from the first floor leads to the main sanctuary on the second, which features a dazzling wall of stained glass designed by Abraham Rattner; entitled "Let There Be Light," it features stylized Jewish symbols and Hebrew letters, including the words of the Shema ("Hear, O Israel . . .") in a blaze of color. Like the Chicago Temple and the new home of Old Saint Mary's Church on East Van Buren, the synagogue serves mainly a transient population of visitors and suburbanites working in the Loop, all of whom have their own permanent congregations. Together with cathedrals, which serve a similar constituency, these chapels – like the preaching orders of the thirteenth century – arose to serve a distinctively new and urban social configuration. Much the same can be said for the nearby Pacific Garden Mission, the scene of revivalist Billy Sunday's conversion; though not architecturally distinctive, it represents a type of urban Evangelical outreach that rose to popularity during the American city's heyday (Lane and Kezys 1981, 202–3, 205).

Although Chicago has always had houses of worship in abundance, the distinctive style of architecture known as the "Chicago School" has typically been associated with secular building, especially emporia such as Marshall Field's and Carson Pirie Scott, and offices such as the early Monadnock Building and the more recent Sears Tower. Although he was shaped by such seminal figures of the Chicago School as Louis Sullivan, who designed only two churches in his career, Frank Lloyd Wright brought his distinctive genius to bear on a great variety of building types. The Chicago region abounds in houses he designed, but one of Wright's most memorable works is Unity Temple in nearby Oak Park, only a block or so away from his own house and studio (see figure 69).

Wright was shaped during his early years in Wisconsin by his religiously liberal Welsh family, including his father, a not-very-successful sometime minister, and his much greater uncle, Jenkin Lloyd Jones, the radical "Western" Unitarian who helped organize Chicago's World's Parliament of Religions in 1893. When he received the commission to design a new Unity Temple for a primarily Universalist congregation whose previous church had been destroyed by lightning, Wright brought a combination of architectural and theological ideas to the task. The result, built on a busy Oak Park intersection from 1906 to 1909, was something revolutionary in American religious building. Wright deliberately rejected the verticality of the Wren-Gibbs tradition exemplified in such latter-day Unitarian churches as Boston's Arlington Street; he regarded temples such as those found in antiquity and contemporary Japan as better prototypes, as well as the New England ideal of the meetinghouse. Using reinforced concrete for the first time in the construction of a public building, Wright created a multi-level intimate congregational gathering space in the auditorium-style tradition, with a social hall incorporated into the complex on the institutional church model. The result, regarded by most critics as among the best of Wright's extensive and diverse work in the religious realm, demonstrated wide possibilities beyond the repertory then possessed by American denominations (Barrie 1996, 107–10; Siry 1991; Siry 1996; Lane and Kezys 1981, 116–17).

As the century progressed, other influences converged in the region to produce yet more innovative forms. Ludwig Mies van der Rohe, known as one of the foremost practitioners of the austere International Style, designed his only church for the campus of the Illinois Institute of Technology (IIT) in 1952 (see figure 70). This brick and glass rectangle blends well into a small, flat campus surrounded by an economically stricken South Side neighborhood; it might be compared both with Eero Saarinen's 1955 Kresge Chapel at MIT, another striking example of contemporary collegiate chapel design, and Bertram Goodhue's Rockefeller Chapel (1926–28) at the University of Chicago, a grand exercise in the Gothic revival in its last stages of popularity for interdenominational Protestant purposes on the model of New York's Riverside Church and the chapel at Cram's Princeton University. (Rockefeller Chapel is here illustrated with a witty imposition of a Michigan Avenue street scene by Chicago photographer Scott Mutter [see figure 71; Lane and Kezys 1981, 182–83, 198; Rettig 1969, 124; Mutter 1992].)

Another major spur to innovation in church design was the Second Vatican Ecumenical Council (Vatican II, 1961–65), which brought about major changes in Roman Catholic liturgy requiring new, less rigidly hierarchical space for worship. Some churches, such as the Chicago and Indianapolis cathedrals, were extensively remodeled to accommodate such changes, drawing on the expertise of non-Catholic architects as E. A. Sovik. In other cases entirely new churches arose to exemplify the new spirit dramatically. Among these were Marcel Breuer's Saint Francis de Sales Church (1964–67) near Muskegon, Michigan, which employs trapezoidal and hyperbolic paraboloid shapes to create something resembling a giant concrete banner (Eckert 1993, 390–91).

The most dramatic concentration of contemporary architecture in the region can be found in the small city of Columbus, Indiana. Located a few miles east of the university town of Bloomington, Columbus achieved considerable prosperity through the presence of several major industries, including Cummins Diesel. The chair of the related Cummins Engine Foundation, J. Irwin Miller, emerged as a patron of architecture on such a scale that he has been called "the Medici of the Midwest" "who has turned his home town of Columbus into a Christian utopia." As a result, this city of about thirty thousand people rapidly became a mecca for connoisseurs of modern architecture, with the city's schools and other public buildings designed by world-class architects under the foundation's sponsorship ("Medici of the Midwest" 1974; "No. 1 Layman" 1960; "Fair and Over-Square" 1961).

Miller was not only an architectural promoter but also served as the first mem-

ber of the laity to head the National Council of Churches. Columbus, accord-
ingly, boasts several churches that rank with its secular buildings in architectural distinction and stand out particularly in contrast with the essentially Victorian older city within which those in the downtown area are sited. The earliest of
these was Finnish architect Eliel Saarinen's First Christian Church (1942), an
austere rectangular structure with attached bell tower and Christian education
facility of similar shapes (see figure 72). Although the design is a clear departure
from the revival styles that had earlier dominated Protestant church building, the
bell tower adds a vertical element absent, for example, in Wright's Unity Temple, and relates it more closely to the Christian tradition than may be at first
apparent. The building is particularly interesting not only for its innovative design but also for the fineness of its craftsmanship, characteristic of the Saarinen
family's work within a distinctively Scandinavian tradition. (A tapestry by Eliel's
wife Loja is featured prominently in the sanctuary area.)

The elder Saarinen's church, influenced by the International Style's emphasis
on a rectilinear, bare-bones functionalism, seems rather conservative when compared with Columbus's later suburban churches. North Christian, designed by
Saarinen's equally distinguished son Eero in 1961, is hexagonal in shape and
culminates in a 192-foot spire (see figure 73). Its interior arrangements are circular rather than rectangular, reflecting a conception of liturgical space very different from its predecessor within the same Campbellite tradition. Harry Weese's
A-frame First Baptist (1965) and Gunnar Birkerts's Saint Peter's Lutheran (1988)
also reflect the playfulness with form, materials, and lighting that characterize
contemporary church design (Taylor 1989, 351–66).

THE COMING OF THE SUBURBS

A final angle on the religious landscape of the Old Northwest states must acknowledge the impact of suburbanization. This demographic process emerged
during the nineteenth century, received a major growth spurt during the economically expansive 1920s, and then in the postwar boom of the fifties achieved a
seemingly unstoppable momentum as the central cities entered what seemed by
the end of the century an irreversible decline. What is usually regarded as the
first planned suburb – a community deliberately intended for middle-class life
with access to but outside the boundaries of a city proper – was Glendale, Ohio,
founded in 1851 on the northern outskirts of Cincinnati. Its curvilinear plan
reflected the Romantic theories of landscape architects such as Andrew Jackson
Downing popular during the era, and its churches reflect this ethos. The board-
and-batten Church of the New Jerusalem (Swedenborgian, 1861) embodies in
picturesque form that denomination's distinctively Romantic theology; nearby
Christ Church (Episcopal, 1869) represents the Ecclesiological Gothicism that
also reflects the era's fascination with symbolism. Both are located at the edges
of a prosperous, well-kept neighborhood of houses of various ages sited on ro-
mantically meandering streets (Clubbe 1992, 442–46).

Later suburban developments that attracted upper-middle-class settlement through an even more lavish program of grand revival-style houses picturesquely sited include Shaker Heights, Ohio, the site of a communitarian settlement demolished for new building, and Grosse Pointe and Bloomfield Hills, Michigan, both favored by the executives of Detroit's automobile industry. The latter community developed a distinctive iconography based on a combination of its topography and a strong dose of Anglophilia, expressed through a fox-hunting motif – "the unspeakable in full pursuit of the uneatable" – in many of its restaurants and shops. (These include Machus Red Fox, where Jimmy Hoffa was last seen alive.) In the religious sphere, the churches of Bloomfield Hills reflect this ambience in names such as Kirk-in-the-Hills (Presbyterian, 1958) and Saint Hugo of the Hills (Roman Catholic; 1936; new building 1988).

The most distinctive feature of Bloomfield Hills, however, is its Cranbrook Institutions, an educational complex financed by newspaper tycoon and philanthropist George G. Booth and named after his family's ancestral English home. Though most of the complex consists of elementary and preparatory schools in the New England Episcopalian "St. Grottlesex" manner, it also features an art academy which gained international fame under the direction of Eliel Saarinen as well as a church. Christ Church, Cranbrook, was designed in 1925–28 by Oscar H. Murray of the late Bertram Goodhue's firm. Its evocation of a Gothic English parish church on spacious landscaped grounds and its lavish interior in the grandest Arts and Crafts manner blend well into the overall atmosphere of opulent philanthropic gentility enriched by a genuine fostering of the contemporary arts (Eckert 1993, 163–67).

MODERN EVANGELICALISM

The less grandly affluent suburbs of northwestern Detroit, such as Troy and Southfield, witnessed a boom of religious building during the 1950s and 1960s, including the Jewish houses of worship cited earlier and a multitude of new Catholic parishes as that tradition's ethnic diversity, represented in Detroit's Hamtramck, joined the exodus beyond the city limits into Warren especially. By the 1970s, another factor had entered into midwestern suburban religious development via the South. On the I-270 beltway that encircles Cincinnati, for example, any number of "interstate temples" began to arise to accommodate burgeoning conservative Protestant congregations reflecting the Fundamentalist, Holiness, and Pentecostal traditions. These began during that decade to attract unprecedented popularity, especially among young families experiencing mobility both out of the South and into the lower reaches of the middle class. These new churches were frequently designed in the less radical modes of the modern styles, such as the A-frame of Tri-County Assemblies of God in Fairfield, Ohio. The main necessities, which could be better accommodated in nontraditional church building styles, were auditorium seating on a large scale; parking and transportation on a similar scale, the latter achieved through school bus fleets and easy

access to interstate exit ramps; and a large physical plant for educational and social
activities. Such churches frequently rejected traditional ecclesiastical language as well as form, often describing themselves as "Christian Life Centers" and re-sembling convention hotels more than traditional Christian houses of worship.

Representative of the latter is the Willow Creek Community Church in South Barrington, Illinois (see figure 74), an affluent northwestern suburb of Chicago. Although it has described as resembling a corporate headquarters, Willow Creek's horizontality and muted earthtones, which blend smoothly into its 120-acre sur-rounding "campus," contrast sharply with the harsh glass-and-steel verticality of nearby commercial office buildings. What *is* distinctive about Willow Creek is the latter-day Puritan aesthetic it embodies. The sprawling plant, built in five "campaigns," lacks any iconography that might identify it as specifically Chris-tian; this absence is a conscious part of its founders' plan to increase the comfort level of potential suburbanite members turned off by traditional religiosity. The plant's horizontality reflects the same strategy, recalling the Old Ship meeting-house, for de-emphasizing sacral associations.

The interior of Willow Creek is similarly "secular." Its scale is vast; up to 12,000 come to worship each Sunday, and its auditorium – equipped with tele-vision monitors for those in its more remote reaches – seats 4650. (Informational services for "seekers" are held on Saturday evenings, and weekdays are filled with extensive programming for all cohorts.) Frequent signage helps to orient the visitor, since the layout contains few obvious landmarks. Other features of the plant include "Promiseland," a Christian education facility with an elaborate system of identifying children to insure their safe return to parents; a "gymna-torium"; a chapel for weddings; a bookstore; and an expansive atrium with ta-bles, chairs, and adjoining food court. The presence of the latter suggests the shopping malls that abound in the same suburbia that Willow Creek exists to serve. The church's moderate Evangelical theology thus comes deliberately pack-aged in the trappings of everyday life, including the elaborate technology with which Willow Creek abounds (Balmer 1992; packet of materials courtesy of George J. Everding at Willow Creek).

Willow Creek and its many smaller emulators belong to a tradition that is a part especially of the midwestern Protestant heritage. The auditorium, Akron, and institutional church plans originated during the latter decades of the nine-teenth century in the ethos of Victorian Protestantism, where the preached word was supplemented by musical performances in elaborate theater-like churches with opera-style seating (that is, individual cushioned folding seats in curved tiers rather than traditional slip pews). Chicago's Moody Memorial Church, already cited as anchoring the intersection of LaSalle and Michigan, is a large-scale ex-ample of this impulse, as is Cincinnati's Covenant–First Presbyterian. A related development was the Akron Plan, originating in that Ohio city's First Method-ist Episcopal Church through the work of manufacturer Lewis Miller and the architect George Kramer after the Civil War. In this scheme, which was largely abandoned after about 1930, rows of modular Sunday school classroom spaces radiated around an auditorium, into which they could be opened so that students could participate in the service. The institutional church, exemplified in Chicago's Fourth Presbyterian, incorporated recreational and educational facilities into an extended plant – of which the worship space itself formed only a portion – in an attempt to involve urbanites in an appealing complex of activities while luring them from dangerous secular alternatives. Cleveland's Pilgrim Congregational Church (1893), which combines Akron Plan divisions, elaborate auditorium church seating, and extensive institutional church facilities such as a gymnasium and bowling alley, is one of the most remarkable examples of this genre still in use today (Armstrong 1992, 226–27; Kilde 1991).

REFLECTIONS

The "churchscape" of the Old Northwest or Great Lakes states is as complex as the region itself. Few religious denominations or theological movements originated in the region, although a number of influential figures, from Dwight L. Moody to Father Coughlin, flourished there. Its most distinctive school of architecture was commercial in spirit, with only marginal spillover into the religious realm. Nevertheless, the region's ethnic diversity and freedom from the past have, despite its reputed cultural conservatism, left it open to innovation – a spirit manifest in much of its religious architecture from the Akron Plan through Unity Temple to today's evangelical "megachurches."

THE OLD NORTHWEST: BIBLIOGRAPHY

Armstrong, Foster, et al. 1992. *A Guide to Cleveland's Sacred Landmarks*. Kent, Ohio: Kent State University Press.

Ball, Rick A., et al. 1975. *Indianapolis Architecture*. Indianapolis: Indianapolis Architectural Foundation.

Balmer, Randall. 1992. "Mine Eyes Have Seen the Glory." Videocassette. Gateway Films/ Vision Video.

Barrie, Thomas. 1996. *Spiritual Path, Sacred Place: Myth, Ritual, and Meaning in Architecture*. Boston: Shambala.

Baskin, John. 1992. "God's Country." *Ohio* 15, no. 5: 114–21, 137.

Blodgett, Geoffrey. 1985. *Oberlin Architecture, College and Town: A Guide to Its Social History*. Oberlin, Ohio: Oberlin College.

Bongartz, Roy. 1978. "The Fruits of 'Utopia' in New Harmony, Ind." *New York Times* Apr. 23: 25.

Butler, Margaret Manor. 1963. *A Pictorial History of the Western Reserve 1796–1860*. Cleveland: Early Settlers Association of the Western Reserve.

Catholic Travel Guide: Indiana. 1995. St. Paul, Minn.: Normandin Publications.

Catholic Travel Guide: Michigan. 1995. St. Paul, Minn.: Normandin Publications.

Catholic Travel Guide: Ohio. 1995. St Paul, Minn.: Normandin Publications.

Catholic Travel Guide: Wisconsin. 1995. St. Paul, Minn.: Normandin Publications.

Cayton, Andrew R. L., and Peter S. Onuf. 1990. *The Midwest and the Nation: Rethinking the History of an American Region*. Bloomington: Indiana University Press.

"Churches to See in Detroit." N.d. Pamphlet. [Detroit]: Detroit Historic Churches Association.

Clubbe, John. 1992. *Cincinnati Observed: Architecture and History.* Columbus: Ohio State University Press.

Coggeshall, John M., and Jo Anne Nast. 1988. *Vernacular Architecture in Southern Illinois.* Carbondale and Edwardsville: Southern Illinois University Press.

Covenant–First Presbyterian Church. N.d. "Historical Highlights." N.p.

Cutler, Irving. 1996. *The Jews of Chicago: From Shtetl to Suburb.* Urbana: University of Illinois Press.

Darden, Joe T. 1984. "Metropolitan Detroit." In Lawrence M. Sommers, *Michigan, a Geography.* Boulder, Colo.: Westview Press.

Davis, Evan E., ed. 1979. *Our Heritage. Early History of Tyn Rhos Welsh Congregational Church and Its Neighborhood.* Oak Hill, Ohio: n.p.

Eckert, Kathryn Bishop. 1993. *Buildings of Michigan.* New York: Oxford University Press.

"Fair and Over-Square." 1961. *Time* Sept. 29: 85–86.

Ferry, W. Hawkins. 1970. *The Legacy of Albert Kahn.* Detroit: Wayne State University Press.

Giglierano, Geoffrey J., and Deborah A. Overmyer. 1988. *The Bicentennial Guide to Greater Cincinnati: A Portrait of Two Hundred Years.* Cincinnati: Cincinnati Historical Society.

A Guide to the Shrine of the Holy Relics and the Retreat House of Maria Stein Center, Maria Stein, Ohio. 1989. Rev. ed. N.p.

Hoying, Louis A., et al. 1982. *Pilgrims All: A History of St. Augustine Parish, Minster, Ohio.* Minster: St. Augustine Press.

Ivey, Paul Eli. 1994. "Building a New Religion." *Chicago History* 23, no. 1: 16–32.

Kantowicz, Edward R. 1985. "To Build the Catholic City." *Chicago History* 14, no. 3: 4–27.

Kilde, Jeanne Halgren. 1991. "Spiritual Armories: A Social and Architectural History of Neo-Medieval Auditorium Churches in the U.S., 1869–1910." Ph.D. dissertation, University of Minnesota.

Lane, George A., S.J., and Algimantas Kezys. 1981. *Chicago Churches and Synagogues.* Chicago: Loyola University Press.

Lloyd, Howell. 1995. Interview. Department of Geography, Miami University, Oxford, Ohio.

McDannell, Colleen. 1995. *Material Christianity: Religion and Popular Culture in America.* New Haven: Yale University Press.

"Medici of the Midwest." 1974. *Architectural Forum* 140: 46–57.

Meyer, Katherine Mattingly, ed. 1971. *Detroit Architecture: A.I.A. Guide.* Detroit: Wayne State University Press.

Mutter, Scott. 1992. *Surrational Images: Photomontages.* Urbana: University of Illinois Press.

"No. 1 Layman." 1960. *Time* Dec. 19: 65.

Perrin, Richard W. E. 1976. *Historic Wisconsin Architecture.* Milwaukee: Wisconsin Society of Architects.

———. 1981. *Historic Wisconsin Buildings: A Survey in Pioneer Architecture 1835–1870.* 2d ed., rev. Milwaukee: Milwaukee Public Museum.

Pierson, William H., Jr. 1978. *American Buildings and Their Architects: Technology and the Picturesque. The Corporate and Early Gothic Styles.* Garden City N.Y.: Doubleday.

Quaife, M. M. 1951. *This Is Detroit: Two Hundred and Fifty Years in Pictures.* Detroit: Wayne University Press.

Rettig, Robert B. 1969. *Guide to Cambridge Architecture: Ten Walking Tours.* Cambridge, Mass.: MIT Press.

Riley-Lockerbie Ministerial Association of Downtown Indianapolis. N.d. *The Art and Architecture of Nine Urban Churches.* [Indianapolis?: n.p.].

St. Florian Parish, Hamtramck, Michigan 1908–1983. 1983? Detroit: n.p.

Schwartz, James. 1986. *Hamilton, Ohio: Its Architecture and History.* Hamilton: Hamilton City Planning Department.

Scroggs, Marilee Munger. 1990. *A Light in the City: The Fourth Presbyterian Church of Chicago.* Chicago: Fourth Presbyterian Church.

Sinkevitch, Alice, ed. 1993. *AIA Guide to Chicago.* New York: Harcourt Brace.

Siry, Joseph. 1991. "Frank Lloyd Wright's Unity Temple and Architecture for Liberal Religion in Chicago." *Art Bulletin* 73, no. 2: 257–82.

———. 1996. *Unity Temple: Frank Lloyd Wright and Architecture for Liberal Religion.* Cambridge: Cambridge University Press.

Slade, Thomas M., ed. 1983. *Historic American Buildings Survey in Indiana.* Bloomington: Indiana University Press.

Struble, Michael T. 1989. "Ty Capels and the Residual Patterns of Welsh Settlement upon the Landscape of Southeastern Ohio." *Pioneer America Society Transactions* 12: 21–27.

Taylor, Robert M., Jr., et al. 1989. *Indiana: A New Historical Guide.* Indianapolis: Indiana Historical Society.

Tentler, Leslie Woodcock. 1990. *Seasons of Grace: A History of the Catholic Archdiocese of Detroit.* Detroit: Wayne State University Press.

Tevesz, Michael, et al., eds. 1990. "Sacred Landmarks of Cleveland." Special issue of *Gamut.* Cleveland: Cleveland State University.

Toker, Franklin. 1986. *Pittsburgh: An Urban Portrait.* University Park: Pennsylvania State University Press.

Vuilleumier, Marian Rawson, and Pierre DuPont Vuilleumier. 1976. *America's Religious Treasures.* New York: Harper & Row.

Writers' Program (Ohio). 1940. *The Ohio Guide.* New York: Oxford University Press.

Young, Mary Ellen, and Wayne Attoe. 1977. *Places of Worship—Milwaukee.* Milwaukee: Past-Futures, 1977.

55. Hauge Norwegian Evangelical Lutheran Church, Dane County, Wisconsin

56. St. Mary the Virgin Chapel, Nashotah House, Wisconsin

57. St. Peter in Chains Cathedral, Cincinnati, Ohio

58. Kirtland Temple, Kirtland, Ohio

59. Sacred Heart Church and Golden Dome, Notre Dame, Indiana

60. Plum Street Temple, Cincinnati, Ohio

61. *Fourth Presbyterian Church, Chicago, Illinois*

62. First St. Paul's Evangelical Lutheran Church, Chicago, Illinois

63. Holy Trinity Russian Orthodox Cathedral, Chicago, Illinois

64. St. Stanislaus Kostka Church, Chicago, Illinois

65. Chapel, St. Mary of the Lake Seminary, near Chicago, Illinois

66. Shrine of the Little Flower, Royal Oak, Michigan

67. Temple Building and First Methodist Church, Chicago, Illinois

68. Chicago Loop Synagogue, Chicago, Illinois

69. Unity Temple, Oak Park, Illinois

70. *IIT Chapel, Chicago, Illinois*

71. *"Untitled (The Aisle)" (Rockefeller Chapel, University of Chicago)*

72. *First Christian Church, Columbus, Indiana*

73. *North Christian Church, Columbus, Indiana*

74. *Willow Creek Community Church, South Barrington, Illinois*

5 : The Great Plains & the Mountains

The area that lies between the Mississippi River and the Rocky Mountains is one of the most difficult to define in terms of culture in general and of religious architecture more particularly. Cultural geographers break it up into a number of regions and subregions but confess doubts about just how this can best be done. Much of this area is usually subsumed under the heading of "Midwest," a term which has the drawback of being so geographically inclusive as to provide little usable information. Fargo, North Dakota, for example, has little in common with Cleveland, Ohio. As a result, I have split off the five eastern states that originally made up the Old Northwest and treated them as a complex but integral unit, and combined the rest of the "Midwest" with the farther West for analytical purposes.

When one crosses the Mississippi heading west, the main cultural and demographic fact is the progressively thinning population. This phenomenon correlates directly with topography: the land changes from fertile, often rolling prairies to flat plains to picturesque but infertile mountains. The line that separates the "prairies" from the "Great Plains" is a forever shifting one, determined by the annual rate of precipitation. The hundredth meridian of longitude is one traditional measure; it forms the eastern line of the Texas panhandle and runs north through the Okla-

homa panhandle, the center of Kansas, Nebraska, and the Dakotas, and continues on through Manitoba. The Rockies and other mountains begin in western
Colorado and Wyoming; much of Nevada and contiguous areas are desert.

The obvious import of this progressively less fertile landscape is that it is unable to accommodate very many people. The sources of wealth – agriculture in
the eastern segment, yielding to ranching in the west and mining in parts of the
west and north – simply cannot sustain a very dense population. As a result, the
part of the nation that lies between the Pacific Coast and the Mississippi is, by
national standards, dramatically underpopulated; it has only a handful of cities
of significant size – Denver, Salt Lake City, Omaha, Kansas City, Minneapolis.
In terms of settlement patterns, most of the region was populated during the middle and later decades of the nineteenth century by a variety of peoples, none of
them in sufficient intensity to sustain a "culture hearth." A preoccupation with,
at best, material prosperity – or, at worst, simply surviving under arduous climac-
tic circumstances – has not usually created a surplus of resources to invest in
"culture." As a result, this entire region can be characterized negatively for our
purposes as one which, though humanly interesting, has produced little distinctive or noteworthy by way of religious architecture (Frazier 1989, 7).

The exception to all of these generalizations is the Latter-day Saints, or Mormons. The history of this religious sect, which rapidly coalesced during the nineteenth century into a "people," runs directly across this region. With brief beginnings in upstate New York and northeastern Ohio, the Mormons attempted
an ambitious colonization attempt on the banks of the Mississippi in Illinois; when
overwhelmed by the force and hostility of their neighbors, they began an epic
trek across country until they found refuge on the Great Salt Lake in the shadow of the Wasatch Mountains. The built environment that issued from these
successive attempts at planting a home was visually remarkable enough to have
captured the eye of Ansel Adams and many other photographers.

Ethnically, the Mormons represent one fairly coherent layer amid several that
have intermixed in the settlement of the prairies, plains, and mountains. The indigenous peoples – the Plains Indians, such as the Sioux – were themselves relative latecomers, moving into the region only after European-introduced horses and
rifles made possible a nomadic way of life based on the hunting of the bison. These
were joined by other Native Americans forced westward by the government prior
to the Civil War, and then still farther westward when what had previously been
set aside as Indian territory was opened for Euro-American settlement. The earlier Plains nomads erected little in the way of permanent habitations; their ceremonies, such as the Sun Dance, could be performed practically anywhere, with an
accessible tree serving as a temporary *axis mundi*. After most of these indigenous
peoples had been militarily defeated or otherwise had come to terms with the
emergent status quo, many lived on reservations – chiefly in arid regions such as
South Dakota – or settled into marginal lives around urban areas such as Minneapolis. The more settled, enduring cultures of southwestern peoples such as the
Pueblo and their accompanying built environments have little parallel here; thus
the Sioux and other native peoples have little further role in this part of our story.

The settlement of the "West" by people of European origin took place during the middle and later decades of the nineteenth century and had both ethnic and sectional overtones. The central and northern tiers of these states were colonized in part by New Englanders, who saw them as promising areas for both investment and, for the poorer and/or more adventurous, physical settlement. Slavery flourished in the border state of Missouri, and Kansas during the 1850s became a major scene of sectional strife as abolitionist-minded Yankees from New England clashed bloodily with southerners intent on spreading their "peculiar institution." Texas, the northern part of which lies within this broad region, was part of the Confederacy, and southern religious institutions and cultural values have continued to permeate it and neighboring Oklahoma.

Ethnicity has also played a significant role in the population of this region. African Americans are not widely distributed here and can be found primarily in the cities of Missouri and other parts of the southern rim. After the influx of those of British birth or descent, including Irish Catholics, colonization of the western frontier was the province of a handful of significant groups: Germans, especially in the east; Scandinavians in the north; and Bohemians and Russians in the center. Jews, primarily an urban people, have never been heavily represented outside the few urban centers, and other groups involved in the New Immigration of the late nineteenth century have only been sporadically important. As a result, the demographic composition of the region differs significantly from that of any other, primarily because of the lack of large-scale opportunity that urban centers elsewhere provided.

BUILDING PATTERNS

During much of the nineteenth century, the region between the Mississippi and the Rockies was the American frontier. It had few permanent white settlers, and native peoples represented a shifting but genuine obstacle to a stable Euro-American presence. The conflict over slavery that was fought out especially in Kansas during the 1850s was another source of uncertainty and even violence. The difficulties even in peacetime of eking out a living once one moved west of the fertile prairie lands of Iowa and Wisconsin also lent to life an aura of tenuousness and precluded large-scale concentrations of settled population. In religious terms, this was mission country, with a settled church presence achieved sometimes decades beyond the time of first settlement. Make-do and innovation were the watchwords for churches as for other aspects of life.

One interesting response to the exigencies of frontier life is shown in a strategy that even the elite Episcopalians resorted to in the Dakotas, then as now a fearsomely difficult place to live. In the early 1890s William D. Walker, the missionary bishop of North Dakota, drew on the backing of Cornelius Vanderbilt and other wealthy sponsors to turn a Pullman coach into what became known as the "cathedral car." With folding chairs, this coach seated eighty at a Book of Common Prayer service. Utilizing this unorthodox but highly utilitarian worship space, Walker visited a circuit of fifty-three small Dakota towns until the railroad balked at providing free locomotive power. Baptists drew on Rockefeller money to provide a similar mission, which was later replaced by Auto Chapel cars (Szasz 1988, 75–76).

Although this latter-day form of circuit riding was not the norm, even for western evangelization, it does emphasize both the awesome distance that clergy in those parts and days faced, as well as the premium placed on utility over aesthetics. The typical pattern, which differed in detail though not in its general contours from other frontier times and places, began with incipient congregations meeting in temporary locales such as private homes, hotels, tents, or stores. The first buildings designed specifically for worship shared the same makeshift character as secular buildings. In eastern regions, where lumber was fairly abundant, log churches were the norm. Among the first such churches built in Kansas, for example, were Indian missions. These were compounds similar to those constructed by the Franciscans in California that aimed at teaching an entirely new way of life, not simply at bringing about religious conversion in the narrow sense. The log cabin of a fur company's agent, for example, served as the first Catholic chapel in Kansas. This was soon replaced by a log structure built by "black robes" for a Kickapoo people who proved largely indifferent to their efforts. Some Indians, however, embraced Christianity, and built their own early churches. Methodist Wyandottes, for example, erected a church of their own of hewn logs filled in with mortar and topped by a clapboard roof. It lasted from 1844 until 1847, when it was replaced by a more permanent church of brick (De Zurko 1949, 10–12; Kalman 1976, 166).

Farther west, where trees were scarce or nonexistent – as in Custer County in central Nebraska – numerous early churches were built of sod instead. New England Congregationalists arriving in Lawrence, Kansas, in the 1850s to establish a bulwark against slavery erected two rows of poles twenty feet apart that extended sixty feet and were joined to a ridgepole at the top. This skeleton was thatched with hay, and the two ends sealed up with sod into which door and window openings were then cut. This curious arrangement only lasted for three years until a more proper structure of limestone, which was abundant in Kansas, could be built. Virtually no such churches survive today, but their memory is an important one in the distinctive history of religion on the Plains (Gebhard and Mansheim 1993, 18–19; Kalman 1976, 166).

The building form intermediate between transient logs and sod on the one hand and sturdier brick and stone on the other was the frame church. Such construction became more commonplace even in tree-scarce areas once the railroad had opened up the region, and lumber or even entire prefabricated structures could be shipped long distances at manageable cost. Differentially between the 1850s and the 1890s, depending on the pace of "civilization," small white frame churches began to dot the prairies, giving rise to a whole subgenre of American religious architecture that became known as the "prairie Gothic" immortalized in secular form in Grant Wood's renowned painting (Szasz 1988, 22–23).

"Prairie Gothic," which subsumes the range of popular church styles from the

Greek revival to the Eastlake and other Victorian modes, dominated the landscape with little regard to ethnicity or denomination. Churches of this sort were
usually designed by a clergyman or local laity who drew on their memories of
the eastern United States or parts of Europe from which they had come for a
few minimal distinguishing stylistic cues. These were usually erected with communal effort. Typically they would stand about 30 feet by 80 feet and were built
with clapboard siding, a gable roof, and a small steeple. Invariably they were
painted white. The interiors were, except in a few cases of Catholic or Orthodox provenance, simple, with wood or coal stoves for heat and light furnished
by kerosene or coal oil lamps. Usually they would seat between one and three
hundred worshipers. Catholic churches would feature a cross; in those of Russian and other Eastern Orthodox congregations, the cross might have a characteristic diagonal member running through it and possibly feature an onion dome
on the top, especially in the prairie provinces of Canada to the north (Szasz 1988,
23).

As in other parts of the country in its early days, these churches carried with
them an iconic significance that captured the imagination of photographers such
as Dorothea Lange in her well-known portrait of three, each a different denomination, in close proximity on the prairie (see figure 75). In the northern reaches, such churches vied for vertical reach; in 1890, for example, the two churches
in Harrison, South Dakota, boasted spires of 68 and 92 feet respectively. Their
bells, often costly and imported from a great distance, provided their communities with the time, notice of the hour of worship, news of births and deaths, and
alarms for fires, Indian attacks, and other occasions requiring collective action.
The bells often outlasted the churches and were removed to other locations when
a frame church came to the end of its lifespan (Szasz 1988, 23–24).

Although these churches closely resembled one another in their overall contours, some variation in composition and structure did occur. Square towers, built
into or abutting the church's front, were frequent features, as illustrated in the
1864 First Congregational Church at Bradford, Iowa – immortalized in the sentimental song "The Little Brown Church in the Vale." (According to legend,
brown was the cheapest color of paint available at the time.) Where the earliest
frame churches in Iowa followed the contours of the Greek revival, which was
in its latter phases as settlers moved into the new area of settlement, "Carpenter
Gothic" soon displaced it as the modish form for rural frame churches. Most
prairie churches lacked the sophistication of an Upjohn plan, and a healthy vernacular eclecticism rather than strict stylistic guidelines once more proved the
rule (Kalman 1976, 164, 166).

Denominational peculiarities had some, though not an overwhelming, impact
on western church design during the early years as well. Episcopalians, as might
be expected, were the most frequent practitioners of the "high style," in this case
that provided by Upjohn. One historian has described these buildings as frequently "dollhouse-like" in their fine materials and attention to detail. Congregationalists were provided by their denomination with a pattern book in the 1850s that
borrowed freely from Upjohn but dampened his high church tendencies with

modified interior plans as well as the eclectic grafting of Romanesque features onto the Carpenter Gothic basic form. Danish Lutherans, whose churches dotted eastern Nebraska during the decades following the Civil War, frequently had broach spires. L-shaped churches seem to have been particularly popular among Kansas Methodists. Quakers, not surprisingly, eschewed ornament almost entirely (Gebhard and Mansheim 1993, 20–21; Bushman 1992, 339; Matteson and Matteson 1988; Fischer 1974, 41).

Wooden churches lasted for many decades in outlying parts of the West, though the shifting population brought about by financial and meteorological vicissitudes often saw them converted to secular uses or abandoned to decay. As the region began to urbanize, a similar pattern of importation of fashion from the culture hearths of the East rapidly prevailed. Kansas City, Omaha, and Denver, as they changed from cowtowns to real cities, began to take on the cultural accoutrements of proper urban centers. Boosters promoted the building of churches, which carried with them an aura of permanence, and railroads were eager to provide free land, particularly to the Protestant denominations.

Not surprisingly, the cityscapes that now began to emerge at wide intervals throughout the urban West did not differ dramatically from those back east. In religious as well as secular architecture, the West for the most part did not turn out to be the wellspring of fresh and dramatic ideas. Rather, western cities were intensely conservative in their built environment, adopting the styles that had already become popular in the cities of the Northeast and the Old Northwest (Szasz 1988, 19).

In Denver, church building sponsored by the city's emergent elite became something of a contest as to who could build the largest and the most fashionable house of worship. The race began with the laying of the cornerstone of St. John's in the Wilderness Episcopal cathedral in 1880, a rather awkward Romanesque cluster destroyed by fire in 1903. First Congregational and First Baptist were launched within the next three years, the latter having a seating capacity of 1200. Trinity Methodist, the successor to the crude Gothic structure that was Denver's first church, was perhaps the grandest of these "cathedrals"; completed in 1887, it is an eclectic mixture of Gothic and Romanesque elements with a corner tower and 182-foot spire. Its organ alone cost more than the entirety of its predecessor. Hemmed in by commercial buildings today, Trinity still remains as a reminder of an age, in Denver as elsewhere, when churches still dominated urban skylines. Central Presbyterian (Richardsonian Romanesque, 1892), Temple Emanuel ("Jewish Victorian," 1898), and the Roman Catholic Cathedral of the Immaculate Conception (French Gothic, 1912) rounded out a "churchscape" in which several major traditions combined religious growth with urban boosterism and denominational competition (Dallas 1971, 161–78; Dorsett 1977, 88–89; Leonard and Noel 1990, 195–96).

During the twentieth century, church building patterns in the West have been unremarkable. Interestingly, at least two examples exist of church designs commissioned from major architects going oddly awry. Louis Sullivan, whose ornate banks and other commercial buildings are among the finest flourishings of mid-

western architecture, designed practically no houses of worship during his career. He did, however, receive the commission for Saint Paul's Methodist Episcopal Church in Cedar Rapids, Iowa, in 1910, and came up with a tripartite
scheme including an Akron Plan–influenced auditorium, a rectangular wing for
classrooms, and a high tower with a hipped roof with some echoes of Frank Lloyd
Wright's Unity Temple. Sullivan, however, was forced to simplify his plans when
all bids came in far over what the congregation was able to afford. The final product was the work of an architect of a competing firm who stepped in to salvage
what Sullivan had abandoned. Sullivan, needless to say, was not amused (Gebhard and Mansheim 1993, 175–76).

Frank Lloyd Wright was another of the region's (and nation's) premier architects of the early twentieth century who only occasionally turned his hand to
church design. In a rare attempt, Wright accepted the commission in 1940 for
the Community Christian Church in Kansas City, located on Main Street not
too far from the city's celebrated art museum and pioneering Country Club Plaza
shopping center. Wright envisaged an auditorium church complex with a hexagonal plan and cantilevered surfaces supported on a "tenuous" steel skeleton with
radically innovative principles of construction he had successfully applied previously in other buildings. These latter proved not to be in conformity with the
city's building codes, and the temperamental Wright withdrew from further participation in building what he had conceived of as "the church of the future."
Community Christian was completed by another architect, but the result is not
nearly as dramatic as what Wright had originally had in mind (Ehrlich 1992, 113–
14; Wright 1977, 507–11).

Not all modern churches in the region were doomed to such at best partial
success. Tulsa, Oklahoma, for example, is known for two religious buildings: the
1967 Prayer Tower at Oral Roberts University (see figure 76), and the Boston
Avenue Methodist Church (see figure 77). The Prayer Tower, sited at the center
of a campus based on the principles of Roberts's faith-healing ministry, is a fu-
turistic affair somewhat reminiscent of Seattle's Space Needle, built for that city's
Century 21 exposition of 1962, or perhaps of the Statue of Liberty's torch. The
200-foot structure is described on an official postcard as symbolizing a twentieth-century cross. In the base, a visitor can witness a multipart "Journey of Faith,"
in which the Oral Roberts story is re-created electronically. Fanning out from
the base is a vertical support for an observation deck, from which obtrude spiny-
like projections intended to symbolize a crown of thorns. From the deck rises a
tall, narrow spire with a flame at the tip (Barth 1986, 148–49; postcard courtesy
of Richard Guy Wilson).

The Boston Avenue Methodist Church, designed in 1926 by Bruce Goff, is
sited high on a hill, and features a 280-foot steel-frame tower covered with limestone, ornamented with polychromed terra cotta, and capped with copper. Where
the tower provides eight floors of office and other space, the main auditorium
accommodates 1800 in individual seats. The overall style is Art Deco, or Moderne, which is generally associated with banks, movie theaters, and other secular
uses; only a few other churches, such as the Shrine of the Little Flower in Royal

Oak, Michigan, adapted the style for religious purposes. Another dramatic use of the Moderne for symbolic expression is Bertram Goodhue's Nebraska State Capitol in Lincoln. Although architectural innovation is not notable in the Plains, perhaps the frontier spirit of Tulsa encouraged these two highly innovative endeavors (Robinson 1929?).

A more recent regional attempt at modernism is the chapel of the United States Air Force Academy at Colorado Springs, designed in 1963 by Walter Netsch of Skidmore, Owings and Merrill (see figure 78). Built of aluminum, glass, and steel, the chapel – which contains separate Protestant, Catholic, Jewish, and interdenominational worship spaces – is deliberately intended to evoke images of flight. The building itself consists of sloping walls which break at a gentle angle to form the pitched roof, rather like an A-frame in general effect. The dazzling effect of the structure, however, comes from the row of seventeen parallel sets of polyhedral forms that combine to form triangular shapes, the point of each of which acts as a spire. Many of the interior details pick up on the flight motif – for example, the pews in the Protestant chapel are sculpted so that the end of each resembles a propeller; their backs are similarly capped by aluminum strips similar to a wing's edge. Just as West Point's fortresslike demeanor seems appropriate in its eastern setting, so do the vertical upthrusts of the USAF Academy chapel admirably echo its mountainous western environs ("Fact Sheet" and photographs courtesy of United States Air Force).

Finally, some note might be taken of the anomalous state of Nevada. Until not very long ago, legal divorce was difficult to obtain in most parts of the United States, and the name "Reno" became synonymous with a refuge for those seeking a speedy marital dissolution. Las Vegas similarly has become symbolic of gambling, an activity also frowned upon in areas where the ethos of Evangelical Protestantism had long prevailed. Even legalized prostitution has not been unknown in the state. Although the religious culture of Nevada has usually been looked upon as something of an oxymoron, an appropriate icon of this elusive entity might be the Wee Kirk o' the Heather Wedding Chapel in Las Vegas, photographed by David Graham in 1988 (see figure 79). This piece of whimsy brings to mind Robert Venturi's slogan of "learning from Las Vegas," though what is to be learned is not entirely clear. This awninged, balconied, and neon-lit domestic-scale structure is at best cute and at worst pure kitsch. It does, however, well signify the differences between Nevada and its prim Mormon neighbor, Utah.

MORMON COUNTRY

The story of the emergence of the Church of Jesus Christ of Latter-day Saints is an intensely American story, and also one intimately associated with the molding of a physical environment. "The Mormon Trail," which runs from the Green Mountains of Vermont to Salt Lake City and beyond, from its beginnings has been shaped by acts of interpretation of the American landscape. A continual molding of that landscape according to the special revelations given to the prophet Joseph Smith and his successors has been a significant feature of the Mormon agenda. It begins with Smith's birthplace in the township of Sharon, Vermont, in 1805, a site commemorated today with a small museum and an obelisk, at which visitors are greeted by loudspeakers broadcasting the Mormon Tabernacle Choir (Burton 1966, 9–11; "Joseph Smith Memorial" n.d.).

By the time the prophet Joseph began to receive his singular revelations, the Smith family had moved from Vermont to the vicinity of Palmyra, New York. Nearby, on farmland that the family had purchased, stands the Hill Cumorah, where the tablets on which the Book of Mormon had been allegedly inscribed and hidden for centuries were revealed to Smith by the angel Moroni; a statue of Moroni now commemorates the event. At this point in the Mormon saga it begins to become clear that the American land itself holds a sacred significance (Burton 1966, 28–29).

Various other sites in the Palmyra area of upstate New York continue to be revered for their historical associations with Smith and his early followers. The first real Mormon settlement, however, was made in 1831 in Kirtland, Ohio, today a suburb to the east of Cleveland. It was here in Connecticut's Western Reserve, a land already distinguished by its New England style of building reflecting the origins of many of its earliest settlers, that Smith and his disciples erected the first of a unique sort of Mormon building, the Kirtland Temple. Maintained today by the Reorganized Church, which split with the larger Salt Lake City group after Smith's death over the question of succession of leadership, the Kirtland Temple resembles in its overall contours a large, latter-day New England meetinghouse, with the pointed-arch windows characteristic of the Gothic revival as its most distinctive feature. A handful of churches with this peculiarly eclectic blend of stylistic traits existed in lower Manhattan prior to this time and may have been the ultimate source of Smith's inspiration. The exterior is also distinguished by its glittering appearance, the result of its sandstone building-blocks being stuccoed over with a mixture of crushed glassware (Andrew 1978, 37–38; see figure 58).

The interior of the Kirtland Temple also reveals the theological and concomitant liturgical innovations that were continually being added to the Mormon repertoire as a result of Smith's ongoing revelations. That this was a "temple" rather than a conventional church is apparent in the lower of the two main levels. At either end is a set of pulpits designed for use by the movement's two priesthoods, the Aaronic and the Melchisedek, the names of which – with the term "temple" itself – reveal the Hebraic restorationism that was a major theme of the new religion. Pews were reversible, so that those in attendance could focus on whichever set of rites was being conducted at a given time. Ropes and pulleys were used to draw or lower "veils" by which the room was sometimes divided (Andrew 1978, 46–47).

Legal difficulties made the group's departure from Kirtland expedient after a few years. Smith had from the beginning viewed the Kirtland community as temporary, and had his eye on a settlement in what is now Independence, Missouri, where advance parties had purchased land. Smith believed that it was here that the Garden of Eden had existed – a place that Smith through revelation knew to have been called "Adam-Ohndi-Ahman" – and that on this same "center spot" the Second Coming would take place and a temple should be built. Hostile "gentile" neighbors, however, ran the Mormon pioneers out, and plans for settlement there were deferred indefinitely. Today, Independence is the national headquarters for the Reorganized LDS, who in 1994 dedicated an impressive spiraling ziggurat-like thirty-six-million-dollar temple very near Smith's "center spot" (Andrew 1978, 8; Burton 1966, 57–60).

When settlement in neither Ohio nor Missouri proved feasible, Smith and his followers acquired land on the Mississippi in Commerce, Illinois, which Smith renamed "Nauvoo" – "a beautiful plantation," in Smith's "revised Hebrew." Over 11,000 Saints assembled here at Smith's call for the "gathering of Zion" – what was taking shape not simply as another religious movement but the establishment of a distinctive people on the model of Israel of old. Reclaiming marsh lands, Smith's followers here set about establishing an entire city according to a grid plan that constituted what Smith called "the city of Zion," akin to the heavenly Jerusalem in Revelation. The result was "a relentless grid pattern of residential blocks," an apotheosis of the rectilinear town plans that had characterized the settling of the Old Northwest into a realization of Eden on earth. Though the earliest residences were log cabins, sturdier brick dwellings characterized by stepped-gable facades or side ends soon gave the town an air of middle-class prosperity (Hayden 1976, 110ff.; Andrew 1978, 56ff.).

Although Nauvoo never achieved an overall centralized coherence, its dominant buildings were the Nauvoo House, intended as both Smith's residence and a hotel, and a new temple. The Nauvoo Temple's architectural roots probably lay in Sir James Gibbs's Church of St. Martin-in-the-Fields, a monumental neoclassical city church well known in America through pattern books and its local derivatives such as Charleston's St. Michael's. Although the overall design was an amalgam of Gibbsian Classicism and the Greek revival, the distinctiveness of the temple lay in its ornamental scheme and its interior arrangements. At the bases of its pilasters were crescent moons with human faces; on the capitals were suns over which were carved hands with trumpets. These various celestial symbols were associated by Smith with the corresponding levels of heaven that were becoming progressively clearer to him. Here was a new iconography, strongly influenced by the Freemasonry which Smith had installed at Nauvoo (Andrew 1978, 71–73, 82–83).

In the temple's basement lay a particularly significant innovation, unknown at Kirtland: a giant baptismal font consisting of an 11-foot tub made of pine that rested on twelve wooden oxen, presumably inspired by descriptions of Solomon's temple. The font replaced earlier baptisms in the Mississippi, and was later itself replaced by one of stone. Here was the material basis for a new and distinctively Mormon sacramental practice – the vicarious baptism of the dead by the living – which continues to this day as one of the principal ritual activities carried on in Mormon temples (Andrew 1978, 79–82).

The future of Nauvoo as the capital of the Mormon Zion came under a serious cloud with Smith's lynching after his imprisonment in 1844. Brigham Young,
who inherited Smith's mantle as the leader of the large majority of the Saints,
hastened to complete and dedicate the temple even while making plans for a
massive exodus across the Plains to the Great Salt Lake. The Nauvoo temple
subsequently fell into ruins while the Mormons embarked on an even more
monumental chapter in their history. The settlement of Utah – known in Mormon language as the "state of Deseret" – involved an even more ambitious and,
in the long run, infinitely more permanent and successful attempt at establishing an extended community based on Joseph Smith's distinctive teachings.

The best-known of the material artifacts that arose in the establishment of
Deseret were two proximate monumental structures, the Salt Lake City Temple
and the nearby Tabernacle (see figure 80). The temple, the general shape of which
was dictated by Young himself, was designed by the Mormon architect Truman
Osborn Angell, who had been involved in the building of the two earlier temples. Begun in 1853 and completed in 1892, the Salt Lake Temple is a definitive
expression of the imperial vision that characterized the Saints under Brigham
Young's leadership. Although Young had originally envisioned its construction
of adobe, the common building material of the desert region, more enduring
granite was soon substituted. Although in its overall profile the temple bears a
certain resemblance to a Gothic cathedral, its use of the Gothic is primarily
confined to its battlements and buttresses. Gothic in spirit, however, is its program of encapsulating a number of central Mormon teachings in material form,
an agenda begun in the symbolic schemes of the Nauvoo temple. Celestial and
Masonic symbolism is also utilized here. Most striking, however, are the three-
tiered spires that rise at either end, expressing the composition of the two priesthoods that had first been accommodated in the liturgical arrangements at Kirtland (Andrew 1978, 97ff.).

These details become significant only upon closer inspection. What is most
striking about the temple is the way in which it dominates the landscape, anchors
the new settlement in an unshakable center, and promises to endure in a way that
earlier Mormon attempts at establishing a permanent presence failed to achieve.
As successive colonies became established along the "Mormon Corridor" that
stretched from Salt Lake City to San Diego, new and similarly imposing temples were designed and erected in the cities of St. George, Manti, and Logan.
These were deliberately sited at high places, symbolizing Mormon success in
dominating a hostile natural environment through tenacity, organization, and
irrigation, as well as defying the broader society that attempted to bring the
Mormons into conformity with its own norms (Andrew 1978, 158ff.).

The architecture of these and the sixteen other temples of the Mormons in
the United States and abroad has changed somewhat over the decades, but in
general has been intended to convey a sense of imposing presence to Mormons
and non-Mormons alike. In addition to size, fashion has played a role in their
design. The Manti Temple, for example, which Ansel Adams captured in a memorable photograph, employed mansard roofs, a distinctive feature of the ornate

Second Empire style favored by society architects such as Richard Morris Hunt during the later nineteenth century. Victorian elegance is reflected in their interiors as well, especially in the larger rooms designed to hold large numbers of people for assemblies or instruction. The Washington, D.C., Temple, dedicated in 1974, comes dramatically into view when one is traveling along the suburbs of the national capital on the encircling beltway. It declares clearly that the Latter-day Saints constitute a significant presence not only in the remoteness of the western desert but in the corridors of power along the eastern seaboard as well (see figure 81; Leone 1977, 54ff.).

In addition to their external, political functions, Mormon temples first and foremost are intended to serve unique cultic functions, beginning with the distinctive baptisms of the dead through living proxies initiated at Nauvoo. Married couples are also sealed here for eternity, and individuals are initiated into the various degrees of the priesthoods through elaborate ceremonies that most likely are indebted to the Masonic rituals which captured Joseph Smith's imagination but were later repudiated by Brigham Young. Although the precise details of these ceremonies and facilities are not supposed to be known to outsiders, it is clear enough that there is a rough division within the temples between public spaces, where initiatory stories about the structure and meaning of the cosmos are revealed through drama aided by murals, and a seemingly endless number of small cubicles in which individual ceremonies are performed. The Washington Temple is particularly interesting not only in its vast size and complexity but also in its hexagonal plan. This mimics the basic structural arrangement of the beehive, a potent symbol to the Mormons for the industriousness and interdependency that these eminently social creatures exhibit. (Brigham Young's house in Salt Lake City is known as the "Beehive House," with a mantelpiece surrounded by a scrollwork beehive [Leone 1977, 51ff.; Workers of the Writers' Program 1941, 243–44].)

Temples are certainly the most dramatic and unique aspect of the Mormon built environment, but they are only the beginning of the distinctive physical landscape that this profoundly American people has created. Once the Salt Lake colony had been established, the Saints were free to experiment with planned settlements and new kinds of religious structures as well as compelled to forge entire communities, quite literally from the ground up. A wide variety of structures emerged that served both practical and religious purposes, a distinction not entirely meaningful for a people every aspect of whose lives was dedicated to broader communal spiritual goals.

One kind of building vividly illustrated in the shadow of the Salt Lake Temple itself was the tabernacle, another Old Testament term appropriated by the Mormons to describe what was fundamentally a large multipurpose auditorium. The one in Salt Lake City is famed for its Mormon Tabernacle Choir, a choral group that for decades has gained favorable publicity for the church through its concerts, radio broadcasts, and recordings. The Tabernacle, which seats 5000, is designed in the form of a massive oval and has been likened in appearance to a giant tortoise. Like Nashville's Ryman Auditorium, it began as a site for specifically religious functions, but authorities were persuaded by the renowned Adelina Patti, an opera singer then touring the West, to allow more secular performances. The subsequent roster of musical virtuosi, presidents and politicians, and other notables who have utilized the facility reads like a list of Victorian and twentieth-century celebrities, especially of the era in which personal appearances were the only means through which large audiences were able to see and hear their favorites (Workers of the Writers' Program 1941, 238–39; Mitchell 1967, 281ff.).

During the period between the establishment of the Deseret community and its forced entry into the American union in the 1890s at the expense of its distinctive doctrine of polygamy, other Mormon institutions and their material expression briefly flourished. The first public structure in a new Utah community would usually be a meetinghouse, a structure which, like its early Puritan prototypes, was intended for multiple uses in a community in which all activities had their sacred meaning. In time these yielded, as they did in later colonial New England, to more specialized structures, which in turn gave way to a consolidation of worship and other communal functions in standardized *ward chapels*. A similar, easy-to-build construct was the *bowery*, an open-air affair consisting of poles supporting roofs of brush and willows that could shelter sizable assemblies. After these initial make-do structures had served their purposes and been dismantled, more permanent buildings followed, built with communal labor to effect communal purposes under the centralized direction of Salt Lake. These included tithing offices, to which tithed produce and other goods were taken for storage and redistribution; meetinghouses of more durable adobe or stone; halls and granaries for the Relief Societies administered by Mormon women; and social halls for recreational and other purposes (Roberts 1975, 303ff.; Francaviglia 1978, 30–32).

The stylistic development of the Mormon built environment can be summarized as a conservative recapitulation of the styles favored by the dominant society during the mid-nineteenth to the early twentieth century. Late Federal and Greek and Gothic revivals dominated much of the nineteenth century. After the achievement of statehood in return for extensive concessions, a period of contraction set in. This was followed by experimentation in which Frank Lloyd Wright's designs, especially that of his Unity Temple in Oak Park, provided the inspiration for a number of temples such as that in Alberta, as well as several Utah chapels. Public response to these was not highly favorable in a generally conservative community, and by the 1920s Mormon architects had generally reverted to Classicism. In 1953, the Church Building Committee, responding to communal taste, a growing degree of centralized administrative control, and the movement's internationalization, imposed what it called an "International" style on new construction of houses of worship – basically an A-frame with adjoining wings. The Washington, D.C., Temple, with its simultaneous echoes of Brigham Young's Salt Lake City and Disneyland, is something of an exception to this principle of standardization (Roberts 1975).

In the course of the settlement of the "Mormon corridor" under Brigham Young's direction, the effects of central planning and shared religious values became clear in the molding of a distinctive landscape that begins with the continuation of the Old Northwest grid pattern employed at Nauvoo and the planting of towns in isolated valleys surrounded by rugged mountains. At stake here was the final realization of what Joseph Smith had seen as the manifestation of the "City of Zion" here in America, at once a recovery of the biblical past and the anticipation of a millennial future. Beyond the erection of buildings with clearly religious or communal functions, students of landscape have identified a collection of distinctive characteristics of which most of the towns in Utah and adjoining areas settled by Mormons partake. Richard Francaviglia lists the following as traits which, when present in sufficient number, virtually insure that a town has been planned by Mormons:

1. Wide streets, an amenity called for by Smith himself;
2. Roadside irrigation ditches, part of Young's program to make the desert blossom;
3. Barns and granaries located in the town itself;
4. Open landscape around each house, with houses located in the town rather than on outlying farmland;
5. The central-hall plan house, a carry-over from the Ohio-Illinois days of origin;
6. A high percentage of solidly built brick houses, reflecting communal values of endurance and permanence;
7. The hay derrick, a simple frame device for lifting hay bales;
8. The "Mormon fence," an unpainted picket fence made up of assorted pieces of leftover lumber;
9. Unpainted farm buildings, reflecting communal values of practicality and scorn for unnecessary ornament; and,
10. An LDS chapel, in recent years usually of simple Georgian revival design, often with a small steeple topped with a needle-shaped spire "resembling an inverted tuning fork," which serves the religious and social needs of a community in which religious pluralism is virtually unknown.

The enduring presence of these communities, which also feature an abundance of Lombardy poplars and fruit trees planted by the early settlers with seeds brought with them on their epic trek, is a testimonial to the way in which a Mormon style developed, largely out of conservative eastern patterns of urban and agricultural life, and has maintained itself to the end of the twentieth century as a distinctive culture with a clearly identifiable built environment (Francaviglia 1978, 25, 63, 67, 69, 81, 83, 89–90).

REFLECTIONS

This survey of the built environment of religion in the Plains and mountains leads to a conclusion that seems to defy the conventional wisdom. Instead of the

West functioning, in Frederick Jackson Turner's image, as a safety valve for the
pent-up energies of the congested East, it has instead seemed content to follow
rather timidly the lead of the eastern region of the nation in the realm of both
religion and architecture. This assumes, of course, that the states that once com-
prised the frontier and the "Wild West" are what we mean by the West; the history of the Pacific Rim will in fact give us a very different and more radical picture of the "western" scene.

The one major novelty that arose in this section of the West for our purposes
has been the Mormons, which serve as something of a rule-proving exception.
The Latter-day Saints, as we have noted, in fact had their roots in New England,
New York's "Burnt-Over District" – the scene of widespread revivals and religious ferment during the 1820s and thereafter – and Connecticut's Western
Reserve in northeastern Ohio. These origins have clearly left an imprint on their
architecture and broader approach to land use and the shaping of space. The
Mormons have been rightly described as both being quintessentially American
in origins and values and also deriving their distinctive identity from the ongoing tension in which they have from the beginning lived with the mainstream of
American religion and society. They have always lived on America's frontiers, both
literally and metaphorically, and their radicalism and its resultant stresses have
manifested themselves in the daring qualities of their temples, from Kirtland to
the Washington Beltway. On the other hand, most of their built environment,
including their ward chapels, have been intensely conservative, drawing on New
England tradition with only a few small twists to demonstrate their departures
from the norm.

In this way the Mormon experience might be taken as more broadly paradigmatic for the country that lies between the Mississippi and the Pacific Coast. For
all of the regional rhetoric about the territory's nonconformity and defiant position vis-à-vis the effete culture of the "Eastern Establishment," most of its culture has proven to be a remarkably tame derivative of the land that was left behind. A few gallant flourishes, such as Oral Roberts's Prayer Tower and the Air
Force Academy Chapel, are only minor distractions from the more mundane
reality of "Prairie Gothic" in the country and derivative Richardsonian Romanesque in the city. Many of these churches are quite handsome, but few are
very original.

THE GREAT PLAINS AND THE MOUNTAINS: BIBLIOGRAPHY

Adams, Robert Hickman. 1970. *White Churches of the Plains: Examples from Colorado.*
    Boulder: Colorado Associated University Press.
Andrew, Laurel B. 1978. *The Early Temples of the Mormons: The Architecture of the Millennial
    Kingdom in the American West.* Albany: State University of New York Press.
Barth, Jack, et al. 1986. *Roadside America.* New York: Simon and Schuster.
Brunvand, Jan Harold. 1976. "The Architecture of Zion: Nineteenth-Century Mormon
    Houses: A Portfolio of Folk Architecture." *American West* 13 (Mar.–Apr.): 28–35.
Burton, Alma P. 1966. *Mormon Trail, Vermont to Utah, Revised and Enlarged.* Salt Lake City:
    Deseret Book Co.
Bushman, Richard L. 1992. *The Refinement of America: Persons, Houses, Cities.* New York: Knopf.

Caldwell, Dorothy J., ed. 1963. *Missouri Historic Sites Catalogue.* Columbia, Mo.: n.p.

Cannon, Hal. 1980. *Utah Folk Art: A Catalog of Material Culture.* Provo, Utah: Brigham Young University Press.

Catholic Travel Guide: Colorado. 1995. St. Paul, Minn.: Normandin Publications.

Catholic Travel Guide: Iowa. 1995. St. Paul, Minn.: Normandin Publications.

Catholic Travel Guide: Kansas. 1994. St. Paul, Minn.: Normandin Publications.

Catholic Travel Guide: Minnesota. 1995. St. Paul, Minn.: Normandin Publications.

Catholic Travel Guide: Missouri. 1995. St. Paul, Minn.: Normandin Publications.

Catholic Travel Guide: Nebraska. 1994. St. Paul, Minn.: Normandin Publications.

Catholic Travel Guide: North Dakota. 1995. St. Paul, Minn.: Normandin Publications.

Catholic Travel Guide: South Dakota. 1995. St. Paul, Minn.: Normandin Publications.

Chamber, S. Allen, Jr. N.d. *The Architecture of Carson City, Nevada: Selections from the HABS Number 14.* Washington, D.C.: HABS/NPS/US/Department of the Interior.

Dallas, Sandra. 1971. *Cherry Creek Gothic: Victorian Architecture in Denver.* Norman: University of Oklahoma Press.

De Zurko, Edward Robert. 1949. *Early Kansas Churches.* Manhattan: Kansas State College.

Dorsett, Lyle W. 1977. *The Queen City: A History of Denver.* Boulder. Colo.: Pruett.

Ehrlich, George. 1992 (1979). *Kansas City, Missouri, an Architectural History 1826–1976.* Rev. ed. Kansas City, Mo.: Historic Kansas City Foundation.

Fischer, Emil C. 1974. "A Study in Types: Rural Churches of the Plains." *Kansas Quarterly* 6, no. 2: 39–53.

Florin, Lambert. 1969. *Historic Western Churches.* Seattle: Superior Publishing Co.

Foerster, Bernd, and the Heritage Commission. 1978. *Independence, Missouri.* Independence, Mo.: Independence Press.

Francaviglia, Richard V. 1978. *The Mormon Landscape: Existence, Creation, and Perception of a Unique Image in the American West.* New York: AMS Press.

Frazier, Ian. 1989. *Great Plains.* New York: Farrar, Straus, Giroux.

Gebhard, David, and Gerald Mansheim. 1993. *Buildings of Iowa.* New York: Oxford University Press.

Gebhard, David, and Tom Martinson. 1977. *A Guide to the Architecture of Minnesota.* Minneapolis: University of Minnesota Press.

Goeldner, Paul. 1969. *Utah Catalog, Historic American Buildings Survey.* Salt Lake City: Utah Heritage Foundation.

Gyrisco, Geoffrey M. 1996. "East Slav Identity and Church Architecture in Minneapolis, Minnesota." In *Perspectives in Vernacular Architecture, VII,* ed. Annmarie Adams and Sally McMurry. Knoxville: University of Tennessee Press.

Hamilton, Charles Mark. 1995. *Nineteenth-Century Mormon Architecture.* New York: Oxford University Press.

Hansen, Eric C. 1990. *The Cathedral of St. Paul: An Architectural Biography.* St. Paul, Minn.: Cathedral of St. Paul.

Hart, Arthur A. 1980. *Historic Boise: An Introduction to the Architecture of Boise, Idaho, 1863–1938.* Boise, Idaho: Historic Boise, Inc.

Hayden, Dolores. 1976. *Seven American Utopias: The Architecture of Communitarian Socialism, 1790–1975.* Cambridge, Mass.: MIT Press.

"Historic Missouri Churches." 1973–80. *Missouri Historical Quarterly* series, vols. 68–74.

Jackson, R. H. 1992. "The Mormon Experience: The Plains as Sinai, the Great Salt Lake as the Dead Sea, and the Great Basin as Desert-cum-Promised Land." *Journal of Historical Geography* 18, no. 1: 41–58.

"Joseph Smith Memorial." N.d. Pamphlet. N.p.

Kalman, Harold. 1976. *Pioneer Churches.* New York: W. W. Norton.

Kansas City Chapter of the American Institute of Architects. 1979. *Kansas City.* Kansas City, Mo.: Kansas City Chapter/AIA.

Koeper, H. F. (text), and Eugene D. Beecher (photography). 1964. *Historic St. Paul Buildings.* St. Paul, Minn.: St. Paul City Planning Board.

Lange, Dorothea, and Ansel Adams. 1978. "Three Mormon Towns." In *Great Photographic Essays from Life,* ed. Maitland Edey, pp. 154–65. Boston: New York Graphic Society.

Leonard, Stephen J., and Thomas J. Noel. 1990. *Denver: Mining Camp to Metropolis.* Niwot: University Press of Colorado.

Leone, Marc P. 1977. "The New Mormon Temple in Washington, D.C." In *Historical Archaeology and the Importance of Material Things,* ed. Leland Ferguson, pp. 43–61. N.p.: Society for Historical Archaeology, Special Publication Series, no. 2.

Lifchez, Raymond. 1976. "Inspired Planning: Mormon and Fourierist Communities in the Nineteenth Century." *Landscape* 20, no. 3: 29–35.

Marchael, James, and George McCue. 1971. *The Architecture of St. Louis.* Exhibition catalogue. St. Louis: City Art Museum of St. Louis.

Matteson, Jean M., and Edith M. Matteson. 1988. *Blossoms of the Prairie: The History of the Danish Lutheran Churches in Nebraska.* Lincoln, Nebr.: Blossoms of the Prairie.

McCue, George. 1981. *The Building Art in St. Louis: Two Centuries.* 3d ed. St. Louis: St. Louis AIA, Knight Publishing Co.

Mitchell, Robert C. 1967. "Desert Tortoise: The Mormon Tabernacle on Temple Square." *Utah Historical Quarterly* 35, no. 4: 279–91.

Neil, J. Meredith. 1976. *Saints and Oddfellows: A Bicentennial Sampler of Idaho Architecture.* Boise, Idaho: Boise Gallery of Art Association.

Noel, Thomas J. 1996. *Buildings of Colorado.* New York: Oxford University Press.

Puderbaugh, Homer L., et al. 1977. *New Architecture in Nebraska.* Omaha: Nebraska Society of Architects/AIA.

Roberts, Allen D. 1975. "Religious Architecture of the LDS Church: Influences and Changes since 1847." *Utah Historical Quarterly* 43 (Summer): 301–27.

Robinson, Adah, et al. 1929? *A Twentieth Century Church.* Tulsa, Okla.: Boston Avenue Methodist Episcopal Church, South.

Shank, Wesley I. 1979. *The Iowa Catalog: Historic American Buildings Survey.* Iowa City: University of Iowa Press.

Sommer, Lawrence J. 1975. *The Heritage of Dubuque.* Dubuque, Iowa: First National Bank of Dubuque.

Szasz, Ferenc Morton. 1988. *The Protestant Clergy in the Great Plains and Mountain West, 1865–1915.* Albuquerque: University of New Mexico Press.

Torbert, Donald R. 1958. *A Century of Minnesota Architecture.* Minneapolis: Minnesota Society of Fine Arts.

Workers of the Writers' Program of the Work Projects Administration for the State of Utah. 1941. *Utah, A Guide to the State.* American Guide Series. New York: Hastings House.

Wright, Frank Lloyd. 1977 (1932, 1943). *An Autobiography.* New York: Horizon Press.

Yarrington, Roger. 1962. "The Saints Build a Temple." *Missouri Historical Review* 57, no. 1: 79–88.

Young, Mahroni Sharp. 1970. "Mormon Art and Architecture." *Art in America* 58, no. 3: 66–69.

75. *"On the Great Plains, near Winner, South Dakota, 1938"*

76. *Prayer Tower, Oral Roberts University, Tulsa, Oklahoma*

77. *Boston Avenue Methodist Church, Tulsa, Oklahoma*

78. USAF Academy Cadet Chapel, Colorado Springs, Colorado

79. *"Wee Kirk o' the Heather Wedding Chapel," Las Vegas, Nevada*

80. LDS Temple (with view of Tabernacle), Salt Lake City, Utah

81. LDS Temple, Washington, District of Columbia

6 : The Spanish Borderlands

The subject of this chapter is something of an anomaly, since the land once covered by the Spanish Empire in what is now the United States overlaps several cultural regions from the Deep South to the Pacific Rim. Furthermore, the area – Arizona, New Mexico, and southwestern Texas – that constitutes this region's heart is by no means exclusively Spanish in its cultural heritage or present complexion. Long before the Spanish were the Pueblo peoples, the Navajo, Apaches, Comanches, and other native groups that endure to this day as a major demographic and cultural presence. After the decline of Spanish hegemony, "Anglos" and their government and technology have wrought irreversible transformations in the colonial life-patterns established by the Spanish. Finally, the presence of the Spanish as a colonizing power was never that decisive, since the country – much of it desert – was sparsely settled, and the handful of friars, soldiers, and other Iberians who ventured this far north constituted only a thin and tenuous tip of an empire whose center was located hundreds of miles south in prosperous and populous Mexico City, the capital of New Spain.

Despite all these qualifications and caveats, there is still a good case to be made for treating the region of Spanish colonial occupancy with a separate chapter in a study of regional religious architecture in the United States. Though thinly stretched and ultimately unsuccessful as a political force, the Spanish did manage to leave a permanent imprint on the region's culture, particularly its built environment. Much of this heritage was left to ruin after first Spanish and then Mexican rule was abandoned during the early nineteenth century; however, and perhaps ironically, its memory was revived with a vengeance during the twentieth for an interesting complex of motives by "Anglos" with no Hispanic genetic or cultural background whatever. In retrospect, it seems clear that what is now the southwestern United States – or, more broadly, those states from peninsular Florida to southern California now often called "the Sun Belt" – did in fact constitute a culture hearth in the establishment of a highly distinctive pattern of religious settlement and building. This pattern, furthermore, was both so widespread and so diverse that it merits a chapter of its own.

The motivation behind the Spanish colonial presence in North America has been alliteratively summarized in three words: Gold, Glory, and the Gospel. The initial ventures into what is now the American Southwest, beginning with Fray Marcos de Niza's expedition of 1539 and Coronado's soon thereafter, were abuzz with rumors of fabulous wealth in such semimythical locales as the Seven Cities of Cibola, which had roots in much more mundane Indian pueblos. Later secular stimuli to a militant Spanish presence were incursions into their sphere by the British and French in the south and southeast and the Russians to the northwest. Ultimately the Spanish found very little profit in these northern borderlands and never succeeded in establishing a presence that amounted to very much in the long run. The large and rapidly expanding Spanish-speaking population in the United States at the end of the twentieth century is almost entirely the result of heavy immigration from Mexico, Central America, Puerto Rico, Cuba, and the Philippines during that same century – all, to be sure, once part of the great Spanish empire, but long since independent (Treib 1993, 10–11).

The work of the evangelization of the northern borderlands was entrusted primarily to the "regular" clergy (the religious orders) rather than the "secular" or parish clergy, who were part of the ordinary ecclesiastical chain of command organized with dioceses and bishops which had been established in Mexico City as early as 1530. With the brief but notable exception of the work of the Jesuits in northern Sonora, including what is now the southern tip of Arizona, almost all of this colonial missionary work was undertaken by Franciscans, of whom Junípero Serra, the founder of the California chain of missions at the very end of the colonial era, was the most notable. After the end of Spanish rule, secularization imposed first by the Mexican government and continued de facto under American rule greatly weakened the presence of these followers of Saint Francis of Assisi, and their work among the native peoples was drastically – and often fatally and permanently – undercut.

With the exception of a few civil or military buildings, such as the Governor's Palace in Santa Fe, New Mexico (1610–14), most of the physical remains of the

Spanish presence is in the form of religious buildings, especially mission churches.
Those that remain are often heavily, even totally, rebuilt after centuries of neglect and natural disasters. Their distribution is uneven. In Florida, nothing survives from the colonial period. The Spanish presence in Louisiana was brief and indecisive, and the colonial history of religious building in that area is dealt with in chapter 3. The religious presence in Texas was sparse and concentrated in two areas: San Antonio, where the mission known as the Alamo is best remembered for other reasons, and the El Paso vicinity, which accommodated the Spanish and their Indian allies fleeing a revolt in New Mexico. In Arizona, the old Jesuit missions lie in ruins, with one spectacular exception: San Xavier del Bac. It is the chain of twenty-one mission stations that run from San Diego to just north of San Francisco that are virtually synonymous with the phrase "Spanish mission." Though heavily and at times entirely reconstructed, these missions remain the fullest physical reminders of the religious, social, and architectural legacy of the Spanish Borderlands.

FLORIDA

Like California, the Florida of today is more mythic than historical. The northern section of the state is culturally part of the Deep South, and its religious history and built environment follow the southern pattern very closely. Peninsular Florida, a creation of the twentieth century beginning with Henry Flagler and his railroad, is a very different story. Largely without history, the region is an amalgam of specialized demographic cohorts that have found the state especially congenial. These include many visitors seeking family amusement at Disneyworld or relief from the cold at motels and hotels along either coast; Cuban refugees, who with their descendants are a major social and political force in Dade County and environs; and New York Jewish and midwestern Gentile retirees, who have established formidable enclaves in Miami Beach and the communities of the Gulf Coast from Tampa to Naples respectively. In all cases, geography has been destiny, in the form of a subtropical climate in a land only a few miles from Cuba and other islands of the Caribbean. For practical purposes, most of these groups have tried to cast off the past, or at least seem sublimely indifferent to their history – except, perhaps, in laminated form in Orlando. Insofar as the regional built environment involves the past, it is as imaginative nostalgia rather than any deeply lived experience.

Ironically, Florida is home to the oldest Euro-American city in the United States, Saint Augustine. Fittingly, perhaps, not all that much of this early Spanish enclave remains intact from colonial days, and some of the more spectacular elements of its built environment are the creations of that great promoter and railroad builder, Henry Flagler. For the lengthy period of time (1513–1763) known as the "first Spanish period," the only major public buildings that remain are the great Spanish fort of San Marcos (begun 1672) and another smaller fort in nearby Matanzas. The main church of the original settlement was destroyed by English invaders in 1702, and worship during much of the eighteenth century took place in smaller, less adequate quarters such as the old Hermitage of Nuestra Señora de la Soledad, which a 1759 ecclesiastical visitor described as being in highly dilapidated condition; the stone chapel of the Franciscan friary; and two hermitages in nearby villages, both built of stone and roofed with palm material and shingles respectively. No serious attempt was made to rebuild the main parish church during the whole Spanish period (Arnade 1961, 149, 156–57).

Today, Saint Augustine is a tourist mecca, combining a handful of structures, mostly domestic, from the Spanish colonial past with artifacts of the heyday of tourism such as the Lightner Museum, built by Flagler as the Alcazar hotel in Hispano-Moorish style in 1888. The city's cathedral, originally built in 1793–97 during the brief second Spanish period of occupancy (between British and American sovereignty), was partially destroyed by a fire in 1887; its facade is in the Spanish Colonial tradition, with four semicircular pierced openings for its bells, but the adjoining bell tower is distinctively Gibbsian. Other notable churches in the city are the Gothic revival Trinity Episcopal (1825), the oldest of that denomination in the state, built originally of stucco with a shingled roof and considerably rebuilt since its first raising; the Renaissance revival Grace Methodist (1887), designed in 1887 by the New York firm of Carrere and Hastings and built of coquina shell, Portland cement, and terra cotta; and the Flagler Memorial Presbyterian Church, erected in 1890 in Venetian Renaissance revival style by the railroad baron as a memorial to his daughter (Federal Writers' Project 1939, 254–55; *AAA Florida Tourbook* 1994, 110; Cushman 1965, 4–5; Reeves 1989, 78–79).

Peninsular Florida is a land in which the hotel rather than the church is the representative building form, so it is unnecessary to engage in a prolonged discussion of its ecclesiastical architecture. Northern Florida, as we have already noted, was an extension of the South during the nineteenth century, and its early frame Gothic revival churches, such as the 1895 Episcopal Church of the Redeemer in Avon Park, are types that can be found throughout the entire region. During the twentieth century the Spanish Colonial revival made its way into the often phantasmagorical assemblage of building that likens the region to southern California. Representative here might be the Church of the Little Flower in Coral Gables (1926), with a great dome at its crossing, and Saint Edward's Catholic Church (1926–27) in Palm Beach. Protestant churches of this type, such as the Coral Gables Congregational Church (1923–24) and Coconut Grove's Plymouth Congregational Church (1916–17), feature Arts and Craft style interiors, with carefully wrought dark wood and metalwork, an interesting contrast with the structures' public aspect. Religious buildings among the newer developments on the Gulf Coast sometimes use traditional regional forms such as white or pastel stucco walls and red tile roofs, but usually do not demonstrate great originality of design. It is perhaps a significant piece of negative evidence that there are no known churches at Disneyworld (or Disneyland, for that matter [Chase 1976, 31 and passim; Hoffstot 1980, 48–49; Patricios 1994, 198–200 and 207–8).

Although the historic Spanish influence on Anglo architecture is a significant part of Florida's religious landscape, Miami's shrine to Our Lady of Charity (see figure 82) illustrates the influence of the continuing immigration of Spanish-speakers to the peninsula. Completed in 1973, this shrine, made of concrete in conical shape, is dedicated to the patroness of Cuba, the land whose exiles have substantially reshaped the life of southern Florida since Fidel Castro came to power in 1959. Spatially aligned with Cuba itself, the shrine is replete with symbolism of history and culture of the exiles' homeland, and serves as a point of orientation for a Spanish-speaking community now several decades in diaspora. Its distinctive tapering shape evokes a Buddhist stupa more than a church, and its waterfront location adds to the drama of the intertwined political and religious statement it makes (Tweed 1997, chap. 5).

TEXAS

Like northern Florida, much of Texas, particularly the highly urbanized south-eastern part, belongs culturally to the South and has been dealt with in chapter 3. Only two small enclaves of missions remain as reminders of its Spanish colonial past. The first mission in the state, at Isleta del Sur near present-day El Paso, was built to accommodate the Indian refugees who had fled New Mexico following the revolt of Popé in 1680, in which many Spanish and those loyal to them were killed. Destroyed by fire in 1907, it was rebuilt as Our Lady of Carmel Church, and features a curved pedimented gable, a dome with a cross, and a single tower on the right. Until recently, at least, traditional dances of a doubtful relationship to orthodox Christianity were performed by local Indians in the churchyard on saints' days (Sanford 1950, 153).

The best-known of the Texas missions were those built in what is now San Antonio as part of the Spanish response to an encroaching French presence. Most famous among these is the Alamo, a nickname derived from the Spanish word for the cottonwood, a grove of which trees grew nearby (see figure 83). Its more formal name was the mission church of San Antonio de Valero, begun in 1744 and abandoned in 1793. By the time of the famed 1836 siege in which Davy Crockett and Jim Bowie lost their lives, it had become a roofless ruin, all that remained of an entire mission complex of buildings in its heyday. Restored by the army in 1849 as a quartermaster depot, it was later transformed into a shrine of regional "civil religion" as the birthplace of Texas liberty (Sanford 1950, 161–62; Pierson 1970, 174).

Seeing the Alamo as a Spanish mission church without the layers of myth and sentiment that its later heroic history has bestowed upon it is something of a revelation. In overall shape it is a cruciform church with buttressed side walls, shallow transepts, and a square sanctuary. The upper part of the facade's center is a stepped and curved gable; the facade's main door is flanked by pairs of spiral columns, each of which frames a doorlike niche. Overall, its design is a simplified version of that found in many earlier Mexican churches. In terms of artistic sophistication, it can be placed somewhere between the adobe churches of New Mexico, built of mud bricks that did not lend themselves readily to the sculptural carving found here, and the much more elaborate *Plateresque* (silversmithlike) churches of Old Mexico. The Alamo, it turns out, is fundamentally a Mexican Baroque church rather than a revolutionary fortress (Pierson 1970, 174–75).

The most architecturally significant of the five San Antonio missions is San José y San Miguel de Aguayo, founded in 1720 but not begun in its present form till 1768. Unlike the Alamo, at which only the church survives, a considerable part of the entire mission compound can still be seen here. The compound consists of a large, completely enclosed quadrangle that comprises eight acres of land. On three sides were eighty-four apartments of stone, described by Governor Barrios in 1758 as each having "flat roofs, parapets, and loopholes. Each apartment consists of a room and a kitchen with its *metate* (stone for grinding corn), water jar, closet, pantry, bed, and dresser." These apartments, which measured 15–18 feet by 12 feet, formed part of the outer wall of the compound. The most trusted Indians lived in rooms adjoining the defensive bastions at each corner; these rooms were fitted with loopholes through which shots could be fired at attacking enemies. Other buildings included a stone granary that had been used as a church in the mission's early days, quarters for soldiers assigned by the local *presidio*, and what may have been the state's first gristmill (Pierson 1970, 176; Sanford 1950, 166–67; not all sources agree on the date of the church).

Architectural historian William H. Pierson, Jr., has called San José y San Miguel "the most authentic surviving example of the European Catholic Baroque in America." In its overall shape the church, which is sited on the north side of the compound, is a long narrow rectangle with one surviving tower on the right side and a hemispheric dome on an octagonal base over the crossing which collapsed in 1868 and was never restored. The central entrance portal of the facade is richly carved in the Churrigueresque manner – an especially elaborate form of the Mexican Baroque style – by the Spanish sculptor Pedro Huizar. In general, there is little evidence here of the folk-art style and construction methods employed in the New Mexico and California missions; San José y San Miguel is fundamentally a Spanish rather than an American church (Pierson 1970, 176ff.).

NEW MEXICO

The American Southwest, and what is now the state of New Mexico in particular, is the one region of the United States in which the native peoples built and lived in permanent dwellings at the time of the coming of the Europeans. The Spanish bestowed upon these Hopi and Zuni the collective name of "Pueblo," for the settled communities in which they dwelt. Earlier peoples in this region, known by later natives as "Anasazi," or "the old ones," originally lived in pit houses dug into the ground. About A.D. 1000 these peoples began to fashion aboveground dwellings which developed into the pueblos, that is, extended collective cellular dwellings, that are still in use today (Sanford 1950, 23–24; Treib 1993, 7).

The pit houses that had originally been used as living space were retained, but took on a sacred meaning as they became transformed into *kivas*. A kiva is a subterranean chamber ranging from ten to forty, or even as much as sixty, feet in diameter and used for ritual purposes (see figure 84). The basic symbolism of the kiva is a representation of the primordial world through which archetypal humans passed on their way into the present world; its significance, in short, is cosmological. The kiva is entered through its roof by means of a tall pine ladder, indicative of the trees growing in the everyday world. Inside is a fire pit and a series of niches along the wall for the safekeeping of ritual objects. During ceremonies, males who have been initiated into the cult emerge from the kiva and perform ritual dances. Larger pueblos, such as the Cliff Palace at Mesa Verde which housed up to 400 people, possessed multiple kivas – in this case, twenty-three. Kivas were the first features of a new pueblo to be built, in order to provide proper ontological grounding for the settlement (Sanford 1950, 25, 27, 30, 33).

The basic material for construction among the Pueblo peoples was adobe, or sun-dried mud mixed with clay and a binder such as straw. Prior to the coming of the Spanish, their building technique was one known as "puddling," which consisted of the piling up of layers of mud without the use of bricks. When the Spanish came on the scene, they had little else to build with except timber from conifer forests in the mountains. Spanish building materials and technology in colonial New Mexico were basically those of the Indians, with the addition of molds for casting adobe into bricks; the use of iron tools for the square cutting of wood, such as the *vigas* or horizontal beams used to support the mission roofs; and wooden doors and windows. Although these novelties permitted the construction of something resembling a European church in its general contours, they hardly were conducive to the sort of sophistication that characterized the missions of San Antonio. The religious architecture of New Mexico, one of the most geographically remote and economically unprofitable stretches of the Spanish borderlands, was thus destined to take on the status of folk art rather than high style (Sanford 1950, 92; Treib 1993, 34).

The royal decree for the settlement of New Mexico was first issued in 1583, more than four decades after Fray Marco de Niza's initial expedition into the territory had resulted in the spreading of extravagant rumors of cities of gold that would lead later explorers to disappointment and even death. In 1598 Juan de Oñate, who had been appointed the territory's governor, set out with an expedition that included five Franciscans, the religious order entrusted with the evangelization of the region's native peoples. Spanish settlement focused on the north central portion of the state, along the basins of the Rio Grande del Norte and other local rivers, where pueblos were already long established. Spanish settlement, in short, was basically an overlay upon patterns of habitation already long established, and the Spanish adoption and modification of native technology and building patterns are indicative not so much of unilateral conquest but a two-way process of mutual cultural adaptation and symbiosis (Treib 1993, 10, 11).

The subsequent development of Spanish missionary Christianity among the

Pueblo peoples was rocky. During the seventeenth century evangelization flourished, although it is not entirely clear how much the conversion of Indians to Christianity, which usually meant their indenturing to the friars under the *encomienda* system, was entirely voluntary. In any case, contemporary estimates put the number of converts by 1617 at 14,000, distributed among eleven churches; by 1630, these numbers had swelled to 60,000 Christianized Indians, twenty-five missions, and fifty friars. Following a prolonged drought, however, a revolt led by the Indian Popé in 1680 focused powerful resentments against the Spanish attempts to extirpate the natives' traditional religion and culture, and resulted in the deaths of twenty-one friars. The remainder together with many Indian followers went into temporary exile in Texas. New Mexico was retaken by the Spanish in 1692–93, but they were never able to acquire complete cultural hegemony in the region. Until the present day, many Pueblo have managed to retain their traditional kiva-based patterns of ritual while coming to terms with the Spanish and Anglo presences only as necessary (Sanford 1950, 102–103; Treib 1993, 15).

Spanish settlement patterns followed two paths. In a few cases, such as the provincial capital established in 1610 at Santa Fe, the principles set forth in the royally promulgated Laws of the Indies were carried out. These were based on ancient Roman city planning principles involving cross-axial grids with two principal roads intersecting at the center. The ceremonial center of the town was the *plaza mayor*, with the governor's palace – which still stands in Santa Fe – in the most prominent position at the north end, and the church, or *parroquía* – replaced in 1869 by the Cathedral of Saint Francis – off to one side of the plaza. This same system of construction of new towns around a central plaza that symbolized the combined power of church and state was also employed at Santa Cruz and Albuquerque (Treib 1993, 18–22; Stilgoe 1982, 34–35).

In most cases the construction of new settlements on the European model from the ground up was simply not practical. It soon became clear that the only serious reason for maintaining a Spanish presence in what was essentially a desert was religious rather than economic or political. Neither Madrid nor Mexico City was interested in subsidizing such a remote outpost very extensively, and supply trains from the south could only be expected to arrive once every three years. As a result, the Franciscans had to go to and live with the native peoples where the latter already were settled, since they could not afford the expense of creating new towns that would be vulnerable to the attacks of nearby Plains Indians who rapidly came to be the common enemy of Spaniard and Pueblo alike. Friars thus went out, alone or in pairs, to already extant Pueblo settlements, and attempted to Christianize their charges through a combination of persuasion and coercion.

The basic architectural unit of Franciscan missionary outreach was not simply the mission church but rather a complex of buildings that provided residential as well as worship facilities. This complex was ideally located in as prominent a place as possible to impress the natives with the power of the Spanish and their God. The pueblos, however, were built incrementally rather than according to an a priori master plan, and the friars usually had to settle for a more peripheral site. They would then enlist native labor to erect a mission church and a *convento* – best translated as "priests' quarters" – which included rooms for the clergy themselves, plus storage rooms, workshops, buildings for livestock, and other support structures that collectively formed a lower-lying contrast with the larger church. Two other spaces were important as well: the *placita*, or courtyard, formed by the complex of buildings, and the *campo santo*, or burying ground, which was usually located directly in front of the church as a transitional area and enclosed by a five-foot wall. A single white cross would sometimes serve as the only grave marker for all those buried within (Treib 1993, 30, 47, 49).

The church, like all the friars' buildings, was constructed by more or less voluntary native labor; according to tradition, the women built the walls while the men confined themselves to woodworking. The basic features of the colonial New Mexico Franciscan mission church included a thick-walled nave made of adobe plastered with mud (or, in a few cases, stone); a flat roof made of horizontal beams called *vigas*, the ends of which protruded beyond the building's ends; and an articulated apse at one end for the sanctuary. The technology employed here did not permit the use of the arch (Treib 1993, 28, 29, 33).

The few small windows were covered not with scarce glass but with hides or selenite; as a result, the long, low nave remained dark. This seemingly primitive quality had its aesthetic uses. As Marc Treib, author of one of the most definitive studies of these churches, has observed, "New Mexico architecture is an architecture of both mass and light." The distinctive masses created by the thick, low, battered (that is, tapered) walls of the mission churches has captured the imagination of many distinguished photographers. Within them, however, is the province of light. Illumination comes not through covered nave windows but rather from a transverse clerestory (row of openings on an elevated level) created by raising the height of the ceiling between the nave and choir areas. As a result, an intense beam of light was directed unto the altar, illuminating it in a way that the architects of the great Baroque churches of Europe of the time would have understood and perhaps envied. Internal decoration – altar screens, lateral flanking paintings, and stations of the cross – were frequently not integrated structurally into the church but rather simply suspended from the walls, as illustrated in Laura Gilpin's photograph of the sanctuary at San José de Gracia de las Trampas (see figure 85; Treib 1993, 41, 172–81).

The New Mexico mission church which had been developed first during the seventeenth century became a veritable archetype, which persisted with various modifications into the nineteenth century and beyond. A few examples might be useful to illustrate some of the variations it has taken over the years. One of the earliest and most unusual is San Esteban Rey at Acoma, the "city in the sky," which stands on a cliff 357 feet above ground level (see figure 86). The Acoma pueblo was bloodily subdued by the Spanish in 1598; in 1629, Fray Juan Ramirez established a permanent Christian presence in the form of the mission church after gaining the confidence of the natives through the rescue of a small child, an action they perceived as miraculous. Building the church was extremely arduous, since the pueblo was practically inaccessible, and logs for *vigas* had to be carried by human power from mountains twenty miles away. Even the *campo santo* had to be built artificially by constructing a retaining wall to fill painstakingly with rock and soil that did not exist naturally on the mesa.

The age of the San Esteban church is uncertain, since the original was badly damaged during the Popé insurrection, and it has never been satisfactorily determined how much if any of the current structure predates its subsequent rebuilding. The church, in addition to being as dramatically sited as any on the continent, is also massive for its kind, measuring 150 feet by 33 feet, with walls ten feet thick. It is essentially a large rectangle with a tapering apse at the rear and two towers at either side of the unornamented facade. In near ruins at the beginning of the twentieth century, San Esteban was restored during the 1920s through a cooperative communal effort (Treib 1993, 304–13; Sanford 1950, 116–20; Federal Writers' Project 1940, 328–33).

Perhaps the most often photographed and painted religious building in the United States is the San Francisco de Asís church at Ranchos de Taos (see figures 87 and 88). Built around 1800, the church was originally part of a fortified plaza, the thick walls of which were intended as a defense against attack by nearby Comanches. The church is cruciform in shape with twin frontal towers, which received pyramidal wooden caps in the 1910s as protection against erosion of the belfries. The main structural interest of the church, which has attracted artists such as Ansel Adams and Georgia O'Keeffe, lies in its buttresses. Two such buttresses, standing at right angles to the building proper with a third diagonal side slanting away from its sparsely ornamented facade, prop up the twin towers. More arresting, however, are a similarly shaped support at the rear of the apse, and two other, almost conical buttresses at the northeast transept. In Dorothea Lange's photograph (see figure 87), as well as in O'Keeffe's 1931 photograph and 1930 painting, these rear buttresses become practically amorphous, taking on a quality more protean than architectural. Fritz Kaeser also provides a dramatic frontal view (Hall 1990, 66–71; Treib 1993, 188–95).

In 1821, Spanish control over New Mexico was yielded to Mexico, and its mission system turned over to secular clergy; by 1840, no Franciscans were left in the area. The first half of the nineteenth century was one of general ecclesiastical neglect of the entire Southwest; church buildings were abandoned, and the intense shortage of clergy and episcopal supervision was filled in part by the emergence of one of the most notorious religious movements in the public imagination of the time. *Los hermanos penitentes* – "the penitent brotherhood" – most likely emerged from the third – that is, lay – order of Franciscans that had been founded in the area. These Penitentes eventually became known for the Baroque extravagances of their Good Friday services that reenacted in quite literal ways the sufferings of Jesus along the *via dolorosa*. Their main contribution to the regional built environment was the *morada*, a small private chapel of little architectural interest that consisted of two rooms used for conducting services, temporary living quarters, and the storage of the large wooden cross and other ritual objects used in Holy Week extravaganzas (see figure 89; Treib 1993, 60–61).

Another aspect of popular piety is illustrated in the *santuario* at Chimayo, lo-

cated along the "high road to Taos" that rises far above the modern four-lane
highway that connects that city with Santa Fe. The chapel was built in 1816 on a site long associated with supernatural events in response to a local following growing around an image of Our Lord of Esquipulas, a healing cult that had earlier developed in Guatemala. Also known as El Cristo Negro – "the black Christ," after the image's coloration – the Chimayo shrine is lavishly decorated with colorfully painted reredoses (altarpieces) and *bultos*, folk-art statues on religious themes that flourished during the nineteenth century before being displaced by mass-produced religious goods. In recent years, another image, Santo Niño de Atocha – the "holy child of Atocha" – has also attained a cultic following, and is said to leave a nearby chapel at night to wander around the surrounding countryside. As in the case of many Catholic shrines throughout the world, the interior of the *santuario* is also adorned with offerings to these images (or to the supernatural powers they represent) in thanks for miraculous cures and other deliverances from evil, ranging from crutches and eye patches to what photographer Douglas Kent Hall reported as "a tiny pair of Big Bird sneakers" for the *santo niño*. Curiously and rather obscurely, a part of the shrine's devotional ritual, which reaches an annual climax during Holy Week, involves the eating of "holy dirt" from the premises. (Recently signs have appeared cautioning "Please! Only small amounts of Holy Dirt per family" [Hall 1990, 48–53; Treib 1993, 162–71; Crawford 1994, 65].)

The *santuario* itself, though built in the nineteenth century, resembles a smaller version of the church at Acoma and other much earlier structures, a testimony to the persistence of the New Mexico tradition. During the 1920s it was rebuilt with a pitched metal roof added as well as caps on the two frontal towers consisting of two intersecting gable-ends. This rather odd transformation, however, is by no means the most extraordinary to occur in the postcolonial period. The commencement of the new Cathedral of Saint Francis by Bishop Jean-Baptiste Lamy – commemorated fictionally in Willa Cather's *Death Comes for the Archbishop* – in 1869 marked the beginning of a new era in New Mexico's history in which the indigenous Spanish-Indian style of church building that had persisted for centuries was now officially challenged by European high style (Treib 1993, 166).

Lamy, who was not Spanish but rather from a part of France rich in Romanesque architecture, imported French architects to build him a cathedral that would in his mind stand for the restoration of Catholicism in the region to the high standards from which it had decayed together with its buildings. The *Parroquía*, the parish church that had been the city's principal church on the plaza since 1713–17, became the framework around which the new cathedral was erected, and was dismantled after it had served its purpose as framework and scaffolding during construction. The result, with its twin never-completed towers, is a decent enough building, but has little relationship to the region's indigenous traditions (Treib 1993, 88–99).

The coming of a foreign bishop was only one of the factors that began to expose those traditions to change. The incorporation of New Mexico into the

United States included it within the network of railroad transport that was helping create a nationally integrated market system, as well as to disseminate information and fashion more rapidly. As a result, new materials such as milled lumber, brick and glass were now readily available for church construction, and stones and logs did not have to be laboriously carted over long distances. The result of these new forces was the modernization of many of the colonial churches in ways that would strike a later, more historically conscious observer as distinctly odd. The church of San Agustín at Isleta Pueblo, which may date back as far as the mission's 1613 foundation, was remodeled in 1910–26 with truly bizarre results: it received a pitched tin roof flanked by turrets with pairs of vaguely Gothic pointed-arch louvered openings and capped by pyramidal spires with crosses (Treib 1993, 67–70, 256–65).

During the later twentieth century, a countermovement set in here as well as elsewhere, placing a premium on authentic historic restoration. In the 1920s the Committee for the Preservation and Restoration of New Mexico Mission Churches was organized, and many local artists and architects lent their talents to this quest to preserve and recapture the regional past. As a result, the Isleta church lost its Gothic apparatus; in this particular case, it was rebuilt not according to its original appearance but rather in a more consistent adobe style with twin towers which, though more comely than their Gothicized predecessors, were nevertheless not part of its historic configuration (Treib 1993, 67–70, 256–65).

ARIZONA

The Spanish colonial presence in what is now Arizona was manifest only in that state's southern extremity, which was acquired by the Gadsden Purchase in 1853. This region south of Tucson is part of the Sonoran desert, which extends southward into the Mexican state of that name. It was here in the late seventeenth century that a missionary endeavor led not by Franciscans but Jesuits took place. Their leader, Eusebio Kino, was one of the outstanding figures among the Borderlands missionaries. Kino established a series of foundations in Pimeria Alta among the Pima Indians, with a stormy subsequent history. After his death in 1711, the Spanish withdrew, being preoccupied with the French presence in Texas. The Jesuits returned in 1732, but were killed or driven out by a native revolt in 1751; after their return, their order was abolished by the Spanish king in 1767 and their work turned over to the ubiquitous Franciscans (Sanford 1950, 174–76).

No physical remains of the Jesuit presence in Sonora and Arizona still exist, and many of the Franciscan mission churches now stand in ruins: six of the nine in Sonora are still in use by Mexicans, while that at Bac in Arizona is the only one in what is now that United States that is well preserved and functional. The other three Arizona churches have long been in the care of the National Park Service, and the ruins at Tumacacori are now a National Historical Park. In 1935 the service organized an expedition of six scholars specializing in relevant disci-

plines such as anthropology and architecture to undertake a thorough study of
the Sonoran missions, which resulted in an extensive report reprinted by the University of Arizona Press in 1993. The report characterized these missions architecturally in the following typology:

1. Solid, massive walls and buttresses, intended to provide structural stability, defensive advantage, and an imposing presence;
2. Arcaded corridors, with arches supported on square piers instead of full columns as they would have been in Spain;
3. An often ornately embellished area around the entrance as the only external decoration;
4. Bell towers, usually of two stories with round-headed openings in which bells could be hung, or an extension of a wall upward beyond the roof to similar effect;
5. Domes;
6. Barrel-vaulted, flat-domed, or flat roofs;
7. Large areas of undecorated wall surface, characteristic of the Mexican Plateresque style;
8. A patio or partially enclosed garden area.

These features, most of them characteristically Spanish, place the Arizona missions of the eighteenth century much more in the Mexican Baroque mainstream of architecture than their counterparts in New Mexico, where the technology for a dome or a barrel vault simply did not exist (Pickens 1993, 13–16).

The major American survivor of the Sonoran missions is one of the most striking religious buildings in the United States. Though rather crude in conception and execution by contemporary Mexican or European standards, the church of San Xavier del Bac, begun in 1772, is a stunning example of how even a building of fairly modest aesthetic pretensions can be transformed by its harmony with its natural setting. Except for the richly ornamented entrance portal, Bac is entirely white, an effect that is sharply intensified by the quality of the desert air and the surrounding landscape. It is cruciform in plan with two frontal towers (one of them never completed), a short nave, and a transept. Particularly distinctive is its system of domes. There are two shallow domes above the nave, one in each transept and the apse, and a high circular dome mounted on an octagonal drum above the crossing. The complexity of forms here is much greater than the equally striking but much simpler shape of the New Mexico mission churches.

Contrasting with the starkly white geometrical forms of the exterior are the ornamental schemes. The entrance portal, the only decorated part of the exterior, is architectural in form and topped with a reverse-curve pediment with unusually large scrolls. It is made of red-orange brick and painted in neutral reds, blues, and yellows, and seems to absorb rather than reflect light as do its surroundings. *Estípite* columns – a distinctively Mexican Baroque innovation – together with broken pediments and volutes create a sense of movement in the Baroque manner. The portal also anticipates the similarly designed *retablo* or reredos within, which is even more intricately carved and dazzlingly bright in its gilding and complex in its symbolism. Also notable are the extensive bold, flat, folk-art-like paintings of saints that adorn the walls and contribute further to the effect of a veritable jungle of ornament. Bac, in short, is unique, a provincial explosion of Baroque forms with distinctively Native American artistic leitmotifs. Two striking photographs – a detail study of the facade by Carleton E. Watkins and a night scene by Fritz Kaeser in which the mission takes on an iconic role in the broader desert landscape – help reveal the imaginative richness of this remote mission church (see figures 90 and 91; Pierson 1970, 185–96; Griffith 1992, 150–59).

Although Bac is the one American Sonoran example of colonial high style, the region also abounds in material artifacts of traditional and folk religion. For the Papago Indians, Baboquivari Mountain southwest of Tucson is the *axis mundi*, or center of the earth, and the focus of their myths of origin. In the same region is the "Children's Shrine," the site where, according to tradition, four children were sacrificed in order to stanch a potentially deadly outburst of water from the earth that had followed a ritual violation. The shrine, which consists of ocotillo stalks and other offerings arranged around a central rock pile, is renewed every four years. Other examples of a sacralized landscape have Christian associations, such as the crosses placed at the sites of highway deaths to invite prayers for those who have died without the last rites and are presumed to be in Purgatory. (The origins of such shrine-building may antedate the Christian presence [Griffith 1992, 15–26 and 100–101].)

Another, more curious shrine that is neither clearly Christian nor traditional can be found on an empty lot in downtown Tucson. It consists of an odd assortment of candle racks and an occasional statue placed in a wall niche. A sign indicates that this site, dedicated to *El Tiradito* – "the little cast-away one" – is a National Historic Landmark that is "the only shrine in the United States dedicated to the soul of a sinner buried in unconsecrated ground." Although the story connected with the site varies with the telling, a common version involves a young Mexican shepherd killed in the 1870s or 1880s by his jealous employer when taken in adultery with the latter's wife. Although the martyrdom celebrated here is not the sort that would win official Catholic approval, the shrine has nevertheless attracted countless petitioners for divine intervention, and has more recently become a symbol of ethnic and neighborhood identity in a city burgeoning with Anglo in-migration and development. Similar "secular" shrines can be found in Mexico south of the border (Griffith 1992, 106ff.).

Still another example of syncretism can be found in the religious built environment of the Papago reservation. Although a Christian presence was inaugurated by Kino, the Papago were not successfully evangelized until the coming of the Franciscans to the region during the late nineteenth century. Thirty-six mission churches were built between 1912 and 1976, usually in the Mission revival style. Prior to the building of these churches, however, the Papagos had erected their own "folk chapels" for the celebration of Christian-influenced rituals they had developed before the Franciscans had systematically introduced them to the faith. These chapels are usually simple gable-end buildings used to store ritual apparatus, such as statues of the saints, utilized in processions and dances held on a nearby open-air dance floor. Accompanying feasts are prepared in an ad-joining outdoor kitchen. Although Catholic masses are said and other "ortho-dox" devotions conducted in the chapels by traveling priests, these structures' origins and other uses represent a syncretism that has been made to coexist peace-ably with religious traditions wholly imported from Europe (Griffith 1992, 75ff.).

CALIFORNIA

California has invited mythmaking from the earliest days its existence was known to Europeans. Already in 1542 the Spanish knew of its balmy climate and good harbors; they also believed some more dubious ideas about the area, such as its habitation by black-skinned Amazons ruled by a Queen Califia. Its remote-ness from the heart of New Spain kept it out of the imperial consciousness until very late in the game of empire, when worries about an emergent Russian pres-ence in the San Francisco Bay area – illustrated in the reconstructed onion-domed Orthodox church at Fort Ross (see figure 92) – in the mid-eighteenth century began to make the colonial government reassess its accustomed neglect of the region (Editorial Staff, Sunset 1964, 14–15; Young 1988, 5).

Jesuits had long been at work in Baja California, and had established fourteen missions there prior to their expulsion from Spanish territory in 1767. The task of the evangelization of Alta California thus fell to the Franciscans, who chose as their president Junípero Serra, a former philosophy professor from Majorca who, at age fifty-five, found himself in San Diego in 1769, beginning the vast task of establishing a chain of Indian settlements along the Pacific coast (Sanford 1950, 183–84; Young 1988, 6).

The enterprise thus begun at San Diego – all the California missions were named after saints or other sacred themes – eventually resulted in a total of twen-ty-one mission stations stretching slightly north of San Francisco, nine established by Serra and eight more by his successor, Fermín Lasuén. The mission was the premier institution of the Spanish colonization of California; a few *presidios*, or military garrisons, were also founded, but their presence was viewed ambivalently by the missionaries, and their impact was not extensive. A small military guard was placed at several of the missions, but the local Indians were generally not very belligerent, and the friars were more afraid of depredations against their native charges by the soldiers than the reverse (Editorial Staff, Sunset 1964, 26, 31, 37).

As in New Mexico, the California missions were not simply chapels for wor-ship but entire complexes aiming at social and economic self-sufficiency – what sociologist Erving Goffman has called "total institutions." San Luis Rey, the larg-est of these compounds, covered thirty square miles in its heyday in the 1820s; within that acreage lived 3869 Indian converts who cared for, among other things, 27,500 head of cattle. A typical mission consisted of an extensive quadrangle formed around an open square. The arched inner arcade connected workshops, priests' quarters, dining and cooking facilities, offices, storage space, and living facilities for young unmarried Indian women. Soldiers' barracks, mills, and tanneries, as well as quarters for married couples, also were part of many complex-es. At Santa Barbara, a two-mile-long aqueduct carried water to a stone reser-voir; at San Buenaventura, a similar structure extended for seven miles. Land-scaping was also important, representing a blend of Spanish, Mexican, and South American flora transplanted into a Mediterranean-like setting: citrus, fig, palm, and pepper trees joined with grapevines and a wide variety of flowers and herbs to produce a cornucopia of natural bounty. Sheep, cattle, dates, olives, grapes, hides, and tallow were among the most important of the missions' products (Goff-man 1961; Barton 1980, 238, 251–52; Editorial Staff, Sunset 1964, 36; Young 1988, 3, 7, 46; Sanford 1950, 205).

The stages of mission construction usually began with the erection of a brush shelter, which would rapidly yield to a slightly less temporary building of wood-en posts covered over with clay plaster and roofed with twigs and mud or thatch. The normative form was soon attained in the use of adobe buildings roofed with red tile. Occasionally, larger buildings might be built of stone or burned brick. Architectural forms, the result of a coming together of the Hispano-Moorish tradition mediated through the memories of the friars, were similar in their gen-eral contours to that of the Arizona missions. Curved, pedimented gables; *cam-panarios* – walls pierced to accommodate bells – or, at times, separate bell tow-ers; long, arcaded corridors with arches supported by heavy brick piers; thick walls; low roofs covered with red tiles; and a patio with fountains and gardens were all found in most of the mission compounds (Sanford 1950, 202, 229).

A brief consideration of three of the missions will give a sense of their variety. San Fernando Rey de España, completed in 1806 near what is now Los Angeles, was one of the larger complexes, and was forced to expand because of its popu-larity as a way station for travelers – a function the missions shared with the monasteries of medieval Europe as well as the Ramada Inns of today (see figure 93). Its quadrangle, of which only the west side remains after substantial resto-ration, is almost the length of a football field. It consists of twenty-one rooms, including a reception area, a "governor's room" for particularly important guests, and a chapel, kitchen, smokehouse, refectory, library, offices, and rooms for the friars (Sanford 1950, 202; Young 1988, 19).

Santa Barbara, founded in 1786, is the only one of the missions never to have left Franciscan control (see figure 94). It is also the only one that is Classical in style, based on a Roman temple facade found in Vitruvius's ancient treatise on architecture. Except for its twin towers it lacks any Baroque features, and thus is something of an anomaly among the California missions. Its interior is richly ornamented by native artists, a common practice among the missions, but in this case with a "thunderbird" pattern also taken from Vitruvius but interestingly compatible with native culture (Pierson 1970, 198–201; Sanford 1950, 204–7; Young 1988, 49–52).

Perhaps the best known of the twenty-one missions is San Carlos Borromeo at Carmel, where Serra himself lies buried and which he had intended as his ec-clesiastical seat and home (see figure 95). The mission church, built under La-suén's supervision, is framed by two asymmetrical towers, the larger of which is

built above the baptistry; the other has spiral steps leading to the choir loft. Made
of ocher-colored sandstone and covered with similarly colored stucco, its flat, bare facade is distinguished by a highly unusual feature: a combined quatrefoil and star cut deeply into the surface. Other distinguishing features are the ovoid dome on the left tower and the parabolic stone arches that make up the frame of the nave's vaulting. The result is a unique effect, provincial in its gross departure from Baroque norms, but extremely interesting and quite appealing in its transmutation of Spanish-Mexican forms through Franciscan supervision of native workmanship (Pierson 1970, 196–98; Sanford 1950, 215–17).

As California passed from Spanish to Mexican and then American hands, secularization became the rule, beginning in 1826 and enforced fully in 1834. The compounds and their lands were sold, often for trivial amounts; the buildings were allowed to decay or turned to profane uses – in one case, as a bordello; and the Indians were scattered. (The illustration of the Carmel mission included here from the Historic American Buildings Survey gives a sense of how these missions appeared in their abandoned state.) The fortunes and reputations of the missions since then have been various. During the middle years of the nineteenth century, "Anglo" observers were generally critical, using their impressions of the friars' authoritarian treatment of their converts to build on the old *leyenda negra* of Spanish brutality. This "Black Legend" had its origins in the early and highly critical accounts of the much earlier Dominican friar Bartolomé de las Casas of the brutal treatment of Latin American natives by the *conquistadores* (Sanford 1950, 232; Young 1988, 7–8; Rawls 1992, 346–50).

Beginning in the 1880s, public sentiment began to undergo a shift as California became more and more Americanized. Influenced by Helen Hunt Jackson's best-selling novel *Ramona* (1884), which romanticized mission life, and the promotional work of Charles F. Lummis, publisher of the periodical *Land of Sunshine*, what has been called the "Mission Myth" began to develop. This rehabilitation of the missions was the work primarily of Protestants from the Northeast now settled in California who were eager for a firmer sense of the past than their newly built society could provide. Not incidentally, the myth proved profitable and became an essential component of regional advertising as "Mission Style" houses and public buildings began to proliferate, exemplified in the Stanford University campus. The friars were now uniformly depicted in textbooks and popular literature as benign patrons of the simple Indians (Rawls 1992, 350ff.; Young 1988, 8).

One happy outcome of this nostalgic appropriation and consequent oversimplification and commercialization of the regional past was a drive to rescue the mission buildings themselves. Beginning in the 1890s, civic groups began to promote the restoration of these buildings. At first, as in New Mexico, restoration work was not deeply grounded in historical reality, but later, more sophisticated efforts have succeeded in returning most to a state at least plausibly akin to the original. Controversy today centers not on the state of the buildings but rather on the reputation of Serra himself, who has been promoted for canonization as a saint by Pope John Paul II. The way in which Serra and his friars treated the California natives, who had previously depended on natural abundance for gathering food and had never developed a complex built environment, began to be compared with the concentration camps of the Nazis. High mortality rates among the Indians, especially during the early years, are firmly documented, though the attrition here was more the result of newly introduced diseases to which they had never developed an immunity. Also clear enough is the stern disciplinary techniques, including whips and chains, that the friars used to punish recalcitrant converts. In the long run, neither the missions as institutions nor the native peoples they were designed to evangelize were to enjoy a very prosperous future (Rawls 1992, 357–60).

REFLECTIONS

The missions of the Spanish Borderlands constitute a remarkable chapter in the history of the built environment of American religion. Ethnologically, they are uniquely American, exemplary of the syncretistic amalgamation that takes place when two cultures come into intimate contact with only occasional overt conflict. From the viewpoint of architectural history, they are a fascinating set of combinations of high and folk styles, ranging from the relative sophistication of the San Antonio missions and Bac to the stark adobe constructs of New Mexico. They are thus a veritable textbook on the nature of vernacular.

As historical artifacts, the missions are more problematic. Viewed *synchronically* – as dimensions of the colonial era – they add a richness of texture to our appraisal of North American colonial life that is usually overshadowed by the English-speaking enclaves along the Atlantic. *Diachronically*, however – from the viewpoint of historical development and causality – they seem to lead practically nowhere. Granted, a Spanish Colonial revival style did emerge in the twentieth century that has been adopted widely from Palm Beach to Santa Barbara for houses, schools, municipal buildings, and a fair number of churches. Hardly any of these latter are individually memorable. Collectively, though, they can be taken as a regional example of the same process the entire nation underwent during the previous century, when the Roman, Greek, Romanesque, and Gothic styles successively provided Americans with historical patterns and associations with which to develop not only a built environment but a mythology with which to interpret themselves. In this sense, perhaps, the architecture of the Borderlands still lives.

THE SPANISH BORDERLANDS: BIBLIOGRAPHY

AAA Florida Tourbook. 1994. Buffalo, N.Y.: Quebecor Printing.

Arnade, Charles W. 1961. "The Architecture of Spanish St. Augustine." *Americas* 18: 149–68.

Austin Chapter, AIA/Women's Architectural League. 1976. *Austin and Its Architecture.* Austin: Austin Chapter AIA.

Baer, Kurt. 1958. *Architecture of the California Missions.* Berkeley: University of California Press.

Barnes, Lavonia Jenkins. 1982. *Nineteenth Century Churches of Texas*. Waco, Tex.: Historic Waco Foundation.

Barton, Bruce Walter. 1980. *The Tree at the Center of the World: A Story of the California Missions*. Santa Barbara, Calif.: Ross-Erikson Publishers.

Brooks, Charles Mattoon, Jr. 1936. *Texas Missions: Their Romance and Architecture*. Dallas: Dealey and Lowe.

Bunting, Bainbridge. 1976. *Early Architecture in New Mexico*. Albuquerque: University of New Mexico Press.

Chase, Elizabeth. 1976. *The Pioneer Churches of Florida*. Chuluota, Fla.: Mickler House.

Connally, Ernest A. 1955. "The Ecclesiastical and Military Architecture of the Spanish Province of Texas." Ph.D. dissertation, Harvard University.

Crawford, Stanley. 1994. "High Road to Taos." *New York Times Magazine/The Sophisticated Traveler* May 15: 63 ff.

Cushman, Joseph D. 1965. *A Goodly Heritage: The Episcopal Church in Florida, 1821–1892*. Gainesville: University of Florida Press.

Dallas Historical Society. 1978. *Dallas Rediscovered: A Photographic Chronicle of Urban Expansion 1870–1925*. Dallas: Dallas Historical Society.

Duell, Prent. 1919. *Mission Architecture as Exemplified in San Xavier del Bac*. Tucson: Arizona Archaeological and Historical Society.

Dunning, Glenna. N.d. *Architecture of the California Missions*. Architecture series A 675. N.p.: Vance Bibliographies.

Eckhart, George S. 1962–63. "Some Little-Known Missions in Texas." *Masterkey* 36 (Oct.–Dec.): 127–37 (part 1); and 37 (Jan.–Mar.): 9–14 (part 2).

Editorial Staff, Sunset Books. 1964. *The California Missions: A Pictorial History*. Menlo Park, Calif.: Lane Book Company.

Ellis, Bruce. 1985. *Bishop Lamy's Santa Fe Cathedral*. Albuquerque: University of New Mexico Press.

Federal Writers' Project. 1940. *New Mexico, a Guide to the Colorful State*. New York: Hastings House.

Federal Writers' Project of the Work Projects Administration for the State of Florida. 1939. *Florida, a Guide to the Southernmost State*. New York: Oxford University Press.

Geiger, Maynard. 1968. "The Building of Mission San Gabriel, 1771–1818." *Southern California Quarterly* 50 (Spring): 33–42.

Goeldner, Paul. 1974. *Texas Catalog, Historic American Buildings Survey*. San Antonio: Trinity University Press.

Goffman, Erving. 1961. *Asylums*. Garden City, N.Y.: Doubleday Anchor.

Griffith, James S. 1992. *Beliefs and Holy Places: A Spiritual Geography of the Pimería Alta*. Tucson: University of Arizona Press.

Hall, Douglas Kent. 1990. *Frontier Spirit: Early Churches of the Southwest*. New York: Abbeville Press.

Hallenbeck, Cleve. 1926. *Spanish Missions of the Old Southwest*. Garden City, N.Y.: Doubleday, Page.

Hewett, Edgar Lee, and Reginald G. Fisher. 1943. *Mission Monuments of New Mexico*. Albuquerque: University of New Mexico Press.

Hildrup, Jesse Stephen. 1920. *The Missions of California and the Old Southwest*. 5th ed. Chicago: A. C. McClurg.

Historic American Buildings: Texas. 1979. 2 vols. New York: Garland.

Hoffstot, Barbara D. 1980. *Landmark Architecture of Palm Beach*. Pittsburgh: Ober Park Associates.

Houston Chapter, AIA. 1972. *Houston, an Architectural Guide.* Houston: Houston Chapter AIA.

Jett, Stephen C., and Virginia E. Spencer. 1981. *Navajo Architecture.* Tucson: University of Arizona Press.

Kelly, Henry Warren. 1941. *Franciscan Missions of New Mexico, 1740–1760.* Albuquerque: University of New Mexico Press.

Kennedy, Roger G. 1993. *Mission: The History and Architecture of the Missions of North America.* Boston: Houghton Mifflin.

Kessell, John L. 1980. *The Missions of New Mexico since 1776.* Albuquerque: University of New Mexico Press.

Kubler, George. 1972 (1940, 1962). *The Religious Architecture of New Mexico in the Colonial Period and since the American Occupation.* Albuquerque: University of New Mexico Press.

McCaleb, Walter Flavius. 1961 (1954). *The Spanish Missions of Texas.* Rev. ed. San Antonio: Naylor.

Miller, Michael. 1991. *Monuments of Adobe: The Religious Architecture and Traditions of New Mexico.* Dallas: Taylor Publishing Co.

Newcomb, Rexford. 1916. *The Franciscan Mission Architecture of Alta California.* New York: Architectural Book Publishing Co.

———. 1925. *The Old Mission Churches and Historic Houses of California: Their History, Architecture, Art and Lore.* Philadelphia: Lippincott.

———. 1937. *Spanish-Colonial Architecture in the United States.* New York: J. J. Augustin.

Patricios, Nicholas N. 1994. *Building Marvelous Miami.* Gainesville: University Press of Florida.

Pickens, Buford, ed. 1993. *The Missions of Northern Sonora: A 1935 Field Documentation.* Tucson: University of Arizona Press.

Pierson, William H., Jr. 1970. *American Buildings and Their Architects: The Colonial and Neo-Classical Styles.* Garden City, N.Y.: Doubleday.

Price, Thomas M. N.d. *Galveston, Texas, Historical District Guide.* Galveston: Historical District Board.

Prince, LeBaron Bradford. 1977 (1915). *Spanish Mission Churches of New Mexico.* Cedar Rapids, Iowa: Torch Press; reissued Glorieta, N.M.: Rio Grande Press.

Quinn, Robert M. 1966. "Spanish Colonial Style: The Architectural Origins of the Southwestern Missions." *American West* 3 (Summer): 56–66 and 93–94.

Ramsdell, Charles. 1976 (1959). *San Antonio: A Historical and Pictorial Guide.* Rev. ed., ed. Carmen Perry. Austin: University of Texas Press.

Rawls, James J. 1992. "The California Mission as Symbol and Myth." *California History* 71, no. 3: 342–61.

Reeves, F. Blair, comp. 1989. *A Guide to Florida's Historic Architecture.* Gainesville: University of Florida Press.

Robinson, Willard B. 1985. "Texas Baptist Church Architecture." *Texas Baptist History* 5: 1–31.

———. 1994. *Reflections of Faith: Houses of Worship in the Lone Star State.* Waco: Baylor University Press.

Sanford, Trent Elwood. 1950. *The Architecture of the Southwest.* New York: Norton.

Savage, Christine E. 1991. *New Deal Adobe: The Civilian Conservation Corps and the Reconstruction of Mission La Purisima 1934–1942.* Santa Barbara, Calif.: Fithian Press.

Schaefer, John P., Celestine Chinn, and Kieran McCarthy. 1977. *Bac, Where the Waters Gather.* Tucson: n.p.

Sheen, Martin, narrator. 1990. *The California Missions.* Documentary film. Berkeley: University of California Extension Media Center.

Steinfeldt, Cecilia. 1978. *San Antonio Was: Seen Through a Magic Lantern, Views from the Slide Collection of Albert Steves, Sr.* San Antonio, Tex.: San Antonio Museum Association.

Stilgoe, John R. 1982. *Common Landscape in America, 1580 to 1845.* New Haven: Yale University Press.

Sumner, Alan R., ed. 1978. *Dallasights: An Anthology of Architecture and Open Spaces.* Dallas: AIA Dallas Chapter.

Thomas, Les, and Bruce Roberts (photography). 1990. "Painted Churches in Texas Shine On." *Southern Living* 25, no. 2: 22, 25.

Treib, Marc. 1993. *Sanctuaries of Spanish New Mexico.* Berkeley and Los Angeles: University of California Press.

Tweed, Thomas A. 1997. *Our Lady of the Exile: Diasporic Religion at a Cuban Catholic Shrine in Miami.* New York: Oxford University Press.

Vernon, Walter N. 1971. "McMahan's Chapel: Landmark in Texas." *East Texas Historical Journal* 9 (Mar.): 72–78.

Wallis, Michael (text), and Craig Varjabedian (photographs). 1994. *En Divina Luz: The Penitente Moradas of New Mexico.* Albuquerque: University of New Mexico Press.

Webb, Todd, and Willard B. Robinson. 1974. *Texas Public Buildings of the Nineteenth Century.* Austin: University of Texas Press.

Weber, David J. 1992. *The Spanish Frontier in North America.* New Haven: Yale University Press.

Williamson, Roxanne Kuter. 1973. *Austin, Texas, an American Architectural History.* San Antonio, Tex.: Trinity University Press.

Young, Stanley (text). 1988. *The Missions of California.* San Francisco: Chronicle Books.

83. Alamo, San Antonio, Texas

82. La Ermita, Miami, Florida

84. Kiva, Nambe Pueblo, New Mexico

85. "Las Trampas Mission Church, the Nave, 1938," Las Trampas, New Mexico

86. San Esteban Mission, Acoma Pueblo, New Mexico

87. "Ranchos de Taos Church, 1922"

88. *"Ranchos de Taos, New Mexico, 1942"*

89. Upper Penitente Morada Chapel, Arroyo Hondo, New Mexico

90. "San Xavier Mission, near Tucson. Facade"

91. "San Xavier Moonrise, 1952"

92. *"Russian Chapel, Fort Ross, California, 1949"*

93. "Old Mission Chapel at Los Angeles, 1899"

94. Mission Santa Barbara, California

95. Carmel Mission, California

7 : The Pacific Rim

The states that border the Pacific Ocean –
California, Oregon, Washington, Alaska,
and Hawaii – are extremely diverse, united
mainly in their closer proximity to Asia than
to Europe. The subregional cultures of this
cluster are more clearly layered than those in
many other parts of the United States. First,
the Native American presence is much stron-
ger and more visible than anywhere except
in contiguous parts of the West. In Alaska,
the direct link with the Eurasian landmass
that was the first conduit for immigration to
the Americas is especially prominent. Hawaii, which is not even part of North America, is another land settled originally by wa-
ter-borne immigrants using traditional
technologies long before the great ocean
steamers and airliners began to bring new
peoples across the seas in the stream of migration that continues to this day.

The next wave of immigration to the Pacific Coast consisted of two streams
that had little effect on other parts of the country until much later: Russian in
the north and Spanish in the south. "Anglo" in-migration was small in scale until
the call of gold at Sutter's Mill and in the Yukon beckoned irresistibly to many
adventurous (or foolhardy) spirits in the northeast at mid-nineteenth century. Following a period of makeshift mining camp life, the Pacific Coast began to attract
different sorts of newcomers. The Northwest, loosely defined as the San Francisco Bay area up to the Canadian border, became a cultural extension of New
England, attracting first both Catholic and Protestant missionaries, then larger
numbers of settlers from New England and other parts of the Northeast. Southern California, which first began to blossom at the turn of the twentieth century, tended to attract midwesterners. Alaska and Hawaii, less readily accessible,
attracted more specialized populations of missionaries and entrepreneurs. The
"New Immigration," though not as dramatic as it was farther east, nevertheless
brought significant numbers of Armenians, Italians, and others especially to
California.

The southernmost zone, which overlaps with the Spanish Borderlands region,
saw an influx of Spanish-speakers beginning around the turn of the twentieth

century, from Mexico and then from Central America as well, arriving first for
economic and then for political motives. In the later nineteenth century, Chinese and Japanese also began to arrive along the West Coast, though their numbers were sharply restricted by punitive immigration legislation, and the confinement of Japanese-Americans to detention camps during World War II further inhibited their presence. Successive American involvement in Asian wars began to increase the flow of settlers from Korea and southeast Asia in particular, so that substantial Chinatowns and other tight-knit ethnic enclaves sprang up in major cities from Seattle to San Diego. The presence of both native Pacific Islanders and Japanese in Hawaii has given those islands one of the most substantial "exotic" ethnic amalgams in the nation.

Climate has also played a role in the emergent culture of the Pacific Rim. Alaska's has been proverbially forbidding, and its population has never climbed much higher than a half-million – somewhere between that of Cleveland and Columbus, Ohio. Hawaii's tropical aura has attracted vast numbers of tourists, though its remoteness has deterred settlers from the mainland. California similarly has long been viewed as an idyllic "La-La Land" and has attracted so many new settlers during the twentieth century that its social and economic systems have become badly strained. The Pacific Northwest, with its mild but rainy climate, has nevertheless drawn many, including considerable numbers disillusioned with California, by its progressive social and political climate, economic opportunities, and attractive rugged coastline.

It is clear from the preceding discussion that the "Pacific Rim" states do not constitute a homogeneous cultural region, but rather consist of several smaller regions which share some important distinctions from the nation as a whole. The consequences for religion and its built environment are similar. Unlike the Plains and Mountain West, the Pacific Rim has been both pluralistic and innovative. In addition to Russian Orthodoxy, Buddhism, and Latino Catholicism, new religious movements, some of them syncretistic blends of Euro-American and Asian elements, have flourished especially in California and have made their own contributions to religious building. Within the "mainline" traditions of Christianity regional architects such as Ernest Coxhead and Pietro Belluschi have provided innovative modern settings for long-established traditions of worship. Even further, aspects of both the natural and "secular" environments, such as national parks and media-based entertainment centers, have generated levels of following that approach the religious in kind and intensity. Overall, the Pacific Rim is one of the richest and most diverse areas of the nation in its broad mix of cultures and in the religious building that has been an intrinsic part of those cultures' expression.

SOUTHERN CALIFORNIA

The "churching" of southern California has gone through several distinctive stages. The Spanish missions, today so important as historical and tourist resources, went into eclipse with the passage of control of the territory first to Mexico and then to the United States, and spent several decades as ruins rather than active churches. The settling of the smaller cities and towns reflected the largely midwestern origins of people moving into the region; many of the churches built in these parts during the late nineteenth and early twentieth centuries greatly resemble the small country churches characteristic of Iowa and Kansas: white gable-end or L-shaped frame structures combining Classical, Gothic, and Victorian elements in various mixes. The main exception to this pattern is exhibited in some Catholic churches of the earlier twentieth century, built of adobe along the stylistic lines of the Spanish Colonial revival then popular in urban areas (Millis and Mord 1990, 189ff.).

Reyner Banham has described Los Angeles, the region's sprawling metropolis, as "the Middle West raised to flashpoint." Architecturally, Los Angeles is a secular city with few distinguished or particularly original examples of religious building. Some of its earliest churches partook of Victorian styles fashionable back east, and the English architect Ernest Coxhead contributed several eclectic churches based on the Victorian Gothic. (His work is even more abundant in the San Francisco Bay area.) One good example of Coxhead's work here is the Church of the Messiah (Episcopal, 1888) in Santa Ana; like many of his churches, it features a massive square shingled tower as its visual center. Standard Victorian Gothic revival churches were reasonably plentiful as well, as were other variants on the "Craftsman" mode associated with the values of the Arts and Crafts movement (Banham 1973, 25; Gebhard and Winter 1977, 434, 644).

The great flowering of southern California building took place in the 1920s, as the film industry blossomed and the region's mystique attained national proportions. Three styles emerged as particularly apt expressions of the region's Mediterranean climate and freedom from the same past that seemed to hold older, less fortunate parts of the nation in its grip. One of these, the Moderne (usually and less accurately known as "Art Deco"), was especially adapted for movie theaters and other commercial enterprises not wedded to tradition. This style was never popular for religious building. In Los Angeles, though, it was occasionally adopted for religious purposes, particularly by denominations that lacked a strong formal liturgical tradition, and often in combination with other, more traditional styles. Examples include the 1929 Community United Methodist Church in Pacific Palisades, where Moderne features modify the Spanish Colonial revival. A similar blend of styles can be found in the Twenty-seventh Church of Christ Scientist (ca. 1948) in Silver Lake. The flourishing of the latter denomination in southern California – satirized in Nathanael West's Los Angeles novel, *The Day of the Locust*, as the "Church of Christ, Dentist" – fits in well with the general preoccupation with physical health and well-being that has been associated with the region for over a century (Gebhard and Winter 1977, 48, 173).

Two other historic revival styles also arose that made more sense in terms of the region's heritage, environment, and self-image. One already mentioned is the Spanish Colonial revival, which features stuccoed walls, red tile roofs, and decorative tiles and ironwork. Kevin Starr, one of the state's major cultural interpreters, has noted how the nostalgia for a largely imagined *Californio* heritage of colonial days produced this stylistic revival in the early twentieth century, which also furthered the emergent myth of the mental and physical salubriousness of the region's Mediterranean climate. A good example of this style is the First Congregational Church in Riverside, designed by Myron Hunt and Elmer Grey in 1914. First Congregational's tower is ornamented in the elaborate Mexican Churriguresque style popularized by Bertram Grosvernor Goodhue, Ralph Adams Cram's sometime partner and architect of Manhattan's Saint Bartholomew's, at the Panama-California International Exhibition in San Diego in 1915. (Goodhue was also responsible for the design of the Los Angeles Public Library.) First Congregational stands on the corner of Sixth and Lemon in Riverside; all of the other three corners boast structures – First Church of Christ, Scientist; Riverside Municipal Auditorium; and Fox Riverside Theater – whose towers combine in a riot of Spanish Colonial exuberant urban display (Starr 1985, 83ff.; Gebhard and Winter 1977, 402, 699–700; Moore, Becker, and Campbell 1984, 88).

The other revival style that proliferated among larger urban churches during the great years of growth in the early twentieth century was the Northern Italian Romanesque. This mode evoked not historical but geographical associations, further enhancing the region's image as a second Mediterranean. It was a style that also ahistorically crossed denominational boundaries, and included Long Beach's First Congregational (1914), Westwood's Saint Alban's Episcopal (1940), and the First Unitarian Church (1930) in MacArthur Park, which incorporates some Moorish features as well. (Moorish elements frequently appear in movie theaters, apartment buildings, and other building forms characteristic of Los Angeles and other cities during this era of urban exuberance [Gebhard and Winter 1977, 85, 114, 189–90].)

Here and there throughout the area are houses of worship designed by regionally renowned architects such as Richard Neutra's Kresge Memorial Chapel (1961) in Claremont; Irving Gill's Saint James Chapel/First Baptist Church (1908) in La Jolla; and Lloyd Wright (Frank Lloyd Wright, Jr.'s) Wayfarer's Chapel (1946–71) in Palos Verdes, a "natural church" of transparent glass designed to disappear into the grove of redwood trees planted around it which have now matured and enveloped it. The one church by a modern architect in southern California known to practically all Americans, however, had its origins in a drive-in theater near Disneyland. Here in Garden Grove Robert Schuller, the television preacher known for his "Possibility Thinking," has built an entire campus dominated by one of the most remarkable houses of worship in contemporary America (Gebhard and Winter 1977, 74, 371, 484; Moore, Becker, and Campbell 1984, 129–30).

Schuller's ministries are conducted from Philip Johnson's 1980 "Crystal Cathedral," a giant glass-and-steel-frame assemblage shaped like a four-pointed star and more formally known as the Garden Grove Community Church (see figure 96). The "cathedral" is unspectacularly sited, located in a California-style suburban neighborhood of ranch houses on grid-patterned streets fashioned from flat land not far from the freeway. The site originally held a drive-in theater, whose owner permitted Schuller to use the property for outdoor Sunday morning services in an innovative ministry to the unchurched. These origins are recollected in the church's giant doors, which open out to enable those seated in parked cars to participate. In addition, services are broadcast nationally on a regular basis, so that Schuller's audience is not simply a large group of mobile suburbanites but potentially the entire nation electronically linked together into a single "parish."

The campus which the Cathedral dominates consists of a variety of other structures, including an earlier, smaller worship space of modern design by the regional architect Richard Neutra (1961) and a fifteen-story "prayer tower" reminiscent of Oral Roberts's creation in Tulsa, designed by Neutra's son Dion in 1967. Books and tapes of Schuller's teachings, which are largely derived from those of his mentor and fellow Reformed Church of America preacher, Norman Vincent Peale, as well as an assortment of inspirational materials in which business, politics, and psychology are inextricably mixed with religion, can be bought at the substantial bookstore. Landscaping is elaborate, with regional vegetation such as olive and live oak trees in abundance. Intermingled with the local flora are a walkway composed of stones inscribed with individual Bible verses, as well as a considerable amount of rather sentimental statuary reminiscent of Forest Lawn Cemetery. Abundant parking lots surround the entire complex.

The Cathedral itself stands in the tradition of the auditorium churches that were widely popular among urban mainline Protestant congregations during the Victorian era, such as San Francisco's First Congregational. Here rows of rectilinear pews divided into individual seats with nameplates are arranged on the main level and in three of the points of the star. The fourth point contains the extensive speaker's platform, from which Schuller and guests such as Peale himself have regularly held forth. A giant organ, an electronic signboard on which announcements and the words of hymns appear, and elaborate audiovisual equipment render the "auditorium" effect up-to-date, though clearly in the tradition of the "princes of the pulpit" of an earlier era. There is much at which to marvel but little of mystery here; architectural critic Robert Benson has noted that this is the one occasion on which Philip Johnson, an architect known for his commercial structures, has turned his hand to a religious building. The easy melding of the secular, particularly the commercial world, with the sacred in Schuller's preaching harmonizes well with a structure that resembles an atrium hotel as much as a traditional church (Moore, Becker, and Campbell 1984, 62–63; "Crystal Cathedral Album" 1984; Benson 1989).

Although the Crystal Cathedral is uniquely southern Californian in its ambience, it needs to be seen in the broader context of the regional culture, which has produced few memorable churches but has given rise to a number of built environments that can be interpreted religiously, or at least symbolically. The Cathedral's proximity to Disneyland, whose Matterhorn and Sleeping Beauty's Castle rise only about two miles away, hardly seems accidental. Both enterprises seem preoccupied with denying the painful reality of life as we experience it and substituting a surrogate existence purged of unpleasantness. Disneyland's Adventureland, for example, features a "jungle cruise" in which mechanical crocodiles and hippos portend menace, but in fact are harmless products of a fertile technology. In truth, Adventureland is no more a jungle than the Garden Grove Community Church is a cathedral; the two partake of their prototypes only virtually, just as nearby Hollywood produces endless imaginative tales on celluloid which have at best a problematic relationship to reality.

Perhaps the quintessence of this flight from the actual is Forest Lawn Cemetery in Glendale, the imaginative product of its founder, Dr. Herbert L. Eaton. Prominent at Forest Lawn is a giant plaque, gazed upon by statues of a boy, girl, and dog, which proclaims the "Builder's Creed" Eaton first articulated in 1917:

> I believe in a happy eternal life.
>
> I believe those of us left behind should be glad in the certain belief that those gone before who believed in Him, have entered into that happier life.
>
> I believe, most of all, in a Christ that smiles and loves you and me.
>
> I therefore know the cemeteries of today are wrong because they depict an end, not a beginning. They have consequently become unsightly stoneyards, full of inartistic symbols and depressing customs; places that do nothing for humanity save a practical act, and that not well.
>
> I therefore prayerfully resolve on this New Year's Day, 1917, that I shall endeavor to build Forest Lawn as different, as unlike other cemeteries as sunshine is unlike darkness, as eternal life is unlike death. I shall try to build at Forest Lawn a grand park, devoid of misshapen monuments and other customary signs of earthly death, but filled with towering trees, splashing fountains, singing birds, beautiful flowers, noble memorial architecture, with interiors full of light and color, and redolent of the world's best history and romances.
>
> I believe these things educate and uplift a community.
>
> Forest Lawn shall become a place where lovers new and old shall love to stroll and watch the sunset's glow, planning for the future or reminiscing of the past; a place where artists study or sketch; where school teachers bring happy children to see the things they read of in books; where little churches invite, triumphant in the knowledge that from their pulpits only words of love can be spoken; where memorialization of loved ones in sculptured marble and pictorial glass shall be encouraged but controlled by acknowledged artists; a place where the sorrowing will be soothed and strengthened because it will be God's garden. . . .
>
> This is the Builder's Dream; this is the Builder's Creed. (Moore, Becker, and Campbell 1984, 304–5; Hancock 1964, 63–64)

Eaton was as good as his word. The resultant Forest Lawn, satirized in Evelyn Waugh's *The Loved One*, is a direct descendent of Cambridge's Mount Auburn Cemetery in much the same way that the Crystal Cathedral's lineage can be traced back to Boston's Trinity Church. Forest Lawn is basically a park or rural cemetery, differentiated from its predecessors by the quantity and quality of art interspersed among the natural landscaping. Included on its grounds are reproductions of several actual churches selected for their inspirational literary or his-

torical associations. These include "the Church of the Recessional," named after Kipling's verse and based on Saint Margaret's in Rottingdean, England; "Wee
Kirk o' the Heather," from Annie Laurie's church in Glencairn, Scotland; "the
Church of the Hills," recalling Longfellow's First Parish Meeting House in Portland, Maine; and "the Church of Our Fathers," modeled on Saint John's Episcopal Church in Richmond, the scene of Patrick Henry's "Give me liberty or give
me death" address. An entire building is given over to an enormous painting (45
by 195 feet) by Jan Styka entitled "The Crucifixion"; a large collection of reproductions of statuary by Michelangelo and other greats also is interspersed
throughout the cemetery. It is here that a whole range of notables from Aimee
Semple McPherson to Chico Marx have come to their final rest (Hancock 1964,
15, 74, 91, 92, 109, 128).

From the early health-seekers who came for the salubrity of the climate to
Hollywood's fans, Schuller's worshipers, Disney's vacationeers, and Eaton's dear
departed, southern California has occupied a special place in the American imagination. Blessed with a lovely physical setting and soothing climate, the region
has generated "California dreaming" that has attempted to transcend the particulars of earthly time and place. When this quest is carried to its logical conclusion, as at Forest Lawn, it leads to the denial of the reality of mortality and
death – only not quite perhaps in the way that Saint Paul had in mind when he
inquired, "Death, where is thy sting?"

THE SAN FRANCISCO BAY AREA

The modern, or "American," history of northern California begins with the
discovery of gold at Sutter's Mill and the influx of hopeful seekers after this most
magical of minerals in 1849. Missionaries of the more evangelical Protestant
denominations had begun to arrive even in the years prior to the Gold Rush, and
were joined by others after a substantial population began to develop after that
fateful year. Early congregations met wherever they could – in hotels, court-
rooms, rented rooms, under tents, and even on ships in the Bay. Before long, not
only Catholics and traditional Protestants but Unitarians, Jews, Swedenborgians,
and devotees of Chinese traditional religions were worshiping as they could, with
makeshift facilities rapidly yielding to the same sorts of respectable Victorian
Gothic and Romanesque revival structures as their counterparts in Kansas City
and Denver (Willard and Wilson 1985, 3–4 and passim).

Victorian San Francisco came to an abrupt end with the earthquake of 1906,
an event as devastating as Chicago's great fire for the built environment. Few of
the city's houses of worship survived the trauma, and most of the city's built environment is postearthquake in origin. Although the Bay Area does boast some
churches of startling originality, the general feel of San Francisco itself is somewhat old-fashioned, even though the structures that create that effect more likely
date from the 1920s than the 1870s. For many of the finest churches in the city
itself, the Classical and medieval revivals are still the norm.

A quick tour of the downtown era and its environs reinforces this conclusion
rapidly. First Congregational Church (1915), for example, occupies a busy corner at the intersection of Post and Mason not far from Union Square (see figure 97). The interior is that of an auditorium church, characteristic of the denomination during the Victorian era. The two faces of the exterior that are visible are similar: Classical revival with ornate Corinthian columns. As Ruth Willard, the foremost chronicler of the city's churches, has observed, "the whole is dignified, discreet; in fact it is sometimes mistaken for a bank" (Willard and Wilson 1985, 30–32).

Two other classic San Francisco churches that reinforce the essentially Victorian image conveyed by the myriad of "painted ladies" – Victorian frame houses painted in bright colors that are characteristic of many of the city's older neighborhoods – are First Unitarian and Grace Cathedral. First Unitarian was the church of Thomas Starr King, the Universalist minister from Boston who arrived shortly before the outbreak of the Civil War and helped keep California in the Union. As the result of his heroic civic efforts, he now represents the state in the national Statuary Hall together with Junípero Serra. The church in which he lies buried was built in 1888; though it suffered considerable damage during the earthquake, it has survived reasonably well and has been augmented by 1968–70 additions that harmonize with its English parish Gothic style but also incorporate some Japanese influences into the ensemble (Willard and Wilson 1985, 48–51; Gebhard 1973, 78–79).

Grace Episcopal Cathedral, standing proudly on Nob Hill, takes its place with New York's Saint John the Divine and the National Cathedral in Washington as one of the largest and most handsome of the denomination's bishop's seats. Its 1860 Gothic revival predecessor was destroyed by the earthquake, and the present structure, begun in 1910, was not dedicated until 1964 – by Bishop James A. Pike, the controversial figure who was tried for heresy and later died in the Israeli desert on a fruitless quest for his dead son, with whom he had tried to enter into spiritualistic communication. Like its East Coast and European counterparts, Grace Cathedral is a *summa*, containing in its stained glass windows and murals a compendium of commemorative information about the history of Anglicanism, the Episcopal church in California, the Franciscan legacy, and the cultural and intellectual accomplishments of the western world. French Gothic in overall conception, it is built of reinforced concrete for protection against future seismic activity rather than relying on the traditional physics of counterthrusts by flying buttresses. Its stunning central doors are cast from the original molds of Lorenzo Ghiberti for those of the baptistry of the Duomo at Florence (Willard and Wilson 1985, 37–42).

San Francisco's other cathedral, about a mile away in the Western Addition neighborhood, is Saint Mary's, the seat of the city's Roman Catholic archbishop (see figure 98). This dramatically modern structure also sits high on a hill, replacing a red brick German Gothic cathedral that survived the earthquake but was demolished by fire in 1962. The construction of the new Saint Mary's, more or less affectionately known as "the Bendix" for its distinctive shape, touched off considerable controversy in the socially minded 1960s when the investment of vast sums in architecture was viewed by many as a betrayal of the needs of poor inner-city dwellers (Gaffey 1984).

The design of Saint Mary's is primarily the work of Pietro Belluschi, the Italian-born architect who gained a reputation for church design in the Pacific Northwest. The basic geometrical form here is the hyperbolic paraboloid; its contours are formed by the intersection of four symmetrical "wings" of this shape at right angles, thus forming for the skeptical the shape of a washing-machine agitator. The cathedral is faced with white marble and its wings supported on narrow piers, creating an effect of lightness and grace. In the center, suspended over the altar, hangs a shimmering baldacchino designed by Richard Lippold which functions as a mobile made up of thin gold and silver cylinders. More representational sculpture in stylized form can be found in the tympanum, the font, and the stations of the cross. The overall effect is one of inexpressible lightness, providing a sublime vista of the city through its windows, and contrasting sharply with nearby First Unitarian and a Lutheran church of Victorian demeanor (Willard and Wilson 1985, 231–35).

A walk through the area readily accessible from downtown, including the churches already discussed, can give a misleadingly conventional picture of San Francisco's religious composition. A few detours into adjoining areas provide a partial corrective, since this is one of the nation's most ethnically and culturally complex cities. Within a few minutes' walk of downtown lie an area of recent heavy Vietnamese settlement, which has not as yet produced very much distinctive in terms of religious building, and the older communities of Chinatown and Japantown, which have. Some of Chinatown's houses of worship, such as Old Saint Mary's Catholic Church, originally the diocesan cathedral and rebuilt several times over the years since its foundation in 1853, are "mainline" Christian, and serve a mixed ethnic constituency, including Chinese. More indigenously Chinese are facilities such as the nearby T'ien Hou Temple on Waverly Place (see figure 99). This temple occupies a room several flights up the stairway in a walk-up tenement, one of a series of similar adjoining buildings decorated in what has been dubbed the "Chinese Renaissance" style – basically the Italianate design of the late nineteenth century with some Asian decorative elements such as "bird's wing" eaves attached. The temple is simply a suite of rooms in which are placed altars to an eclectic assortment of deities in this syncretistic combination of Confucian, Buddhist, Taoist, and traditional folk religious elements. Offerings for individual or family purposes may be placed here, with no collective ceremonials carried out and no priests officiating. This highly individualistic religious observance stands in sharp contrast with traditional western expectations, as does the secular ambience of apartment dwellings, commercial establishments, and fraternal organizations in which the temple is situated (Willard and Wilson 1985, 42–45).

Japantown, a former Victorian enclave recently and dramatically modernized, stands just beyond the Western Addition area where reside Saint Mary's Cathedral and First Unitarian. Here can be found the Soto Zen Mission (1989) and the Konko Church (1973), a Shinto offshoot, both in traditional Japanese temple style, which today harmonizes well in a broader built environment that has been heavily influenced by the simplicity of traditional Asian design. An older, more Victorianized manifestation of Asian religiosity in this heavily Asian city can be found almost literally around the corner at the Buddhist Church of San Francisco (1914), maintained by the Pure Land sect and founded originally by Japanese missionaries in 1898. Built in Roman Baroque style, only the stupa on its roof reveals an Asian connection (Willard and Wilson 1985, 168–69, 236–37).

In addition to more recent and ethnically based versions of Asian religion, reminders of the exotic attraction that such beliefs and practices had exerted on Victorian-era San Franciscans still persist in the region. Strikingly archaic is the onion-domed old headquarters (1905, 1908) of the Vedanta Society on Webster Street, described by one observer as "a meeting of the mysterious East and the uninhibited West" (see figure 100). Rosicrucian Park in San Jose, an hour or so south of San Francisco, is similarly wonderful to behold. In the middle of an older suburban residential enclave lies a block of Egypt, consisting of very literalistic reproductions of Egyptian architecture as the home for a society dedicated to promulgating the esoteric lore of a vanished civilization (Willard and Wilson 1985, 168–69; Gebhard 1973, 46).

Finally, a survey of Bay Area religious building should acknowledge the creativity of the region's architects, many of them newcomers to the area themselves, who helped to create a distinctive style, capitalizing especially on the possibilities of working with wood that have given California crafts a distinctive character. Noteworthy here are the churches – mostly Episcopal – of Ernest Coxhead, the British architect who enjoyed the patronage of Bishop William Ingraham Kip and designed a plethora of diminutive Victorian churches incorporating Arts and Crafts touches such as shingling and eyelid dormers. The results, though aesthetically very appealing, risk the appellation of "cute" for their size and preciousness. One good example is Saint John's Episcopal Church (1891) in Monterey. Unfortunately, many of Coxhead's larger urban churches were demolished in the 1906 earthquake or subsequently (Gebhard 1973, 446; Longstreth 1983, 47–50, 96–106).

An excellent example of innovative architecture in the region with which to conclude this section is Bernard Maybeck's First Church of Christ, Scientist (1910), in Berkeley (see figure 101). Maybeck was a highly innovative turn-of-the-century "Progressive" architect who had designed the vast and exotic Palace of Fine Arts for the Panama-Pacific Exposition in San Francisco in 1915. (It has since become an "Exploratorium.") His Christian Science church in Berkeley is very different, and can be located squarely in the California regional love for craftsmanship in wood. Located next to "People's Park," the scene of a long-term clash between the University of California and students and local residents, the church is small in scale, and blends neatly into the local landscape. Although at first glace it appears to be in the Arts and Crafts tradition in its attention to detail, a closer examination reveals runaway eclecticism. Romanesque-inspired freestanding columns along the exterior support pergolas, so that the vegetation that surrounds the building becomes part of its texture. The pergolas themselves combine with the three-level pagoda-like roof to suggest an Asian element. On the interior, the Greek cross plan, suspended lights, and thronelike screens give a Byzantine effect, though one complemented by Romanesque piers supporting massive girders ornamented with fanciful Gothic tracery. Such a stylistic mixture could have been disastrous, but Maybeck nevertheless turned it into something rich and strange, nestled unobtrusively in the shadow of a great university. Very California (Gebhard 1973, 41, 265; McCoy 1975, 24–36; Jordy 1972, 300–312).

THE PACIFIC NORTHWEST

The northwesternmost region of the continental United States is divided by mountains into two distinct regions. That to the east of the Cascades is sparsely settled and primarily agricultural, with Spokane as its major city. The western coast is much more heavily urbanized; in addition to logging and fishing, its cities, especially Seattle, have attracted considerable heavy industry. Although social and cultural differences are considerable, with the western part known for its liberal and tolerant political spirit, both are products of the process of frontier settlement, and their religious composition and built environment reflect this process.

Virtually nothing of the built environment of the region's aboriginal peoples now survives. The first Euro-American settlers of the Pacific Northwest were missionaries to the natives, most notably the Jesuit Pierre Jean De Smet, Jason Lee in Oregon's Willamette Valley, and Marcus and Narcissa Whitman in what is now Washington State, in the 1830s and 1840s. The Whitmans' missionary compound has been partially restored and is now a historical museum. After the earlier missionary and pioneer days, the economic boom years that followed 1880 and the substantial immigration from central and southern Europe began to swell the region's population, bringing with it not only American Protestants but a wide variety of New Immigration peoples as well (Woodbridge and Montgomery 1980, 4, 426; Pearson and Pearson 1980, 3, 8).

The nineteenth and early twentieth centuries saw considerable prosperity but little cultural innovation. For practical purposes, the Pacific Northwest on both sides of the Cascades during this period can be considered together with the broader forces chronicled in our discussion of the Plains and the mountains. Clergy were scarce, and the entire region was the province of missionary preaching rather than settled parish life. Religious building was similar, and the region's churches during its first several decades followed the contours of "Prairie Gothic" – white frame churches built by clergy, carpenters, and congregations according to folk memory or following patterns provided by Methodists and other evangelizing denominations.

A typology of the region's churches closely resembling that seen in Kansas, Colorado, and other frontier states can be described. Churches were generally

small in size, frame in material, and rectangular in plan. They had steeply pitched
gable roofs, with a steeple or belfry centered at the front end and an entrance similarly located. Roofs were of cedar shingles, and windows came in a variety of shapes. Steeples were the main occasion for variety and experimentation in form. Siting was catch-as-catch-can, with corner lots permitting formal variations such as corner towers or L-shapes. In raw frontier towns, churches were generally located a block or so away from the main street and its array of saloons. On the whole, these churches were conservative in plan, echoing their New England origins as filtered through the Plains (Pearson and Pearson 1980, 13–15; see also Freeman 1976).

The array of denominations represented was not radically different from that farther east, but it did reflect the role of foreign as well as internal immigration in the region's population. Catholics, Methodists, Congregationalists, Episcopalians, and Lutherans were most numerous, while Baptists, Disciples, Presbyterians, and Eastern Orthodox were significantly represented as well. Even such rather unusual groups such as Christian Scientists, Jews, Polish National Catholics, and African Methodists were making an occasional appearance by the turn of the century. Religion and ethnicity were quite heterogeneous, but building styles were dictated more by financial limitations and cultural expectations than the flourishing of imagination (Freeman 1976).

As Seattle, Spokane, and Portland began to develop into urban centers, a process of church construction similar to that further east also prevailed. The Gothic in its various manifestations was the style of choice for urban churches, while the Richardsonian Romanesque was relatively scarce. The variation possible within the Gothic idiom is well illustrated by Washington's two Episcopal cathedrals. Where Spokane's Saint John's (begun 1926) is traditional English Gothic, Seattle's Saint Mark's (1926–30), made of poured concrete, has Byzantine features as well (Clark 1983, 102; Woodbridge and Montgomery 1980, 158, 412–13).

The architectural interest and distinctiveness of the region lie not in its appropriation of traditional styles originating in the Northeast and spread throughout the entire country but in the convergence of three factors also characteristic of northern California that express the spirit of the Pacific Rim: wood as a basic material, Arts and Crafts movement–inspired love of detail, and an aesthetic compounded of indigenous Modern influences as well as ideas imported from traditional Japan and contemporary Scandinavia. The love of wood, of course, is natural in a country that prides itself on the export of "Oregon toothpicks" (giant logs); many of its earliest buildings, religious and otherwise, were log constructions. Saint Paul's Catholic Mission in Kettle Falls (1847) and Saint Andrew's Episcopal Church (1898) in Chelan, both in Washington, are two good nineteenth-century examples. The New Deal's WPA also encouraged the creative use of indigenous wooden construction; its massive Timberline Lodge on Mount Hood inspired a spin-off in tiny Saint John the Evangelist Catholic Church (1937), of artfully primitive log design in nearby Zig Zag, Oregon (Pearson and Pearson 1980, 132–33 and 148–49; Clark 1983, 190–93).

The love of wood used simply and organically has become a staple of modern

Northwestern design, manifesting itself across the denominational spectrum in structures such as Seattle's Congregation Ezra Bessaroth (1914), built of rough dark-stained cedar boards, and Paul Hayden Kirk's University Unitarian (1960), of similarly striking simplicity. Although the Asian influence is manifest in a few structures with specific ethnic connections such as Seattle's Japanese Presbyterian Church (1963), its pervasive appeal has come about within the religious "mainstream" through the work of equally "mainstream" regional architects. Prominent among these was Italian-born and Portland-based Pietro Belluschi, already seen through his New Saint Mary's Cathedral in San Francisco, and eventually well known throughout the entire country for his work especially in religious design (Woodbridge and Montgomery 1980, 188, 190).

Belluschi's aesthetic development can be traced through a variety of convergent influences, including Bernard Maybeck and the Arts and Crafts movement, Frank Lloyd Wright and Prairie School modernism, Zen Buddhism, and the contemporary Finnish designers Alvar Aalto and the Saarinens. Beginning with the Morninglight Chapel of the Finley Mortuary in Portland (1936–37; demolished 1985), Belluschi began to design worship spaces that combined the principles of austerity, love of natural materials (especially wood), good craftsmanship, geometrical shapes, and harmony with the environment. Some of these followed fairly traditional plans, such as his Saint Thomas More Catholic Church in Portland (1939–40), a small rectangular building with a double-pitch roof, distinguished principally by its dominating shingled broach spire resting on a complex but unornamented multistage steeple base. Much of the effect derives from his treatment of building materials, here unfinished knotty pine boards and red cedar shingles. Inside, the altar in the elevated chancel is highlighted in an almost Baroque fashion by light from the lantern contrasting with the dimly lit nave (Clausen 1992, 14, 15, 17, 19, 20, 42, 48–51).

At least two other of Belluschi's Oregon churches deserve mention here. Central Lutheran Church in Portland (1948–50) is a much larger urban church on a busy residential neighborhood corner. The solution to the needs of this congregation came in the form of a series of connecting rectangles of brick and wood. The overall plan of a longitudinal processional space leading to a stagelike chancel is standard for a liturgical church; the innovation is apparent in such details as the open timberwork tower that adjoins the narthex. Even more distinctive, perhaps, is Belluschi's First Presbyterian Church (1948–51) in Cottage Grove, near Eugene, Oregon (see figure 102). Here was a congregation that did not want a church that asserted its social status but rather one that would emphasize the uses of the lumber that was the community's economic base. One stipulation was that a cluster of honey locust trees on the site not be disturbed, a provision with which Belluschi sympathized wholeheartedly. The result was an unobtrusive L-shaped wooden church with a Japanese-style garden, ornamented Zen-like with rocks, through which the congregation entered. The nave, which is simple and focused on an austere communion table, features a row of plate glass windows through which worshipers may see both the church's garden and, beyond it, the broader community in which they are collectively engaged in social concerns. First Presbyterian is thus a quintessentially regional church; it embodies twentieth-century Christian liturgical and social concerns in a physical environment that reflects both the local natural setting as well an aesthetic derived in part from the Asian thought patterns that constitute one of the Northwest's major cultural overlays (Clausen 1992, 64–67, 70–75).

THE FINAL FRONTIERS: ALASKA AND HAWAII

In the two newest American states, little remains of any distinctively aboriginal religious building. The cultures of the Alaskans were such that religious and "secular" uses were not formally distinguished. In a phenomenon with parallels among the Navajo and other indigenous peoples, the Tlingit built houses with cosmological implications. The house plan was square, reflecting the overall shape of the cosmos. The floor represented the earth and the roof the heavens; the fire at the center corresponded to a similar point in the broader scheme of things. Entry through the shape of a carved animal constituted a symbolic rebirth (Hoagland 1993, 19).

Such symbolic building became increasingly rare as the native peoples, who themselves had migrated over the Bering Strait from Siberia over ten millennia previously, adapted first to Russian and then "Anglo" occupancy. Christian churches beginning in the late eighteenth century became the normative religious structure as Orthodox, Roman Catholic, Anglican, and Protestant missionaries served both indigenes and more recent arrivals. Since the climate and terrain prohibited permanent settlement by all but the hardiest, the range of denominational expression in Alaska has never been very great; Presbyterianism has been the major player among Protestant groups, and few other than those already mentioned have erected houses of worship worthy of particular note.

Alaskan natives had been converted to Russian Orthodoxy by fur traders – *promyshleniki* – even before the coming of monks as missionaries in 1790. Early churches reproduced with logs some of the classic features of the Russian tradition, including octagonal shapes and cupolas. By 1860 the Orthodox had built nine churches and thirty-five chapels. None of those constructed before the territory's acquisition by the United States – "Seward's Icebox" – in 1867 survive today. The eighty churches that now exist and serve some 20,000 members echo the same distinctive architectural features of their predecessors – not surprisingly, perhaps, for a religious community in which tradition plays a very powerful role (Hoagland 1993, 31, 32, 35–36, 40, 43).

Alaska's Russian Orthodox churches share a number of common characteristics, many but not all of which are also partaken of by their counterparts in the "lower forty-eight." First, they are built on an axial three-part plan which is deeply rooted in the distinctive liturgical theology of Eastern Orthodoxy. At the west end – these churches are consciously oriented – is the narthex or vestibule, a transitional zone that links the profane outer world with the inner sacred world of the church. Intermediate is the nave, in which the congregation stands for the duration of what is usually a rather lengthy service, with the exception of the elderly for whom benches are provided. Finally, at the east end, is the sanctuary, which is set apart from the remainder of the church by an *iconostas* (*-stasis, -stasion*), a screen covered with icons, or sacred images, arranged in a prescribed pattern, and penetrated by royal doors in its center. Women are forbidden from the sanctuary, which can be entered only by the priest and his assistants (Hoagland 1993, 43–44).

This traditional internal arrangement is paralleled on the exterior, where the liturgical components of the church are structurally differentiated. The sanctuary is usually rectangular or polygonal; the nave rectangular, octagonal, square, or cross-shaped; and the narthex rectangular. The rectangular form is probably derived from that of the *izbou*, a traditional Russian dwelling; the octagonal shape is a survival of archaic Russian tent-roof churches. Other standard elements include the hipped roof, the bell tower, an interior dome, and, most distinctive, the onion dome, sometimes explained as a symbolic representation of a flame. Not all domes are the familiar onion-shape; in many cases, towers are capped with pyramids or other geometrical figures. Siting of these churches, which are usually designed by priests, is frequently on an elevation a short way from the village proper. Finally, in Alaska, virtually all Orthodox churches are brightly colored and built from wood, a traditional but not unique material in Russia (Hoagland 1993, 43–47).

Although generally much smaller than their Russian counterparts, Alaska's Orthodox churches do vary somewhat in size and style. At Sitka, for example, is Saint Michael the Archangel Cathedral, rebuilt in 1966 after a fire had destroyed Bishop Innocent's original 1848 structure (see figure 103). Constructed of more durable steel and concrete rather than the logs of the original, the rebuilt 67-foot by 97-foot church is arranged in the shape of a Greek cross – with all four arms of equal length – an unusual arrangement in Alaska. Saint Michael's also features a large square tower with an octagonal drum and tall, attenuated onion dome surmounting it (Hoagland 1993, 185–87).

At the opposite end of the size spectrum is Saints Sergius and Herman of Valaam Chapel on Spruce Island, which measures about twenty feet square and has no electricity, heat, or water. It has a hipped roof and a small porch with stairs ascending to the front door. Nearby stands the frame cabin of Father Gerasim (1888–1966), who had been a devotee of Herman of Valaam. It is preserved as a shrine together with a complex of other buildings associated with his life, including a chapel built on the site of his cell (Hoagland 1993, 285–86).

Most of the remainder of the religious buildings of Alaska that can be described as having a distinct architecture are Roman Catholic and Anglican. The majority are rather small, of wood frame construction, and frequently have a rustic rather than a high style appearance. Immaculate Conception Roman Catholic Church (1904) in Fairbanks is one of Alaska's larger churches; it features a tall central bell tower, steeply pitched gable roof, and a pyramid-capped belfry. More typical perhaps of the region is Saint Matthew's Episcopal Church (1948), also in Fairbanks, which replaced an earlier church of similar design. It consists of a

main body and a smaller adjoining narthex, both made of logs sawed flat on three
sides, with steeply pitched rooflines that almost form an A-frame. A small belfry sits upon the narthex under the peak of the church's gable. A Presbyterian church that fits into this same regional stylistic mode is the United Protestant Church (1936–37) of Palmer, built on land donated by the Alaska Rural Rehabilitation Corporation with the stipulation that all construction be of logs. Logs are thus used here in a wide variety of decorative patterns to constitute what has been described as "the epitome of romanticized rustic architecture" (Hoagland 1993, 132, 215, 222).

Although the traditional religion of Hawaii has become attenuated to the status of folklore, some remains of its physical apparatus can still be found in the islands. The forerunners of that religion were introduced with the first Polynesian settlers, possibly in the sixth century A.D. Captain James Cook, the first European visitor to the islands, was impressed with the similarities its religion bore to that of other Polynesian lands in the late eighteenth century. Just as Hawaii was opening up to European and American settlement, the ascension to the throne of Liholiho in 1819 brought about a disestablishment of the official cult that his father, Kamehameha I, had presided over as head of a unified society. Congregationalist missionaries from New England began to arrive at this exact time, and they and their more commercially minded descendants introduced Christianity as the first of the novel cultural elements that would transform Hawaii into one of the most pluralistic enclaves in the United States (Luomala 1987).

The principal physical structure for carrying out the cultic activities of traditional Hawaiian religion was the *heiau*, an open-air center whose complexity varied considerably according to the power of the chief who had constructed it. Larger *heiaus* might include terraces, an altar, refuse pits, consecrated images, an earth oven, and, unique to the islands, a tapa (bark) covered oracle tower. William Ellis, an English missionary of the early nineteenth century, has left us the following description of a *heiau:*

> After breakfast, I visited the large heiau or temple called Bukohola. It stands on an eminence in the southern part of the district, and was built by Tamehameha [*sic*] about thirty years ago, when he was engaged in conquering Hawaii, and the rest of the Sandwich Islands. . . . When he had overcome those who had rebelled, he finished the heiau, dedicated it to Tairi, his god of war, and then proceeded to the conquest of Oahau. Its shape is an irregular parallelogram, 224 feet long, and 100 wide. The walls, though built of loose stones, were solid and compact. At both ends, and on the side next the mountains, they were twenty feet high, twelve feet thick at the bottom, but narrowed in gradually towards the top, where a course of smooth stones, six feet wide, formed a pleasant walk. The walls next the sea were not more than seven or eight feet high, and were proportionally wide. The entrance to the temple is by a narrow passage between too [*sic*] high walls. As I passed along this avenue, an involuntary shuddering seized me, on reflecting how often it had been

trodden by the feet of those who relentlessly bore the body of the human victim an offering to their cruel idols. The upper terrace within the area was spacious, and much better finished than the lower ones. It was paved with flat, smooth stones, brought from a distance. At the south end was a kind of inner court, which might be called the sanctum sanctorum of the temple, where the principal idol used to stand, surrounded by a number of images of inferior deities.

Although the *heiaus* and the human sacrifices carried out in them have not been an active part of Hawaiian culture for many decades, some have been preserved as historic relics, for example, at Pu'uhonua O Honaunau National Historical Park on the island of Hawaii (Luomala 1987, 215; Ellis 1974, 96–97; Morgan 1983, 125; *AAA Hawaii Tourbook* 1994, 48).

The transition of the Hawaiian Islands from a traditional Polynesian society to part of the modern United States was mediated by nineteenth-century missionaries, particularly Congregationalists, though Episcopalians, Roman Catholics, and others participated as well. Perhaps the best known missionary presence was Father Damien, the "leper priest" of Molokai at the leper colony at Kalawao on the Kalaupapa Peninsula. Saint Joseph's Church, which Damien built before his ministry to the lepers, still stands on Molokai's south coast. It is a small white frame gable-end structure with a pointed-arch door, a tall louvered steeple and polygonal spire surmounted by a cross. Another interesting example of a Catholic mission church is Saint Benedict's, sited on the slope of the Mauna Loa volcano. On the exterior, Saint Benedict's is also a plain frame structure with a later addition of "Carpenter Gothic" ornament. What is noteworthy is its interior, the walls of which are covered with a series of murals by a Belgian missionary priest, Father John Berchmans Velghe. These murals, painted around 1900, include both Old and New Testament scenes as well as representations of sinners in Hell, together with inscriptions in Hawaiian. Together they constitute a striking example of the combination in medieval fashion of art and architecture as a catechetical aid (Morgan 1983, 253; Shimoda 1981).

Christian churches in the islands range considerably in style and scale, beginning with the diminutive Ka Ekalesia O Jerusalem Hou-Hoomana O Ke Alii Ona Alii Ka Haku Ona Haku (Jerusalem Hou, Congregational Church of the King of Kings and Lord of Lords), built in 1948 in Halawa Valley, Molokai, which echoes in stylized form the "Carpenter Gothic" of the nineteenth century. Kawaiahao Church (1842; see figure 104) in Honolulu, built of coral blocks, stands on the site of an earlier thatched hut used by the first missionaries to the islands; its round-arched windows, four Doric columns, and crenelated central clock tower echo in eclectic fashion such earlier New England churches as Alexander Parris's United First Parish Church (1824) in Quincy, Massachusetts. Central Union Church (1924) represents the work of the ubiquitous Ralph Adams Cram, here working in a neoclassical idiom in homage to Sir James Gibbs (Morgan 1983, 200, 254; Fairfax n.d., 56, 80).

Other Congregational churches attempt to combine the Anglo-American

Christian heritage with the Asian ambience of the islands in strange and wonderful ways. Makiki Christian Church, for example, is patterned after Japan's
Himeji Castle; it is characterized by a cascade of roofs, with a tiny pavilion at the
topmost story of the resultant tower. The First Chinese Church of Christ (1929)
incorporates into a traditional church design a doorway with upswept hornlike
corners based on a Chinese gate, which in traditional Chinese culture would have
been symbolic of hierarchy and power and provided entry into a place of religious or governmental importance. Attached at one corner is a pagoda-like bell
tower with three stages, a function never played by Asian pagodas. Yet another
example is Saint Luke's Episcopal Church, which has upswept "bird-wing" eaves
in the Chinese manner, as well as an adjoining *obon* tower used in Japanese Shinto-
Buddhist eclectic religion as a ceremonial platform for dances to entertain the
gods. This also has been domesticated into a bell tower surrogate. Finally, Waikiki
Baptist Church (1916) is an odd combination of a small-scale eclectic wooden
Victorian church with a Russian Orthodox-like onion dome (Morgan 1983, 201–
2; Fairfax n.d., 78, 97; my thanks to my colleagues Ann Cline and Alan Miller
for their valuable advice on East Asian religious architecture).

The third major layer of Hawaiian religion and culture is that provided by
Asian, especially Japanese, immigration. Scattered throughout the Islands are a
number of Shinto shrines with their *torii* gates and protruding crossed decorative finials at either end of the roofline. Buddhism is represented in Oahu by
Bodoyo-in, a replica of the similarly named shrine outside Kyoto, the oldest extant
piece of Japanese architecture from the Heian period (ca. A.D. 800–1185). Its
erection in 1968 commemorated the centenary of the arrival of Buddhism in
Hawaii. In a very different vein, the Soto Mission Temple in downtown Honolulu is a modernized eclectic version of Tibetan Buddhist architecture with a hint
of India, featuring a stupa-like pagoda tower capped with a finial symbolizing
spiritual aspiration (see figure 105; Morgan 1983, 203–5).

REFLECTIONS

The religious buildings of the Pacific Rim are in many ways emblematic of
the distinctive cultures that have developed in those states. In southern California, the Crystal Cathedral represents the erosion of the lines between sacred and
secular and the movement of traditional religion into an alliance with worldly
forces that promise escape from mortality and redemption from finitude in a
"virtual" reality of natural beneficence and human manufacture. Northern California and the Pacific Northwest share many characteristics. For them, San
Francisco's Grace Cathedral might be taken as a symbol of urban Victorian civic
presence and power, while Pietro Belluschi's First Presbyterian stands for a more
modest quest for harmony with nature and responsibility toward the social order. Alaska's frame Orthodox churches bespeak an exotic presence in a hostile
environment, never fully assimilated into the broader patterns of national life and
tenaciously clinging to an independent frontier tradition. Finally, Hawaii's Chris-

tian churches, designed with elements borrowed from the Chinese and Japanese, denote the one American subculture where races have extensively and successfully intermingled, perhaps a portent for the broader national future in an increasingly global society.

THE PACIFIC RIM: BIBLIOGRAPHY

AAA Hawaii Tourbook. 1994. Buffalo: Quebecor Printing Buffalo.

Andree, Herb, and Noel Young. 1980. *Santa Barbara Architecture from Spanish Colonial to Modern.* Santa Barbara, Calif.: Capra Press.

Banham, Reyner. 1973. *Los Angeles: The Architecture of Four Ecologies.* Harmondsworth, Eng.: Penguin.

Benson, Robert. 1989. "The Garden Grove Community Church: Religious Imagery in the Late 20th Century." Unpublished paper, American Academy of Religion, Anaheim, Calif.

Bernhardi, Robert. 1977 (1972). *The Buildings of Berkeley.* Oakland: Holmes Book Co.; reissued Oakland: Forest Hill Press.

———. 1979. *The Buildings of Oakland with a Section on Piedmont.* Oakland: Forest Hill Press.

Churches along the Oregon Trail: A History of Churches Identified with the Central Pacific Conference of the United Church of Christ. 1976. Portland, Ore.: Central Pacific Conference of the United Church.

Clark, Rosalind, et al. 1983. *Oregon Style: Architecture 1840 to 1950s.* Portland, Ore.: Professional Book Center.

Clausen, Meredith L. 1992. *Spiritual Space: The Religious Architecture of Pietro Belluschi.* Seattle: University of Washington Press.

"The Crystal Cathedral Album." 1984. Garden Grove, Calif.: Robert Schuller Ministries.

Ellis, William. 1974 (1842). *Polynesian Researches: Hawaii.* Reprint. Rutland, Vt.: Charles E. Tuttle Co.

Fairfax, Geoffrey W. N.d. *The Architecture of Honolulu.* Honolulu: Island Heritage.

Freeman, Olga Samuelson. 1976. *A Guide to Early Oregon Churches.* Eugene, Ore.: Freeman.

Gaffey, James P. 1984. "The Anatomy of Transition: Cathedral-Building and Social Justice in San Francisco." *Catholic Historical Review* 70, no. 1: 45–73.

Gebhard, David. 1967. "The Spanish Colonial Revival in Southern California (1895–1930)." *Journal of the Society of Architectural Historians* 26, no. 2: 131–47.

Gebhard, David, and Robert Winter. 1977. *A Guide to Architecture in Los Angeles and Southern California.* Santa Barbara, Calif.: Peregrine Smith.

Gebhard, David, et al. 1973. *A Guide to Architecture in San Francisco and Northern California.* 2d ed. Santa Barbara, Calif.: Peregrine Smith.

Hancock, Ralph. 1964. *The Forest Lawn Story.* Los Angeles: Angelus Press.

Henderson, John D. 1971. *AIA Guide San Diego.* San Diego, Calif.: A.I.A., San Diego Chapter.

Hoagland, Alison K. 1993. *Buildings of Alaska.* New York: Oxford University Press.

Jordy, William H. 1972. *American Architects and Their Buildings: Progressive and Academic Ideals at the Turn of the Twentieth Century.* Garden City, N.Y.: Doubleday.

Longstreth, Richard W. 1983. *On the Edge of the World: Four Architects in San Francisco at the Turn of the Century.* Cambridge, Mass.: MIT Press.

Luomala, Katharine. 1987. "Hawaiian Religion." In *The Encyclopedia of Religion*, ed. Mircea Eliade, vol. 6, pp. 214–19. New York: Macmillan.

McCoy, Esther. 1975. *Five California Architects*. New York: Praeger.

Millis, Bette R., and Jeanne Mord. 1990. *Sentinels of Love: Rural Churches of California*. Santa Barbara, Calif.: Fithian Press.

Moore, Charles, Peter Becker, and Regula Campbell. 1984. *The City Observed: Los Angeles*. New York: Random/Vintage.

Morgan, Joseph R. 1983. *Hawaii: A Geography*. Boulder Colo.: Westview Press.

Pearson, Arnold, and Esther Pearson. 1980. *Early Churches of Washington State*. Seattle: University of Washington Press.

Portland, Oregon, Chapter, A.I.A. 1968. *A Guide to Portland Architecture*. Portland: Portland, Oregon, Chapter A.I.A.

Renaissance of Religious Art and Architecture in the San Francisco Bay Area, 1946–1968. 1985. Berkeley, Calif.: Regional Oral History Office of the Bancroft Library.

Shimoda, Jerry Y. 1981. *The Painted Church at Honaunau, Hawaii; St. Benedict's Church*. Honaunau, Kona, Hawaii: Restoration Committee, Saint Benedict's Church.

Spokane A.I.A. 1978. *Spokane's Historic Architecture*. Spokane: Eastern Washington State Historical Society.

Starr, Kevin. 1985. *Inventing the Dream: California through the Progressive Era*. New York: Oxford University Press.

Steinbrueck, Victor. 1953. *Seattle Architecture 1850–1953*. New York: Reinhold.

Upton, Will Oscar. 1940. *Churches of El Dorado County, California*. Placerville, Calif.: Old Hangtown Press.

Vaughan, Thomas, and George A. McMath. 1967. *A Century of Portland Architecture*. Portland: Oregon Historical Society.

Willard, Ruth Hendricks, and Carol Green Wilson. 1985. *Sacred Places of San Francisco*. Novato, Calif.: Presidio Press.

Woodbridge, Sally B., and Roger Montgomery. 1980. *A Guide to Architecture in Washington State*. Seattle: University of Washington Press.

96. Crystal Cathedral, Garden Grove, California

97. First Congregational Church, San Francisco, California

98. St. Mary's Cathedral, San Francisco, California

99. T'ien Hou Temple, San Francisco, California

100. Vedanta Society Headquarters, San Francisco, California

101. First Church of Christ Scientist, Berkeley, California

102. First Presbyterian Church, Cottage Grove, Oregon

103. St. Michael the Archangel Cathedral, Sitka, Alaska

104. Kawaiahao Church, Honolulu, Hawaii

105. Soto Mission Temple, Honolulu, Hawaii

CONCLUSION

Wallace Stevens may have had more ways of looking at a blackbird, but there are many points of view from which American religious architecture might profitably be considered. *Liturgy* provides one vantage point, focusing on interior arrangements and decoration and how they conduce to the celebration of particular rituals. *Style* is another: what are the components of a particular architectural mode, and from where do they derive? *Ethnicity* has been a continuous factor, as one group after another has come to these shores and attempted to reproduce its memories of ancestral building patterns in a New World context. *Social history* offers yet another perspective: what does a religious building tell us of the social status and aspirations of its builders? All of these have been major vantage points for our reading of the physical artifacts that surround us and our trying to reconstruct the tales they tell.

The organizing principle of this study, however, has been *regionalism*, an interpretive principle shared mainly by cultural geography and American studies. That there have been, and still are, regions in the United States that have been culturally, socially, and at times politically significant is intuitively obvious. What, after all, was the Civil War fought over? How have electoral votes divided in recent elections between the "Sun Belt" and the "Rust Belt"? Despite the effects of a nationally integrated market economy and mass media, many Americans still identify as southerners, westerners, and the like, and the demographics of religious distribution, though slowly changing, still do not constitute a nationally homogeneous picture. Similarly, building styles associated with New England or California, though sometimes a bit vague, are hardly contentless.

One way we might have organized this study is in terms of a succession of styles, both "high" and vernacular. To speak of "high style" exclusively is to load the dice against the importance of regionalism. The Wren-Gibbs style, the Roman, Greek, Gothic, and Romanesque revivals, and the Modernism of Frank Lloyd Wright and his successors have all been transregional and frequently national in their appeal and impact. Of these, only Wright's "Prairie Style" had its inspiration in a regional landscape, and had very little effect on religious building.

It is when we address the vernacular that religious building comes into closer harmony with regional contours. The early meetinghouses of New England were distinctly vernacular – New World adaptations of medieval European patterns in an age when they had been long since superseded in fashion. The dominance of the Wren-Gibbs meetinghouse that emerged in the eighteenth century and triumphed in the nineteenth was, to be sure, closely associated with a region, but hardly confined to it – as St. Michael's in Charleston illustrates effectively. Arguably, it is in its most domesticated – that is, most vernacular – form that the Wren-Gibbs church was most New England and least national.

The same argument might be made about other high style fashions during the nineteenth century especially, when regional isolation was breaking down as transportation and communication networks increased and denominations became more and more national phenomena. The Greek revival as high style was a national fashion; in its most basic, stripped-down, vernacular form, however, it became a virtual icon of the popular religion of the South. Upjohn's "Carpenter Gothic" had similar, though somewhat more complex, ramifications. In one form, it became the distinctive mark of elite religiosity in the South; as "prairie Gothic," hybridized with the Greek revival in innumerable humble but self-respecting white frame churches, it was an architecture not so much of one region but of the frontier, which increasingly meant the ever-advancing West.

What became clear during the nineteenth century is that certain styles were well adapted for widespread distribution along certain transregional lines where the traditions with which they were associated flourished, while others of colonial origin were destined to persist only in gradually altered fashion. In the "culture hearths" of New England, Philadelphia, Alaska, and New Mexico, for example, distinctive colonial styles were intimately associated with a particular religion in closely constrained physical and social circumstances, and representative of uniquely American blendings of Old and New World motifs. These never actually disappeared, but gradually tended to assimilate to the dominant revival styles of the age.

The relationship of ethnicity with region and religious architecture also emerged as an important variable as the "New Immigration" unalterably changed the nation's social complexion. Although Patrick Keeley's French Gothic provided a norm for the Irish-dominated national Catholic church, variants in the Polish neighborhoods of the Great Lakes cities, the German Catholic counties of western Ohio, and the Cajun parishes of southern Louisiana provided important variations on a national theme. Jewish building during this period was more uniformly of the Moorish medieval variety, but was localized primarily in the cities of the Northeast where Jewish population was concentrated. The humble but intriguing temples of the small cities of the South provide an instructive parallel here with the Catholic regional experience.

Among Protestants, the trend was toward national homogeneity. Presbyterians, Methodists, and Episcopalians after the Civil War all gravitated toward certain national fashions – primarily variants or amalgams of the medieval revivals – so that the "churchscapes" of San Francisco, Denver, Birmingham, Chicago, and New York became increasingly difficult to distinguish. L-shaped Methodist urban churches were distinctive to that denomination, but Methodism had become so widely dispersed by that time that any regional association had been lost.

In the twentieth century, both "high" and "medium" styles – the latter a good word, perhaps, to describe the building patterns of Methodists and other prima-

rily middle-class denominations and congregations – continued to be national
rather than regional in character. The issue, however, is complex. The Spanish Colonial style is a distinctively twentieth-century mode that is definitely a "medium" style and associated with the broad region – or interregion – that has come to be known as the Sun Belt. The latter-day Colonial revival is favored heavily by southern Evangelicals, and has spread beyond the South as Evangelicalism has become a national and middle-class phenomenon. Pietro Belluschi's distinctively northwestern churches have gained popularity throughout much of the nation, and most of his later work was national rather than regional in scope.

It would be gratifying to be able to end this study with a firm and unambiguous conclusion: regionalism has – or has not – continued to be an important factor in American religious design. Some distinctively regional phenomena, such as the Quaker meetinghouse, have virtually disappeared as contemporary forms, though historic examples continue to exist and are even utilized regularly in the Philadelphia area. Others, such as New England's Wren-Gibbs style, have achieved a new popularity with a very different religious and cultural significance in the South. For the liturgically avant garde, whether Catholic, Anglican, Protestant, or Jewish, historic – including regional – styles have largely disappeared in favor of liturgical renewal and Modernism; even here, though, the popularity of Belluschi's regionally inspired work suggests a caveat. Let us conclude, then, on a firm note of ambiguity: regionalism *does* persist in American religious architecture, but in a convoluted fashion that reflects the ambiguity and multifariousness of American religion, society, and culture themselves.

PHOTOGRAPHIC CREDITS

CHAPTER 1: NEW ENGLAND

1. Congregational church, Tallmadge, Ohio. Courtesy of Library of Congress/Historic American Buildings Survey.
2. Old Ship Meetinghouse, Hingham, Mass. Photograph by Edmunds E. Bond, ca. 1930. Courtesy of the Boston Public Library, Print Department.
3. Old North (Christ) Church, Boston, Mass. Courtesy of Old North Church.
4. Old South Meetinghouse, Boston, Mass. Courtesy of Old South Association, Boston.
5. First Baptist, Providence, R.I. Courtesy of First Baptist Church in America, Providence, R.I.
6. Center (First) Church, New Haven, Conn. Author.
7. "Village of East Corinth, Vermont." George Tice, photographer. Courtesy of George Tice.
8. First Congregational Church, Madison, Conn. Marjorie Jephson, photographer. Courtesy of the Rev. Gordon M. Rankin, First Congregational Church.
9. "Church in New England (Lancaster, New Hamphire)," 1936 (St. Paul's Episcopal Church, Lancaster, N.H.). Arthur Rothstein, photographer. Courtesy of Indiana University Art Museum: Henry Holmes Smith Photo Archive.
10. First Parish Church, Brunswick, Maine. Courtesy of First Parish Church, Brunswick, Maine, Archives.
11. "The Old Church—Built 1792" (stereoview 1878) (Shaker Meetinghouse, Canterbury N.H.). W. G. C. Kimball, photographer. Courtesy Lee Marks Fine Art, Shelbyville, Ind.
12. Touro Synagogue, Newport, R.I. John T. Hopf, photographer. Copyright John Hopf Educational Serives. Courtesy of John T. Hopf and Touro Synagogue.
13. "View of the Mother Church and Christian Science Center," 1973 (Christian Science Mother Church, Boston, Mass.). Nicholas Nixon, photographer. Courtesy Zabriskie Gallery, New York.
14. Trinity Church, Boston, Mass. Author.
15. New Old South Church, Boston, Mass. Author.
16. All Saints Episcopal Church, Ashmont (Boston), Mass. Author.

CHAPTER 2: THE MID-ATLANTIC REGION

17. Arch Street Meetinghouse, Philadelphia, Pa. (exterior). General Meetinghouse Picture File. Courtesy of Friends Historical Library of Swarthmore College, Swarthmore, Pa.
18. Same, interior. Same source.
19. Mennonite Meetinghouse, Lancaster, Pa. Photograph by George A. Tice. Courtesy of George Tice.
20. Ephrata Cloister, Ephrata, Pa. Courtesy of the Pennsylvania Historical and Museum Commission.

21. Old Swedes' (Gloria Dei) Church, Philadelphia, Pa. Courtesy of Library of Congress, Historic American Buildings Survey.

22. St. George's Methodist Church, Philadelphia, Pa. Courtesy of Library of Congress, Historic American Buildings Survey.

23. Lovely Lane Methodist Church, Baltimore, Md. Author.

24. Basilica of the Assumption, Baltimore, Md. Author.

25. "Old Dutch Church—Tarrytown," ca. 1910–25 (Dutch Reformed Church, Sleepy Hollow, N.Y.). Wallace Nutting, photographer. Courtesy of William and Gretchen Hamann Collection.

26. St. James the Less Episcopal Church, Philadelphia, Pa. Author.

27. "Trinity Church and Wall Street Towers, New York, 1933" (Trinity Episcopal Church, New York, N.Y.). Berenice Abbott, photographer. Courtesy Berenice Abbott/Commerce Graphics Ltd., Inc.

28. St. Thomas Episcopal Church, New York, N.Y. Author.

29. St. Bartholomew's Episcopal Church, New York, N.Y. Courtesy of St. Bartholomew's Church.

30. St. Patrick's Cathedral, New York, N.Y. Author.

31. "Untitled (One woman kneels at the still-closed church on the way to work)" (Holy Name of Jesus Catholic Church, New York, N.Y.). Weegee, photographer. Courtesy of the Stephen Cohen Gallery.

32. "Synagogue," 1938 (Pitt Street Synagogue, New York, N.Y.). Walter Rosenblum, photographer. Courtesy of Walter Rosenblum.

33. St. Peter's Lutheran Church, New York, N.Y. Brad Hess, photographer. Courtesy of Brad Hess, 146 Castle Heights Ave., Upper Nyack, N.Y. 10960 (914-358-4434).

34. National Cathedral, Washington, D.C. Photograph by Franz Jantzen. Courtesy of Franz Jantzen.

35. Washington Mosque, Washington, D.C. Photograph by Franz Jantzen. Courtesy of Franz Jantzen.

36. Shrine of the Immaculate Conception, Washington, D.C. Photograph by Franz Jantzen. Courtesy of Franz Jantzen.

CHAPTER 3: THE SOUTH

37. Aquia Church, Stafford County, Va. Francis Marion Wigmore, Photographer. Courtesy of the Pictorial Archive of Early American Architecture, Library of Congress.

38. Old St. Luke's, Isle of Wight County, Va. Courtesy of Library of Congress, Historic American Buildings Survey.

39. St. Peter's Episcopal Church, New Kent County, Va. Courtesy of Library of Congress, Historic American Buildings Survey.

40. Bruton Parish Church, Williamsburg, Va. Courtesy of Bruton Parish Church, an Episcopal church in continuous use since 1715, located in Williamsburg, Va.

41. St. Michael's Episcopal Church, Charleston, S.C. Courtesy of Library of Congress, Historic American Buildings Survey.

42. First Baptist Church, Charleston, S.C. Courtesy of Library of Congress, Historic American Buildings Survey.

43. Temple Beth Elohim, Charleston, S.C. (exterior). Courtesy of Library of Congress, Historic American Buildings Survey.

44. Same, interior. Same source.

45. Unitarian Church, Charleston, S.C. Courtesy of Library of Congress, Historic American Buildings Survey.

46. "Ram Looks Down on the Symbols of the Past" (St. Louis Cathedral, New Orleans, La.). Clarence John Laughlin, photographer. Courtesy of the Historic New Orleans Collection #1981.247.1.237.

47. All Saints' Chapel, Sewanee, Tenn. Charley C. Watkins, photographer. Courtesy of All Saints' Chapel, University of the South, Sewanee, Tenn.

48. Wooden Church, Beaufort, S.C., 1936. Walker Evans, photographer. Farm Security Administration photograph. Courtesy of Hallmark Photographic Collection, Hallmark Cards, Inc., Kansas City, Mo.

49. Church Interior, Alabama, 1936. Walker Evans, photographer. Courtesy of Prints and Photographs Division, Library of Congress.

50. Bethlehem No. 2 M.B. Church, Miss. Tom Rankin, photographer. From *Sacred Space* by Tom Rankin c. 1993 University Press of Mississippi. By permission of the publisher.

51. "Throckmorton Street, Fort Worth, Texas, 1976" (First Christian Church, Fort Worth, Tex.). Stephen Shore, photographer. Courtesy of Stephen Shore.

52. Sixteenth Street Baptist Church, Birmingham, Ala. Courtesy of Birmingham Public Library Department of Archives and History.

53. Ryman Auditorium, Nashville, Tenn. Courtesy Bill LaFevor, Gaylord Entertainment.

54. Downtown Presbyterian Church, Nashville, Tenn. Courtesy of Library of Congress, Historic American Buildings Survey.

CHAPTER 4: THE OLD NORTHWEST

55. Hauge Norwegian Evangelical Lutheran Church, Dane County, Wis. Courtesy of Library of Congress, Historic American Buildings Survey.

56. St. Mary the Virgin Chapel, Nashotah House, Wis. Michael Tolin, photographer. Courtesy of Michael Tolin.

57. St. Peter in Chains Cathedral, Cincinnati, Ohio. Author.

58. Kirtland Temple, Kirtland, Ohio. Courtesy of Library Archives, Reorganized Church of Jesus Christ of Latter Day Saints, The Auditorium, Independence, Mo.

59. Sacred Heart Church and Golden Dome, Notre Dame, Ind. Courtesy of University of Notre Dame Archives.

60. Plum Street Temple, Cincinnati, Ohio. Courtesy of Archives, Isaac M. Wise Temple Library.

61. Fourth Presbyterian Church, Chicago, Ill. Micah Marty, photographer. Courtesy of Fourth Presbyterian Church, Micah Marty.

62. First St. Paul's Evangelical Lutheran Church, Chicago, Ill. Author.

63. Holy Trinity Russian Orthodox Cathedral, Chicago, Ill. Author.

64. St. Stanislaus Kostka Church, Chicago, Ill. Courtesy of the Archdiocese of Chicago Archives and Records Center.

65. Chapel, St. Mary of the Lake Seminary, near Chicago, Ill. Courtesy of the Archdiocese of Chicago Archives and Records Center.

66. Shrine of the Little Flower, Royal Oak, Mich. Courtesy of the Shrine of the Little Flower.

67. Temple Building and First Methodist Church, Chicago, Ill. Courtesy of Chicago Historical Society (ICHi–22300).

68. Chicago Loop Synagogue, Chicago, Ill. Hube Henry of Hedrich Blessing, photographer. Courtesy of Chicago Historical Society (HB–24526).

69. Unity Temple, Oak Park, Ill. Courtesy of Library of Congress, Historic American Buildings Survey.

70. IIT Chapel, Chicago, Ill. Courtesy of Art Wise/Illinois Institute of Technology.

71. "Untitled (The Aisle)" (Rockefeller Chapel, University of Chicago). Scott Mutter, photographer. Copyright 1986 Scott Mutter, from *Surrational Images*, 1992, University of Illinois Press. Courtesy of Scott Mutter.

72. First Christian Church, Columbus, Ind. Hedrich-Blessing, photographers. Courtesy of Chicago Historical Society (HB–07052-I2).

73. North Christian Church, Columbus, Ind. Hube Henry (Hedrich-Blessing), photographer. Courtesy of Chicago Historical Society (HB–27503-A).

74. Willow Creek Community Church, South Barrington, Ill. Copyright William Favata, photographer. Courtesy of Willow Creek Community Church.

CHAPTER 5: THE GREAT PLAINS AND THE MOUNTAINS

75. "On the Great Plains, near Winner, South Dakota, 1938." Dorothea Lange, photographer. Copyright the Dorothea Lange Collection, The Oakland Museum, The City of Oakland. Gift of Paul S. Taylor.

76. Prayer Tower, Oral Roberts University, Tulsa, Okla. Courtesy of Oral Roberts University.

77. Boston Avenue Methodist Church, Tulsa, Okla. David Halpern, photographer. Copyright 1988 David Halpern. Courtesy of David Halpern.

78. USAF Academy Cadet Chapel, Colorado Springs, Colo. U.S. Air Force Photo. Courtesy of United States Air Force Academy Public Affairs.

79. "Wee Kirk o' the Heather Wedding Chapel," Las Vegas, Nev. David Graham, photographer. Courtesy Lawrence Miller Gallery, New York.

80. LDS Temple (with view of Tabernacle), Salt Lake City, Utah. Courtesy of Utah State Historical Society.

81. LDS Temple, Washington, D.C. Author.

CHAPTER 6: THE SPANISH BORDERLANDS

82. La Ermita (Our Lady of Charity), Miami, Fla. Author.

83. Alamo, San Antonio Tex. Courtesy of Library of Congress, Historic American Buildings Survey.

84. Kiva, Nambe Pueblo, N.M. Courtesy of Library of Congress, Historic American Buildings Survey.

85. "Las Trampas Mission Church, the Nave, 1938," Las Trampas, N.M. Laura Gilpin, photographer. Gift of Fritz Kaeser, The Snite Museum of Art, University of Notre Dame.

86. San Esteban Mission, Acoma Pueblo, N.M. Courtesy of Library of Congress, Historic American Buildings Survey.

87. "Ranchos de Taos Church, 1922" (San Francisco de Asís, Ranchos de Taos, N.M.). Dorothea Lange, photographer. Copyright the Dorothea Lange Collection, The Oakland Museum, The City of Oakland. Gift of Paul B. Taylor.

88. "Ranchos de Taos, New Mexico, 1942." (San Francisco de Asís, Ranchos de Taos, N.M.) Fritz Kaeser, photographer. Courtesy of the Indiana University Art Museum, gift of Mrs. Fritz Kaeser.

89. Upper Penitente Morada Chapel, Arroyo Hondo, N.M. Courtesy of Library of Congress, Historic American Buildings Survey.

90. "San Xavier Mission, near Tucson. Facade" (San Xavier del Bac, Ariz.). Carleton E. Watkins, photographer. Courtesy of the Bancroft Library, University of California, Berkeley.

91. "San Xavier Moonrise, 1952" (San Xavier del Bac, Ariz.). Fritz Kaeser, photographer. Courtesy of the Indiana University Art Museum, Gift of Mrs. Fritz Kaeser.

92. "Russian Chapel, Fort Ross, California, 1949." Harold Allen, photographer. Courtesy of Harold Allen.

93. "Old Mission Chapel at Los Angeles, 1899" (Mission San Fernando Rey, Los Angeles, Calif.). Detroit Photographic Company. Courtesy of Etherton Gallery, Tucson, Ariz.

94. Mission Santa Barbara, Calif. Courtesy of Library of Congress, Historic American Buildings Survey.

95. Carmel Mission, Calif. Courtesy of Library of Congress, Historic American Buildings Survey.

CHAPTER 7: THE PACIFIC RIM

96. Crystal Cathedral, Garden Grove, Calif. Author.

97. First Congregational Church, San Francisco, Calif. Author.

98. St. Mary's Cathedral, San Francisco, Calif. Courtesy of Rev. Milton Walsh, Pastor of St. Mary's Cathedral.

99. T'ien Hou Temple, San Francisco, Calif. Author.

100. Vedanta Society Headquarters, San Francisco, Calif. Author.

101. First Church of Christ Scientist, Berkeley, Calif. Ross M. Selmeier, photographer. Courtesy of Ross M. Selmeier.

102. First Presbyterian Church, Cottage Grove, Ore. Courtesy of Oregon Historical Society (OrHi 46751).

103. St. Michael the Archangel Cathedral, Sitka, Alaska. Courtesy of Alaska State Library/ Winter and Pond Collection/PCA87/1520.

104. Kawaiahao Church, Honolulu, Hawaii. Courtesy of the Hawaiian Historical Society.

105. Soto Mission Temple, Honolulu, Hawaii. Nancy Bannick, photographer. Courtesy of Hawaii State Archives

Several of the author's photographs included in this work were made possible by a series of grants from the National Endowment for the Humanities.

INDEX OF PERSONAL NAMES

Other Buildings and Sites

Other Sites with Religious Associations

Nonreligious Buildings

PETER W. WILLIAMS is Distinguished Professor of Religion and American Studies at Miami University in Oxford, Ohio, and regularly leads tours of historic religious sites at academic conferences across the nation. He is the author of *Popular Religion in America* and editor of the series Studies in Anglican History, both published by the University of Illinois Press.

University of Illinois Press
1325 South Oak Street
Champaign, IL 61820-6903
www.press.uillinois.edu